IF STONES COULD SPEAK

I. ST. STEPHEN'S GATES

From a plaque by Moray Smith, reproduced by courtesy of
Morgan's Brewery Co. Ltd.

[*Frontispiece*

If Stones Could Speak

AN INTRODUCTION TO AN
ALMOST HUMAN FAMILY

by

R. H. MOTTRAM

Republished
EP Publishing Limited
1973

Reproduced 1973 by EP Publishing Limited
East Ardsley, Wakefield
Yorkshire, England
by permission of the Copyright holders
© Estate of the late R. H. Mottram

This book was first published in 1953
by Museum Press Ltd., London
This is a reprint of that edition

ISBN 0 85409 810 0

Please address all enquiries to EP Publishing Ltd.
(address as above)

Reprinted in Great Britain by
Scolar Press Limited, Menston, Yorkshire

CONTENTS

ILLUSTRATIONS

Plate No. 1 is reproduced by permission of Morgan's Brewery Co. Ltd.; No. 2 by permission of the *Eastern Daily Press*; Nos. 3, 4, 5, 6, 8, 9, 16 and 17 by permission of Mr. G. C. Le Grice; No. 7 by permission of Lord Mackintosh; Nos. 11, 12, 13, 14, 15 by permission of Mr. A. H. Mottram; and No. 10 by permission of Mr. Alec Cotman.

I

TOMBLAND. THE DISPOSSESSED ELDEST OFFSPRING

WHERE shall we begin to make the acquaintance of this family of Norwich streets that Time and Place have bred? Surely with Tombland, the eldest, the first offspring that graced the union, the shambling, rather unkempt, obviously very ancient trackway that broadened out and became the first meeting-place of the citizens. It is hardly a street. The metalled roadway, to this day, runs diagonally across it, between cobbles amid which trees have been planted and market-stalls stand.

Its character leaps to the eye. Who has not heard the parents of some large family say of the eldest: " He—or (even more probably) she—will have to make herself useful! " Who does not know that elder child, tolerant and easy-going from not expecting too much, handy and made-use-of, from long custom of being sent on errands or told to hold some younger brother or sister?

Just such a one is Tombland. Possibly still the busiest street in Norwich, it has the air of never having a moment to spare to brush its hair and wash its hands. A medieval churchyard has encroached on its once-symmetrical shape. It is completely overshadowed and dominated by its younger relative, the Cathedral Close, that stands immediately east of it and has taken half the light and deprived it of half its original space. Indeed, its very name is a nickname, a malpronunciation, just as some elder daughter, christened Elizabeth, has become " Liz . . . fetch this . . . take that! " so Tombland has nothing to do with tombs. The hasty tourist who crosses it unheeding, to look at the Cathedral, dismisses it: "Ah, the monks' graveyard, no doubt! " That is what it looks like so obviously, but how did such a state of things come about? For anyone who looks at a street map—nay, anyone who tries to drive a car across Norwich, to get to somewhere else—soon discovers that Tombland is still the centre at which the main

roads, north, south, east and west, converge. They do not
lead to the modern City Hall, nor to the Railway Station, the
Bus Station, or the main bridge of the nine bridges that now
span the River Wensum as it winds through the ancient, hap-
hazard city. They lead to Tombland. That is why, in
parenthesis, the traffic problem of Norwich, if less heart-
breaking than that of Cambridge or Oxford, is more per-
manently hopeless. It would be comparatively easy to move
Nuffield's Works or Cambridge Station. It is quite impossible
to shift Norwich Castle and Cathedral.

Far more important, however, is the basic reason of the
curiously distorted plan of Norwich. It is not a lack of plan,
nor a bad plan. The early plan of Norwich was not that of a
Roman military or civil centre. It was a natural growth
suddenly and violently distorted. The resulting plan of
Norwich is a crime. That is exactly what the motorist feels,
as he halts at the traffic lights and sees them turn green, and
red and green again, before he can pass. That is what the
driver of heavy night-riding goods-traffic by road feels, when he
comes down the magnificent half-mile elm avenue of Newmarket Road from London, or the wide Dereham Road from
Lynn, Peterborough and the North, and loses himself in narrow
tangles of one-way streets. That is what the traveller by rail
feels when he realises that Norwich stations are termini. You
have to back out and go round about.

It all began very long ago, in the age of crude violence, and
deceptively "Tombland" derives its contortion, its air of
overworked neglect, from bloodshed and piracy. As anyone
may guess from its name—a corruption of NORTH-WYCK—
Norwich was a settlement, literally a settling down, of men
who had come overseas, to take what they could get, what they
must have if they were to live—land, water, living-room.
The history book calls them "Saxons", and the later strain
that overlaid them "Danes". In fact, those misleading if
convenient labels do not hide the real identity of those people
from anyone who surveys Europe in 1952. They were what
we call "displaced persons", mixed up with all the hungry,
unscrupulous hangers-on of the years we dimly discern as the
Dark Ages. They may have come from what is now Saxony,
and the later wave of them from what is now Denmark. But

so far from being anything like the laborious and orderly operatives and peasants of those districts today, the Saxons and Danes who made Norwich out of NORTH-WYCK were pirates. That is the plain word for them. They came to kill and plunder and sail away again. The particular local focus of their attacks was not at modern Norwich at all, but three miles to the south-west, where, on the banks of the little Tas stream, a tributary of the neighbouring Yare, there remain today the massive walls of the Roman administrative and marketing centre. Wrongly called " Caistor ", as if it were a Roman Camp like Chester or Exeter, it was Venta Icenorum, the clearing made by the Iceni in the woods and swamps. The Romans adopted it as their district base. It may have been the rude capital of Boadicea, that chariot-riding virago who nearly stopped the Romanisation of Britain altogether. That, however, is another story, and its only connection with Norwich is the old rhyme, true enough in its vagueness:

> Norwich was built of Caistor stone,
> Caistor was a town when Norwich was none.

Centuries after Boadicea (or Bou-dyk-ya, as her primitive companions probably called her) was disposed of, some sort of Romanised colonial society dwelt and flourished there, rich enough to attract the starving, desperate crews of the open boats that came across the North Sea.

" Caistor " was thoroughly dug in the nineteen-twenties, and furnished meagre if sufficient evidence of why this should be so. The people who lived there, of whom perhaps some spoke Latin and had been to Rome (just as some of the in-habitants of a minor market town in India might speak English and have been to school in Britain), had glass and pottery (which they doubtless called Samian, as we call the produce of Staffordshire " china "), baths and drains, and better heating systems under their tessellated floors than most Norwich buildings had in A.D. 1900. Of course the " Saxons " were attracted, though they had no use for glass, and ivory door-hinges, bronze horse furniture, and hypocausts. So far as could be ascertained, they seem to have burned the place twice, and the skulls of the last survivors were found in a position that suggested they had taken refuge in a heating-

chamber. Anyhow, Venta Icenorum perished, and the hazy
memory of what it had been led to its being called " Caistor "
centuries later. It was no easy conquest. The latest in-
vestigation of the subject, I believe, suggests that the raiders
were fought off, more or less successfully, for perhaps two
hundred years. There is no legend in East Anglia of any
semi-fabulous " King Arthur ", but it now seems to be thought
that local chiefs, with who knows what tradition of what the
Roman armies had once been, rebuilt and walled their town,
and its conquest must have been long and costly. Haverfield
says the " Saxons " had no arms or armour save pikes and
occasional helmets. But they persisted. Probably they could
not help it, had nowhere else to go, and in the very long run
they won.

What happened then? Nothing. We do not know. The
next thing that archæologists dug up is the trace of a " Saxon "
settlement, where Norwich stands today.

Why? Presumably there was no one left to fight, and
instead of going back to the dangers and discomforts of their
boats, the rough crews settled down. But not to any great
extent at Caistor. It may have been because of bad con-
sciences. They had blood on their hands. Or, more likely,
the little Tas was not much use to their sea-going craft. They
were a water-borne people, had been so for longer than they
could remember. That is why the site of Norwich suited them.
That is why Tombland was born. It happened to be opposite
the lowest crossing or ford of the Wensum river. It is also the
highest point to which sea-going vessels could go with comfort.
The fuel for the Power-station at Norwich still comes in sea-
going ships. They settled down, then, in the elbow of the wide
sweep of the Wensum, where the ground is firm enough, near
where the General Post Office stands in Norwich today.
Between them and the river-bank, north, east and south-east
of them, was the " Tum "—or vacant—land, part meeting-place
for what may have been separate crews of pirates, and eventually hamlets of little one-room wooden shanties, built like
boats turned bottoms upwards; part market-place for such
primitive commodities as they had to exchange.

Thus was " Tum-land " born, first of all Norwich tracks, or
rather, open spaces. The settlers had no use for the Roman

Road that runs under the Castle Mound and was discovered
there in the nineteen-hundreds; they had no traffic that did
not go by water.   So they made some kind of a fort, perhaps
where the Castle Mound stands today.   Round " Tum-land "
they gathered.   The Romans may have left them a ford, for
piles of undeterminate antiquity were found under what is now
Fye Bridge.   These Saxons had wooden churches, St. Mary
in the Marsh, St. Mary Coslany; their saints were Etheldreda,
the daughter of one of the first Christian kings, and people like
Swithin and Botolph.   Sooner or later their chieftain, or earl,
built himself a rather more pretentious place where the Inland
Revenue offices are today, on the southern side of Tombland,
and there are indications that he had stone vaults beneath it.
Near by was the Motte-stowe or Committee-mound, at which
they governed themselves, as much as they ever were governed.
They prospered in their slow, independent, beer-swilling, pig-
keeping way, became incorporated in that loose, ever-changing
system, called by history books the Heptarchy, eventually
became important enough to have a Mint and issue coins with
the figure-head of King Athelstan.

It was not all such smooth going as that may sound.   A
fiercer, better-armed type of pirate was pushing them about.
These Danes, infiltrating wherever there was plunder, settled
among them.   The dedications to St. Olaf (" Tooley " Street
as it became called) and St. Vedast (St. " Faith " was what they
made of it) show a Scandinavian rather than Friesian or Rhine
delta origin.   The " Saxons " resented these incursions, and a
great massacre, in A.D. 1001, drew Sweyn, King of Denmark,
to attack the place.   " All this Burgh he over-harrowed and
down burnt," says the compilation called the Anglo-Saxon
Chronicle.

It recovered with remarkable speed and completeness.   It
takes more than that to obliterate Norwich.   Sweyn would
be surprised to see it today.   It is as though some middle-aged,
tough, unimaginative person, being tipped out of a gig and
summarily thrashed by the roadside, replies by getting up and
going on with the next business, as if nothing had happened.
We know little or nothing owing to the almost complete
absence of records as to how it was done, but there seems no
other explanation than abundant vitality.   Almost the only

certain fact is that, a little more than sixty years after Sweyn had done his worst, Tombland was again so prosperous, so obvious a prize, that the Norman invasion fell on it with a heavy hand which has left its mark on the townscape we see today.

Tombland was plainly the administrative and commercial centre of the district, and the Normans made no mistake about it. The severity of their treatment may have been connected with the fact that it was a Godwin stronghold, a centre of the slow-moving, obstinate and primitive Saxon Kingdom.

This time Tombland did not merely get, as it were, a couple of black eyes and a shaking. Its neck was finally and, as the Normans supposed, fatally wrung, and the place was left for dead.

The Norman invaders not only heightened and strengthened with some sort of stockade the old primitive mound which may have existed, where the Castle now stands, to block the ancient Roman trackway. The market, whatever may have been what the desultory Saxons called " market " (one pictures a collection of adjustable booths where various simple wares were exposed for sale), was transplanted bodily, a quarter of a mile, and planked down where the present Provision Market extends, on the other side of the little stream that ran under the Castle walls, where the alley called " Back of the Inns " stands today; that gave the garrison command of supplies and an immediate domination of the tough, rebellious, unsubdued market-people. But Tombland itself was dismembered. The See was transferred from Thetford (which had been, on the whole, a more important town) and taken from the " Saxon " bishop, Stigand, and given to a Norman, Herbert de Losinga, who forthwith proceeded to build right across Tombland the wall of his great Cathedral enclosure. Tons of stone imported from Caen, a whole Holy garrison of Benedictine monks— foreigners, at least the first sixty of them—were parked there as an army of occupation, and a Holy one at that, so that they were doubly fortified, by stone, and by the anathema ready to fall on such as attacked the Church.

Why were the Normans so vindictive? The answer is easy: they were insecure. And they were quite right. Within a hundred years the language they imported to their new " French " quarter beyond the new market had died out. By

1194 Norwich people forgot that they had ever been Saxons,
Danes and Normans, called themselves " English " and
demanded of the King the right to govern themselves. They
got it. Almost the only sign of the savaging of Tombland is
the " French " names of the Saints to whom the western
quarter churches were dedicated : Peter, Stephen, Giles. The
Lord in the Castle, the Bishop in his Palace, became English.
The rooted tenacity of a population, bedded in layer after
layer of absorbed invasion, absorbed the Normans too.

Tombland got on its feet again. Maimed, truncated, robbed,
it succeeded in re-establishing itself as a market. Provisions
might go to the " new " place beyond the Castle, but the
growing trade in beasts stuck to Tombland. The Charter
of the great Horse Fair at Easter is still called " Tombland
Fair ", though in A.D. 1738 it had been transferred gradually
to the Castle ditches because it was too prosperous to be contained in the restricted limits left to Tombland.

That is why Tombland has its present appearance. That is
why it looks as if it belonged to the Cathedral Close, which
has elbowed it out of half its original area. That is why the
four main roads meet on its broad bosom and not at what is now
the City Hall. That is why special round, flat biscuits,
flavoured with ginger, or with lemon, are still called " Tombland Fair buttons " and should be bought and eaten in pairs.

Since the day when it recovered from its operation, as some
garrulous old woman would love to tell, it has seen history
enough. It has actually profited by the incursion of the Close,
which was intended to settle its fate for good. It is now the
most-photographed street in Norwich, which is saying a good
deal. Containing two magnificent gateways to the Close, one
of Norwich's thirty-five parish churches, several government
offices, good hotels and restaurants, it has never relinquished
the smaller, busy shops that must be direct successors of its
first market. Rebellions and Royal Processions have outraged
or graced it. Robert Greene, who was Shakespeare's rival,
was born on it. Winston Churchill crossed it in face of a
yelling mob. Finally, when the City Corporation felt bound to
stabilise the type of stall that had evolved from the old two-
planks-under-a-canvas-tilt type, the Norwich Society got on its
hind legs and defied the new move, in the High Court of Justice,

and established the fact that the cobbles of Tombland are the inalienable Open Space belonging to the citizens, and never shall be built upon, even with the very best intentions.

Yet nothing can arrest the passage of time or smooth out the wrinkles that use begets in all of us. So Tombland today, in contrast to the still and silent dignity of the Cathedral Close to which it leads, looks what it is, a place so used that it hardly has time to get swept. It is an awful warning to invaders, dictators and their like. Something moves in the habit of the human mind that is stronger than all of them. I will not hesitate to prophesy that if ever Norwich were destroyed, Tombland would survive.

2. TOMBLAND BY JOHN THIRTLE

3. THE LOWER CLOSE

4. CASTLE DITCHES

5. PULL'S FERRY

II

THE CATHEDRAL CLOSE. THE CLERIC AND HIS " FOREIGN " EDUCATION

THE next member of the family of Norwich streets is a very different thing—or rather person—from the older Tomb-land. It is more usual in France than in England to find the second son of the family entering the Church. But it was not so when the great Cathedral of the Holy Trinity was founded— or " born ", if you wish to follow my image. There can be no mistake as to *these* stones " speaking " or what they say. The Close as we call it, the Monastery enclosure as it became in A.D. 1096, elbowed old Tombland out of the picture, usurped, to all appearance, its place as the most prominent feature of the summarily subdued " Burgh ". That is not merely my notion : it is what the citizens themselves felt about the matter, and the evidence is not far to seek.

I said " to all appearance " the Cathedral and its enclosure became more important than Tombland and its market. Today, nine hundred and fifty years after, the Cathedral is the first thing that strikes the eye as one approaches Norwich, even more so than the Castle, for it is much higher, and its enclosure occupies more space. Tombland remains the scarcely articulate meeting-place of the Saxons and Danes. The Cathedral has not only its appearance. It has, and had far more vividly when it was first built, a kind of prestige due to the odour of sanctity surrounding it, and forming, as I have suggested, a fortification additional to its great walls and the professional retainers of its Prior, the only regular soldiers besides the Castle garrison. It has managed to maintain its original purpose while its nearest relative, the Castle, has become first gaol and now Museum and Picture-gallery, and has not been taken seriously as a Castle these five centuries.

The citizens, however, had another reason for resenting this incursion. There was something in those days about the community serving the Cathedral and occupying the Close which had an odour other than that of sanctity. As one turns over the voluminous records, the centuries-long account-books of the Benedictine Monastery, it is difficult to believe that one is perusing the documents of a religious organisation. They read more like those of some modern government-controlled monopoly. The community was one of the largest land-owners for many a mile, rivalling the comparable foundations of the Abbey of St. Benets at Holme and St. Edmundsbury. It drew tribute—rent in plain language—from far and wide. It carried out large-scale operations in farming and breeding, kept open house, not merely as a Christian institution giving doles to the poor, but as the only travel and lodging agency of the place and time. It is now calculated that anything up to two hundred persons sat down to the main meal of the day in the great hall, the ruins of which still stretch from the great west door to the business offices, kitchens, cellarer's and chancellor's premises, which today form Nos. 63–68 The Close. Canon Hudson's learned description in the eighteen-nineties was that it might have been called the " County Hotel ". In the year 1281 no fewer than 132,500 eggs were bought in three months for Easter. Anything from the friendly visits of relatives of members of the community, to those who had taken the vow, up to Royal Progresses, could be catered for. The charity to the poor was kept separate, and was dealt with through the less important " Ethelbert " Gate giving access to the Almonry. Class distinctions were observed. The scale of the kitchens shows something of the scope of the under-taking, with its " lardar " and porkery, its communars' chamber and buttery. It was moreover a self-supporting unit. As one passes, nowadays, down the main street that leads east from the Ethelbert Gate, one leaves the " Upper " Close, and sees northwards a building labelled " Probate Registry ". It stands on the site of the Infirmary chamber where the monks were regularly bled by the " groom ". Passing a substantial modern house, we find ourselves looking up at the southern elevation of the great church, just where the south transept breaks the long line of the nave, and above it the tower, upon which the spire is superimposed, gives such a sensation of dizzy height that it is difficult to believe that the gilded weathercock is only 316 feet above the ground—a mere hundred yards. Now we see, between the transept, the nave and what was the great Hall, the square of the cloisters in which the monks spent most of their working hours, the elders in the northern walk, where the sun struck, the naughty little novices near the porter's lodge, over the " dark entry " at the south-eastern corner.

That is why the infirmary stood there, beyond the refectory. Over the ground floor of the cloisters was a library, still in use, and an armoury for the Prior's servants. The great square of the Lower Close was the farm-yard. The grey buildings on its north, now numbered 51 to 56, were the " garner " or granary, the brewery and bakery and steward's houses. On the southern side opposite were stables, swannery and the ruins of the church of St. Mary in the Marsh, one of those suppressed and incorporated in the establishment of the Cathedral. The eastern wall of the enclosure can still be traced in the fabric of the house at the corner. Behind what is now No. 34 adjoining was the quayhead of the canal that then ran from the water-gate now called " Pull's Ferry ".

There was originally no road leading to the south face of the transept past the Deanery, that has taken over what was the Prior's lodging. Where it runs today was filled with chambers, with the dormitory over them, domestic offices, then, near the south door, the Chapter House, of which the only trace remains in the three open arches in the outer cloister wall that give a fascinating glimpse of the Cloister Garth. Then, where the modern road winds below the three chapels of the apse, was the monks' cemetery, and here, in " Life's Green ", lies all alone Edith Cavell, a native of Norfolk and hospital matron, shot by the Germans in Brussels in 1915 on the grounds that she was helping her patients to escape. " Patriotism is not enough," she is reported to have said, and went to her death with grim resolution. Beyond again, as the private lane winds out to the street called Bishopgate, that must have been diverted to hug the wall, were a horse-mill, a " plumbery ", a gardener's house, and north of the sacred church edifice, the " hall " of the manor which de Losinga, the Bishop who began the building of the Cathedral, made his palace. Its magnificent gate confronting St. Martin's-at-Palace Plain breaks the line of the best-preserved remaining portion of the wall, which, encircling the whole enclosure, justifies, I think, my description of the original Close as a " Holy Fortress ".

Anyhow, that is what the citizens thought. I do not know if anybody knows precisely what it was that caused them to break in from Tombland in A.D. 1270 and fight a pitched battle in which monks and retainers were killed, and some citizens, and portions of the conventual buildings, and even a part of the Cathedral Church, were burnt.

What aroused such fury, centuries after the Norman Conquest was not only an established fact, but a forgotten one? The citizens who behaved in this outrageous manner—for just think what it meant in those ages of Faith to attack and burn a super-church—were not actuated by the old quarrel between Saxons and Danes on one hand and Normans on the other. They had ceased to think of themselves in such a light. What the scanty records of the time tell us is that the monks, or their military retainers, had mounted the artillery of the period—some kind of gigantic crossbow or arbalest—on their " clocher " or bell-tower, which stood just inside the Erpingham Gate, as we call it. This " clocher " was intended to house the bells, at a date when men had no means of hanging them in the present belfry below the spire. It was a very solid piece of masonry, and thus would stand the strain of firing this engine.

But still, why? What an unlikely-seeming story! Indeed it may not be true, or at least unbiased. Yet we do learn that there was a chronic quarrel between the civil and ecclesiastical powers about the right to tax the trade of that day. The Priory authorities claimed the right over various areas and certain trades. Moreover, they had means to enforce their claims. The Bridge we call " Bishop's Bridge " was really the Prior's Bridge. The old tower that stands in Great Hospital meadows, north-west of the Cathedral, known to the present generation as the " Cow " Tower, because for centuries it has served no purpose but that of a huge rubbing-post for beasts at pasture, was in fact the collecting point for river dues.

The whole subject is buried in ancient and complicated dispute, upon which I would be the last person to pretend to pass judgment. I doubt, in fact, if any really satisfactory conclusion can be come to or that it is worth much time or trouble. What I think is beyond doubt is that the citizens felt they were being unjustly treated by a power which might have a Holy side, but which was, most days of the week, a very unholy and oppressive business corporation, encroaching on their means of livelihood. Their view may have been wrong. It may be quite untrue that the Prior's soldiers fired the first shot. But anyone who reads the account-books of the Cathedral Priory will find it hard to dismiss the citizens' case as being without some foundation.

That is how it was treated in the year 1270. The Priory authorities appealed to the King, and he came down into East Anglia with armed force, deprived the citizens of the " liberties " they had been granted by the charters of his predecessors, condemned them to pay 3,000 marks—a swingeing fine—and put the Provost (he was not called a Mayor then) in the Tower, as a sort of security or hostage. When he was released, eventually, the citizens gave him a new hat.

This was by no means the only contention between the citizens and the Priory, but I think it gives some idea of the feeling in the family, so to speak. The Priory was still considered an intrusion. It was, in fact, as we can see from the Cathedral accounts, a means of drawing off a certain amount of local wealth, for a proportion of whatever rents and taxes the Priory acquired went into the Papal coffers, for Crusades and other projects for which the citizens felt that they did not receive an adequate return, and they may or may not have been right.

Now, all this is very long ago, and the interesting point arises, how did such an institution as the Priory is shown to be, at any date up to A.D. 1500, come to be the Cathedral and Close of A.D. 1950, a prime mover in the new Welfare State, a section of Norwich much admired by visitors from all over the world, presided over by men of learning, piety and exemplary public renown? There is no better answer, I fear, than that, given a chance, human institutions do develop and improve. The dramatic contrast is between the attitude of the citizens in the great strife of A.D. 1270, and that of their descendants in A.D. 1950 who have just subscribed, at a time of grave economic disturbance, a sum of over £35,000 for the repair of the fabric.

The answer in full is too long, and perhaps not all of it relevant. Let us grant that the Close, or the Priory enclosure, was a rather overbearing member of a large family. It then becomes evident that the personality of the place has changed. It has taken centuries, but in the very long run it has been accomplished, and we are face to face with the decorous atmosphere, beautiful outlines, mellow sounds of the Close we know. Many of the Bishops were statesmen, one at least, Despencer, was a first-rate soldier, and showed it in the suppression of one of the numerous rebellions of turbulent Norfolk, when, in 1381, he charged the insurgent trenches at North Walsham at the head of the royal troops, put the enemy to flight, captured the leader, Litester, shrived and executed him on the spot. For the rest the long line of Bishops were often posted near to the throne, with advice and counsel and service. The Priors were continuously employed in caring for the great House of God which was their charge. No one would pretend they were all excellent or even moderately good men, but the sum total of what they were stands before us today, and whatever else Norwich means, it means that.

The seeds of change began inside the church itself. Not only were there Lollards, outside, singing hymns of which, or of the singing of which the Church could not approve, but within were new bodies: Friars of all kinds, with their particular buildings and thoroughfares, as we shall see, came to join the family of Norwich streets, and so it went on to the Reformation.

Most people who want to know what that was and why it was, will find plenty of controversial matter on the subject, but as to its effect on the Norwich handed down to us, we find the answer in the fact that the last Prior of the Benedictine community became the first Dean of the Protestant Cathedral. The clerical member of the Norwich family, in fact, changed his clothes, his mode of speech, and presumably many of his convictions. Much that was then destroyed we may well lament, much that was changed, has changed again. It has not changed back to what it was. Human affairs seldom do. The twentieth century has some difficulty in re-becoming the sixteenth, and only a few people alive today want it to do so.

In brief, decorations and ornaments disappeared, relics were no longer exhibited. Emphasis changed. Instead of falling upon the singing of certain services, as we should call them, it fell upon preaching. North of the great west doors, on what is now the playground of the Grammar School, was set up an open-air pulpit on the " preaching green ". The "carnary " that had received the bones from all the churchyards became diverted to the use of the Grammar School of King Edward VI. The Cloisters became the resort of noble families, who painted their armorial devices on the walls. The ordinary life of the town invaded what had been an exempt jurisdiction. (The private prison and workhouse of the Diocese occupied the dismantled infirmary and dormitory well into the eighteenth century.) A little row of shops ran from the great west doors to the Erpingham Gate, many trades entered the precincts and inns were opened for the refreshment of the public. The most notable was the inn at the ferry, which came to be known as " Sandlin's " and finally " Pull's Ferry " in later years, when the canal from the water-gate was filled up, and the road running from the Ethelbert Gate to the stairs and ferry-boat became a short cut to the neighbouring suburb of Thorpe, until, in the nineteenth century, the present Foundry Bridge was built to give access to the " new " railway. This ferry service lingered until the early years of the twentieth century, and it was one of the treats of my childhood to be taken across the deep, slow-flowing water, by the laconic old ferryman who " quanted ", Norfolk fashion, with a long pole; he did not row. And when landed safely on the other side, what fun it was to sit on the grass of the tow-path of those days and watch the slow but capacious wherries go gliding by.

But the conversion of the Close into a trading part of the community was also only a passing phase and one so long past that I do not remember it. By the time, in the eighteen-nineties, that I was taken down to the water-gate and ferried across, and sat to see the wherries, the great revival of religious observance, of serious decorous conduct, at least outwardly and on the part of the upper and professional classes, had taken place.

The " Courts Christian " ecclesiastical jurisdiction that made the Bishops and the Dean into local authorities, all passed away. The beautiful old Infirmary which had housed the Close Work-house was evacuated and demolished in spite of the protest of (among others) Sir Robert Peel. In the mood of the nineteenth century the place became the preserve of the low-church but devout clergy pictured by Trollope, equally removed from the conventional atmosphere of the fifteenth century as from that of a trading quarter of the town. One's footfall became hushed, one did not play one's childish games while passing through it. Tradesmen's carts proceeded at a walking pace from the residence of one canon to that of another. The bawling newsboys, muffin-men with bells and other street hawkers intruded no more than the ordinary horse traffic of the streets. Indeed, it could not become a thoroughfare, for there was a " bar ", generally padlocked, which closed the eastern exit into Bishopgate and made it a " cul de sac ". Some of the clergy kept conveyances, but otherwise the chimes reverberated in an atmosphere of silence so strictly preserved that when bicycles came in, the Dean's gardener, sweeping its gravelled alleys, bade one dismount and walk beside one's machine.

So we come to the latest phase of this, the Cathedral Close, nearly the oldest of Norwich by-ways, for a by-way it must be. It can lead nowhere on this earth. Its signpost is the spire, pointing vertically upwards, to whatever may be there. But something else has happened, an economic rather than a political or social revolution. Wise financial advisers had pointed out that clergy cannot possibly pay the rates, or provide for the repairs, on the houses of the Close. Consequently, one by one, these have been vacated by resident canons and others, and have been occupied by the offices of lawyers, accountants, local authorities and government and professional offices, which can afford what is today an " economic " rent. The feeling one has as one passes through the Close today is one of high probity, good manners and a surprising modernity.

Finally came the war, in which not even so sacred a spot, so far removed from all previous battlefields these four hundred years, was spared. As I went my rounds in the bombardments of 1942 I always had a look at the Cathedral, outlined against the humming sky by the light of great conflagrations. The opinion has been advanced that few things would have affected the morale of Norwich more deeply than any damage to the Cathedral spire. It escaped. Incendiaries set light to the roof of the transepts on each side, but they were extinguished and it has remained intact.

It looks today as any elderly but virile cleric may look, who has had to change his habits violently in middle life and now, very far from young, has had to be called from his study to take decisions on financial matters, and finally has had to take off his coat, roll up his sleeves and learn to use a stirrup pump. What he may have been in extreme youth is all forgotten. What he was in days when the profession of religion carried with it social privilege has been forgiven. He may cut an outmoded figure today, but it is one of dignity. And from the ends of the earth come tourists—even for three years soldiers—who photograph him respectfully. That is the story of the clerical member of the Norwich family.

III

THE CASTLE DITCHES, OR SOLDIER TURNED TRADESMAN

THE next personality among the streets of Norwich is a complete contrast. One might describe " Castle Meadow ", as the street that skirts the base of the mound is now called, as " a soldier demobilised ". In spite of its imposing width of four lines of traffic, and its central position, leading from the main railway station through the heart of the town along which buses roar, it is still overlooked by the Castle, perched up there on its mound, these eight hundred and fifty years. And not all the vigorous and hopeless attempts at improving the traffic scheme of old Norwich will ever make " Castle Meadow " anything else than the ditch round two sides of that fortress.

Its origin is wrapped in mystery. We know something about the beginning of Tombland, and that of the Cathedral Close is circumstantial and documented. But of the Castle mound and ditch we know only that the former is artificial " made " earth, so that, in spite of dire need in 1939, it could not be tunnelled for an adequate air-raid shelter. Moreover, some years ago, during some repairs, a Roman trackway, unmistakable with its rammed earth, was found to run right under it, at the natural level of the soil. " Castle Meadow " is quite unmistakably military, then, the ditch from which some chieftain, in the dark ages, dug the soil to make a primitive strong point. It used to be fashionable, in the more confident histories of a century ago, to ascribe this activity to " Uffa ", whoever he may have been, nor does it matter much. The Normans found something of the sort there, improved it, and presently built their typical cube-shaped keep on the summit, where it has lasted to this day after eight hundred and fifty years. It is still a dizzy business to stand at the western brink and peep down the perilous drop, into what was still called, in all directories of a hundred years ago, " Castle Ditches ", with much greater exactness.

The modern name " Meadow " is misplaced. The ditch did not run right round the mound. The Norman keeps were

26

places of garrison and refuge, but for ordinary peacetime police work, overawing of rebellious Saxons and neighbouring potentates in their " keeps " at Bungay or Thetford or Bucken-ham or Castle Rising, it had on its south and east a wide, kidney-shaped " bailey " or castle yard, for horses and cattle, which could be driven under the stone walls, or even perhaps into the ground floor in case of need. That " bailey " received the overflow from too-prosperous and restricted Tombland, at least as early as Stuart times, and by 1744 the great cattle market, still called, at its principal Easter Saturday meeting, " Tombland " fair, was transferred hither. This bailey was in fact the Castle " Meadow " properly speaking, and its increasing use, in the nineteenth century, with the construction of Prince of Wales Road from the railway, has caused the name to be applied to what, in spite of all modern improvements, is plainly a dry ditch of an early fortification.

I have called it a military street " demobilised ", for it has seen active service. One of the first things that happened after that " conquest " of which the Normans were so uncertain, was that the command of the Castle was given to Ralph de Guader, a Breton follower of William the Norman; he had married the daughter of the Norman Governor of Norwich and it is said that at the wedding he and others, perhaps in their cups, bragged themselves into some sort of a conspiracy against their new and heavy-handed if insecure master. Whatever plans they made were upset, their forces dispersed, but the heroic Lady Emma held the Castle against besieging royal troops for three months and was allowed to march out with military honours. This, by far the most brilliant incident of the long history of the Castle, it is now thought took place in the original timber-and-stockaded building, the present edifice, of stone from Caen and from West Norfolk, being built in the early eleven hundreds, after Emma had gone.

These old stones are what the visitor now sees from the inside of the Keep, for the outside was so decayed by 1834 that it had to be refaced. The dwelling-rooms of the garrison were at the height of the present museum gallery, and were divided by a wall on the site of the present arches of masonry. On one side lived the Governor and his family, on the other the sixty or so regular soldiers. The basement, at ground level, held the stores and perhaps, at a pinch, horses. There is a fine stairway and a very beautiful Norman door for the main or state entry, a well going plumb down through the mound into the natural earth beneath. The battlements are reached by corkscrew staircases in two of the angles, and the series of passages and tiny six-foot chambers in the thickness of the wall would have delighted Harrison Ainsworth or any other writer of romances about the supposedly glamorous Feudal Age to which the building belongs. I find it interesting in a different way. The queer little chambers I am now told were probably lavatories, and in fact, what I remember most vividly of the occasion when my father took me in 1893 to watch the work of reconstituting the interior of the building for its present use is the stench of centuries of undrained sewage. Even if it were not so, the living conditions within such a place stagger the imagination. What sort of a life can it have been for the women of the Governor's family? Perhaps they lodged outside somewhere, normally. Yet when one struggles up to the remodelled battlements what a scene meets the eye! The whole of Norwich lies at one's feet, and miles of fertile, undulating Norfolk beyond, including Mousehold Heath, which Crome painted and Borrow described. It is the fifth largest keep in England of its particular type of building, and many have been the American G.I.s I have led up to see that view, and heard them exclaim "Gee!" I spent the night of 21 June 1941 on duty there, watching for German parachutists.

Well, this is the building that was held by Louis of France in 1216 against King John, but after the building of the walls of Norwich it gradually became useless except as a prison. Its stones are scratched with heart-rending inscriptions of poor wretches incarcerated there without hope and sometimes, they thought, without justification. It passed at length from the Royal hands to those of the county magistrates, and finally was purchased by the City.

Its last days as a prison saw added to it the comparatively modern outbuildings that now contain only show-cases of famous scientific collections. But there is connected with the place one memory of an eye-witness which I heard from his own lips, for he was my father, and lived at No. 20, Castle Meadow, as it is now numbered.

In 1849, on a certain day he was bidden not to go out. It was the day of the execution of James Bloomfield Rush, a bestial and dishonest farm bailiff who had murdered Jeremy, the Recorder of Norwich, and his son and wounded two other people on account of some alleged ill-treatment. The magnitude and brutality of the case made it a *cause célèbre*, and the " swell mob " of London chartered a special train to come to Norwich to join the eleven thousand people who crowded the neighbouring Cattle Market to see the condemned man strung up, in public, at the foot of the Castle Bridge. Incidentally their train was stopped at Attleborough and they were sent back. But the orgies of drunken, sadistic delight in the hanging were duly enjoyed by the vast crowd. Nice little boys like James Mottram did not participate but saw the crowd. It was the last public execution in Norwich.

In 1894 the Duke of York, whom we remember better as George V, opened the Castle as a Museum, to house a local collection largely formed by that foremost inhabitant of Norwich, Sir J. E. Smith, who had brought the Linnean Collection from Sweden. That collection Norwich did not retain, but, with its Victorian outbuildings, the Castle houses today the largest general collection in the provinces, and is supported by a separate Folk Museum at the merchant's house called Strangers Hall, a Craft Museum at the ancient Bridewell and an ecclesiastical one in St. Peter Hungate, the church used by the Pastons near by. Such is Norwich Castle, the building that sticks in the centre of Norwich like a knot in a piece of wood, and just cannot be moved, tunnelled or avoided. Above all, it gives the character to the street that runs half round it and once formed its ditch.

I do not need, then, to apologise for calling it a " demobilised " street, a soldier turned tradesman. Its long history is surprisingly like that of many a man of my age in Norwich today. It began as many of us began, in all innocence as a very ordinary street, just as we were very ordinary individuals, children of a long era of Peace, or, more exactly, of unawakened contentions that slept under an appearance of diplomatic good manners and industrial development. Just so Castle " Meadow " was the place near which some kind of Roman track ran from one settlement of that early civilisation to another. What the birds and creatures, and perhaps one or two primitive cultivators, thought when Uffa, or whoever it was, began some sort of rudimentary mound to block the Roman track we shall never know. He wanted to make sure it was never used as a means of attack upon the pirates who had retired from their ravaging conquest of the remote Roman province of the Iceni and founded what we call Norwich. These new people from overseas, who congregated around Tombland, used iron swords, and not flint hatchets. But the original inhabitants and their conquerors soon had to think hard enough when yet another set of pirates called Normans fell upon the prosperous place, pulled down several one-room houses (as we know they did, for the traces have been found at the edge of the mound) and built a regular fortress. What had been open country beside a neglected trackway, became part of this new state of things, the ditch of a castle. It must have struck them much as the war of 1914 struck us. The sillier probably thought they could avoid being dragged into a quarrel they little understood, just as the sillier of us, in 1914, thought that the Russians, the Prussians and all the rest of the comic continental people could get on without disturbing us with their war. There probably were, in 1066, some people who saw that something was coming, though they did not know what. Similarly, there were those of us, in 1914, who enlisted in the belief that the war would be " over by Christmas ", feeling rather virtuous that we made such a sacrifice to help it along. We certainly had not any idea that we should still be in a state of partial mobilisation in 1952, and perhaps it was just as well.

We survived. At least some of us did. It seemed improbable, very often, that we should, but we did, and we returned to what we fondly supposed was the state of things from which we had so gallantly torn ourselves in 1914. That is what we had enlisted for (apart from a good deal of rather vague sentiment in popular songs), that was what " Keep the home fires burning " meant. It took us several years to get used to the idea that we had blown or helped to blow a great hole in human history and that there was no getting back across it. Just such was the fate of Castle " Meadow ", as it had come to be called. It had survived that war very well, quite undamaged. It had survived too well. It had remained a narrow, tree-shaded lane, along which two lines of tramway rails had been forced in 1900, because there was no other means of laying them in such a place as Norwich. The old-horse-drawn transport had cursed but yielded. The horse fair that used to sprawl across the roadway learned to confine itself to the higher ground. There were fewer horses to sell. The old Bell Yard, in which the ditch once ended, was shorn through. But the street remained a country field by-way, trams or no, and for twenty years the congestion caused by the new motor traffic the war had let loose mounted and mounted, until buses replaced the trams. The street was more than doubled in width, and at the expense of several fine forest trees and thousands of tons of earth, the base of the mound was shorn away several yards, and an imposing modern street made to lead from Prince of Wales Road, hitherto the only thoroughfare capable of taking four lines of traffic, into what had once been the old cobbled rookery called the " Goose & Gridiron ", after an inn of that name. This network of little streets still interposes between the main road crossing on Tombland and the road from London, which enters the city by the magnificent elm avenue of Newmarket Road (for that is how Norwich thinks of it, having more interest in Newmarket than London). That was how Uffa (if it was he) had planned Norwich. That was how the Normans had wanted it to remain. And so in 1930 the now enormous expense of drastically altering that basic plan appalled and halted the citizens. There is still, in 1952, no means of driving from the improved and busy Castle Meadow to the London exit without encountering one-way streets, diversions and awful congestion that a wide ring road, designed to take heavy long-distance vehicles round and not through the city, does not entirely solve.

Such was the state of things when the Second World War fell upon us, and Castle Meadow, like the citizens who used it, became inured to black-out and austerity—wore, so to speak, a Civil Defence, Home Guard aspect. Hitler did his worst. He machine-gunned the endless stream of transport, and blew a great hole in the Goose & Gridiron, which we had taken to calling " Orford Place ". But as in everything else, Hitler was a failure. It takes more than machine-guns to alter

Norwich, and the hole was a hole, and not quite in the right place. Norwich people are like that. They will not be hustled for their own good, much less pay out good money to be " improved ".

So here we are, well typified by our -" Castle Meadow ". Shocked Town Planners and impatient Americans tell us that our lay-out is worse than that of Oxford or Cambridge, hoping that we may be persuaded. But it would be child's play to shift Nuffield's Works or Cambridge Station in comparison with the task of shifting Norwich Castle, and Cathedral, to do the job properly, and lay down a road that would incorporate Castle Meadow in a First-class Highway from London to Yarmouth, with links to Peterborough on one side, and the rail and port on the other.

Castle Meadow has grown old like any one of us. Elderly and obstinate, forcibly modernised (look at the half-dozen fine Georgian houses it still contains), we are by no means sure that an increase in the speed at which it might be possible to drive through Norwich would make up for the loss of character we should suffer if we made it possible. The Castle Mound is now planted with a great variety of spring flowers that make its ancient grassy sides a fragrant spectacle for weeks together. Next, the lilacs round the Shirehall come out in scented mauve and pearl. After them the turn comes of the roses which line the coping of the new wall above the sidewalk, so that sweet-smelling petals blow about the line of parked cars. The wide pavements and sometime Horse Fair give a rare point of vantage for witnessing Royal Progresses and Festivals of Britain. Modern shops, especially the great stores, are replacing the little old houses of the professional people who used to live here. And these features perpetuate the quality that is perhaps the proudest, and most legitimate boast of Norwich to be a City of Gardens. There are trees all the way, not only immediately overhead, but in the distant view, whichever way you engage in it.

Yet along its northern and western curve are still to be found the series of little passages by which alone what was once the exempt jurisdiction of the Royal Castle, a foreign country, a bit of Windsor or the Tower of London in the midst of Norwich, used to communicate with the City that surrounded

6. ST. ANDREW'S HALL—THE CHURCH OF THE DOMINICAN FRIARS

7. ST. MARTIN'S GATES BY GEORGE VINCENT

it. The first, as you come from Prince of Wales Road, ran through the garage of Barclays Bank, sensibly rebuilt to retain the George II features of the original building. Then, one that was called " Devil's Alley ", where sedan-chairs used to stand for hire, has been widened and re-named after Amelia Opie, the beautiful girl who married the Court painter and became so strict a Quakeress. Others can be seen, some incorporated in big business premises. One, miscalled Davey Steps, is the place where Parson Woodforde used to descend to his inn, the King's Head, the sign of which still hangs below. Another leads under a shop, and one more divides the last houses before you come to Orford Hill. It is as though one of us who have lived through so much consented to don a new suit, but insisted on keeping the waistcoat button-holes of another age.

I sometimes wonder if, in the roar and vibration of the mechanical movement that passes along it most days of the year, I can hear the hoarse, uncouth laughter of Uffa, or whoever it was who first made a mound to stop anyone from using the trackway the Romans made. He did his work well, and the semi-circle that Castle Meadow makes is probably the oldest memorial in Norwich to any of her former inhabitants, older than Castle or Cathedral. He may well laugh.

C

IV

THE NEW PROVISION MARKET THE NORMANS MADE, OR PROTECTED DOMESTICITY

GRIMACE and posture how we may, the original basic motives of our acts wear through, and become visible, like the grain in wood, the stitches in material, the baser metal behind the plating.

The Provision Market of Norwich is no exception. It has suffered many changes since it was an open and rather large, remote " croft " called " Magna " on the farther bank of a little stream (hence " Mancroft ", the parish). The Normans created a new market-place in it, for military reasons. It was the first deliberately planned item in the growth of their Norwich. Since their day it has become the civic centre, ousting the older one on Tombland. Round it assembled new inhabitants who spoke a kind of French. And today, in spite of the rolling centuries, and the introduction into it of the first municipal, or, as we should call them, " local government " buildings, neither ecclesiastical nor military, it still has a slightly foreign air. Travelled visitors compare it with the wide market-place of some continental town. The twentieth century has lined its western side with a great City Hall such as the medieval ages never dreamed of, unless it were the Cloth Hall of Ypres or the Rathaus of Bonn. It is the sort of rectangular central *Place* you find at Lausanne or Leipzig. Those ranks of open stalls, with a great church at one end and a " Guildhall " where you paid your " geld " at the other, are not quite English today. Certainly the Cattle Hill on the other side of the Castle is far more characteristic of Norfolk. Inherent characteristics never die out. Of all the parts of Norwich, this one plainly had a foreign education. It is a place not merely where things are bought and sold : it is a place where buying and selling are regulated. Arising from that it became the place from which the citizens' lives were regulated.

That was the foreign thing. It is always risky to theorise about racial stocks (think of Hitler), but I believe it will not be

seriously denied that all south-eastern England, and patches of
Scotland as far north at least as Aberdeen and the Orkneys and
Shetlands, are peopled by folk called " Saxons " and " Danes "
in history who derive their main characteristics from the
Friesian and Scandinavian sources from which they came.
Those who came from parts as far south as Holstein and Friesia
share those characteristics. The strongest one is a kind of rest-
lessness. I do not know how early it is now thought that they
reached Iceland, Greenland and perhaps America. The thing
they never seem to forget is that they are a water-borne people.
They have always at the back of their minds the notion that
they can get into a boat and go somewhere else. They have
never known the awful overcrowding that haunts the fate of
all central Europe, and they resent the strong central government that it demands.

That is why we first hear of them as the people who fought
the Romans. That is why they joined eagerly enough in the
almost immediate rebellion against the " new " Norman Conquerors, who were in fact little enough different from them as
far as race goes. It was not so much the Normans they fought,
as Government. I need not make a list of their various anti-
government outbreaks down the ages. It is enough to recall
that G. B. Shaw, a man of a different habit of mind, noticed
this characteristic and pointed out that his friend, Lord Pass-
field, for all his learning, would never understand it, because
he was, by blood, to some degree a Central European. The
strongest proof, however, of what I am trying to advance is that
in 1952 these are the only people whose daily habit is regulated
by an unarmed police force, as it never is in Dublin. They
won't have gendarmes at any price. The history of Norwich
Provision Market is, then, the history of the sustained attempt
to keep the citizens in order, and in the main it has been a
failure.

The Provision Market was put there so that it was dominated
by and supplied the garrison in the Castle. In about three
generations the citizens were asking for what would be called
today " Local Government ". They got it, and precious feeble
it was. Norwich is lucky in possessing the day-to-day records
of what the Provost, as the first civil governor—a kind of mayor
—elected by the arms-bearing males, had to contend with.

He was soon superseded by four " Bailiffs ", elected one for each of the four wards: Conisford, southward along the river; Mancroft, the western ward, which had already in the early twelve-hundreds ceased to speak French; Wymer, the crowded southern bank of the Wensum where it divides the City; and Over the Water, to the north. These four men met in a timber-and-mud or clay-lump " Tolbooth " on the site of the subsequent Guildhall, and must have cursed the day when they had been put in the irksome position by their fellow citizens. For the daily record is one of continuous endeavour to avoid being governed at all. The most frequent offence was " not being in tything ". These great-grandsons of pirates had always had their queer voluntary system of little police committees, by which every ten or twelve heads of families all watched each other, and which they seem to have brought with them in their boats. It is as though those cut-throat crews had always been divided among themselves into " watches ". When they decided to " go no more a-roving " and to settle down in their " North wyk ", they seem to have kept this system. It was the heads of these " tythings " who elected the Bailiffs in some rudimentary fashion, with probably no end of shouting and perhaps fisticuffs. Not that they meant to obey the Bailiffs they elected. They seem to have had an instinct that the Bailiffs would be easier to disobey than some Governor in the Castle, whose two or three score of professional soldiers would make no bones about slaughtering anyone who was a nuisance.

So from " Monday next after Ash Wednesday in the 16th year of the reign of King Edward " (the First—that is, 1287–9) anyone who wants to know can read how a place such as Norwich governed itself, or rather, made a pretence of doing so. The Bailiffs had no regular soldiers at their command and could only fine delinquents and put the less obstreperous in gaol, in the cells below the Tolbooth. The system of " tything " by which the citizens were bound together and distinguishable from " foreigners " (i.e. folk from some other " hundred ") was sketchy in the extreme. In fact a large number of the charges brought before the Bailiffs on that Monday morning, and the subsequent mornings, nearly seven hundred years ago, were precisely that various citizens had dodged the obligation of being " in tything ". It is quite understandable. If you had yourself properly " registered " (as we may call it, though there were probably few if any written documents or lists), you became responsible for collaring some rowdy neighbour and dragging him to justice. He might hit back or get you into trouble. Also, if you were a known member of a tything it was easier to tax you. Indeed, as one tries to picture it, the wonder is that the system actually worked for nearly two hundred years, until, about A.D. 1406, a new Charter made Norwich into a municipality not dissimilar in structure from that in which it is organised today. The Mayor and Council began to have a certain number of whole-time officials, and enough money, as the City became rich, to hire armed force if needed.

But in the early days a simple primitive voluntary system actually supplanted military occupation. This is the sort of thing that confronted the Bailiffs that Monday. I give the English translation of the dog-Latin in which the original is written, and abbreviate:

" The Capital Pledges " (headman of the tythings of the South Conisford sub-ward, twelve of them, with occupational surnames such as " Boatman " or place names like " de Southgate ") " present on their oath that Ernald de Castro wounded Hugh de Bromholm and drew blood contrary to the peace." " Nicholas le Jay wounded a certain clerk, a stranger." And so on. Half a dozen crimes of violence. Fingers were cut off and citizens beaten. A rough house! Can one picture it? The grey, chilly spring day, the muddy track between one-room wooden shacks, with holes in the thatch for chimneys and shutters over the window-openings. Shouts and running, and the ringing of the bell in the wooden steeple of St. Peter de Southgate. Clatter and cries and a splash of blood in the gutter which was also the sewer. The constable of the ward was wounded " and the hue was raised, the said Nicholas was taken and imprisoned, and Ernald escaped ". Further, treasure trove was concealed, while the " hue and cry " was being raised without proper cause. What a tale-telling there must have been among the gossips!

There was a black market in corn and in beer " by which the Bailiffs lost their custom or Toll ". The chest of the late John,

Dean of Norwich (whom we should call Rural Dean), was broken into and gold and silver, £40 or more, carried off. There were larcenies and nuisances. Roger of Morley, " obstupavit viam regalem ", blocked up the King's highway with a muck-heap, and the Cellarer did not mend his shutters, so that it seems they flapped in the faces of passers-by. Imagine going down such a lane as Conisford must have been in the dark and being hit in the eye by a swinging shutter! Then there were miscreants who mixed bad whelks with fresh ones, for sale, and others who sold " measley pork ", " porcinas superseminatas ". The fines ranged from sixpence up to half a mark, but could not always be collected (" debet "), or were forgiven (" condonatur "). More serious was the fact that the " Borough " contained all kinds of " exempt jurisdictions " as it were, bits of foreign countries, including the liberty of the Castle, which was the King's, all ecclesiastical and conventual enclosures and the Jewry, into none of which the Bailiffs could penetrate, and in which their writ did not run. Thus one ruffian who had committed a theft, cut the leather thong of the church bell to stop the hue and cry, and escaped into the Castle ward; another thief took goods and hid them in the Jewry. But the Bailiffs struggled on, and it is a fascinating thought, that when the magistrates take their seats on the Bench, any day of this year of grace (1952), they do so on the same spot, though in a later building, as their forerunners in the thirteenth century. And their record is continuous with that I have quoted, although nowadays it is mainly concerned with traffic offences and contraventions of the endless regulations we now accept, but with the ancient bad grace.

That is how Norwich was governed by its elected Bailiffs, from the Tolbooth in the Provision Market. The story does not end there. Not only the citizens' private lives, but their trades were regulated to an extent that the twentieth century would find irksome. The rows of wooden " selds " or stalls, rather more substantial than the ones we see replacing them today, for they were permanent and some of them had two storeys, were ranged according to trades. If you were a goldsmith or " lorimer ", your shop was situated on the lower part of the Guildhall Hill, and so forth.

When the Bailiffs looked out from their Tolbooth southwards across the market-place, they saw orderly rows of stalls, running north and south.   Those on the upper or western edge were selling bread, barley and grain, even mustard, on the ground covered by the steps of the present City Hall.   Nearer St. Peter's Church were drapers, who also occupied part of what is now the churchyard, until the Black Death of 1348 made graves more important than shops.   Adjoining these, northward, were the needlers and soapmakers.   The centre of the market contained butchers and poulterers who seem to have been superseded, perhaps naturally, by dealers in hides, tanners and the white-tawers, or those who dressed skin with alum instead of bark.   Spicers were connected with herbs and unguents.   The footgear and clothing trades held the eastern edge, with saddlers and spurriers in what is now White Lion Street.   In the midst of all were the market cross and a water conduit.   Beyond the east end of St. Peter's Church the specific commodities seem to have changed more frequently. Nets and timber, beasts and honey congregated here, but seem to have acquired markets of their own as these trades grew in importance.   Like everything else in the ages of Faith, about which we know so little, there was an under current of constant change beneath the superficial regimentation.   The purpose of the close organisation of the market seems to have been taxation.   It was, at least at first, an offence to form a Guild or association.   It seems to have been felt that such a body might try to manipulate prices.

Such was the picture before the Bailiffs, and one must respect the valiant efforts they seem to have made to keep order, collect taxes and pay their dues to the King, and run the city government they had thus purchased.   They had little enough scope. They kept their precious documents, charters and such, with the White Friars or Carmelites, away in the north ward; it seems that these holy men had safer coffers than anything existing at the Tolbooth.   The very meetings at which the Bailiffs were elected were held at the other end of the town, in the great hall of the College of St. Mary, where the Assembly House stands today.   The Bailiffs had no place of their own half so commodious.   Finally, about A.D. 1400 the whole system broke up.   The citizens, growing richer and more independent, forgot that they had ever been governed by the soldiers in the Castle. They clamoured for a proper constitution like London and other great places.

Under the Charter of Henry IV they got it. Royal power was declining, that of the Church sub-divided by every class and kind of Friar and endless varieties of special establishments set up by the wealthy and devout. The citizens emerged (and this was a hundred years before the Reformation brings the Middle Ages to their formal close) with a sort of little parliament of their own. Sixty common councillors were elected for the smaller sub-divisions or little wards, and sat under a " Speaker "; the Aldermen, a sort of upper house, sat separately, under the Mayor. It was at this time that they built themselves the present Guildhall, with its Council Chamber, its Magistrates' Court, its cells dug deep into the soil below, its little Chapel dedicated to St. Barbara and its armoury in the roof.

Although some of it was badly built, and fell down, although much of the new dispensation the Charter granted was spoiled by the most shocking political corruption, beside which Tammany Hall seems innocent and harmless, the municipal structure then set up lasted until 1835, when its flagrant condition caused it to become the object of the salutary Municipal Reform Act. The building remained the seat of local administration until 1938, when the new City Hall was opened by King George VI and his Queen. The Petty Sessional Court is still held in it every day, and Her Majesty's Justices still begin the Assize with formal pomp there, though they immediately adjourn to more adequate premises. The lovely old Council Chamber with its carved screens and stained-glass windows, its portraits of bygone worthies and its air, laden with the dust of five centuries of half-forgotten disputes, is now used only for the meetings of charitable and learned societies.

So there it stands, the Guildhall of Norwich, in the Provision Market in which for all these centuries Norwich has done its shopping, ever since it became a County Borough with a municipality, and ceased to be a village of retired pirates round Tombland. The Guildhall is the most human of all the larger stone buildings of Norwich, and it is the one of which one says perhaps most readily " If these stones could speak ". One may say that equally of the Castle or the Cathedral, but both of them stand a little above or apart, in their own separate enclosures. The Guildhall stands knee deep, as it were, in the daily life of Norwich. Itself the harbinger of change, the new thing in the life of the place, it seems now, in its old age, as its faculties desert it, to have changed less than the others. The Cathedral has been built on to and embellished century after century; indeed, its eastern chapel has been added since 1920. It has been refurbished and beautified since 1930. The Castle has come to be something quite unimaginable by its builders. It would be interesting to tell Dame De Guader that the spot she defended so stoutly has become a Museum. But the Guildhall does today what it was built to do and has always done. Around it everything else has changed. The great church of St. Peter Mancroft is encased in the architectural improvements of the eighteen-sixties, as though your grand-mother had suddenly put her hair in curl-papers or assumed a crinoline. The very stalls in the market place run differently. Yet, under the shadow of the immense new City Hall the Guildhall remains, so little changed; a clock and cupola are the chief additions.

Perhaps one can see best what has happened if one visits the Lord Mayor of Norwich in his beautiful new parlour in the City Hall. There he sits in his handsome robes, very much the same in colour and cut as any time these five hundred years. He may be our friend Mr. Jones the grocer, or, more probably today, the executive of some great manufacturing or transport combine, or a Trades Union official. He may be wearing a pullover underneath all that finery, but there it is, the robe of office of the Chief Citizen, neither an ecclesiastic nor a soldier, though he may have been either in private life. He is sur-rounded by typewriters and telephones. But he is to be seen receiving royalty or Lord Justices, proclaiming a new Monarch or making a declaration of Peace or opening a Festival, admitting a new Freeman, or attending the funeral of a notable. As what? As the elected representative of a body of people, living together in a County Borough and governing themselves.

It has not been so simple as it sounds. It is only during these last hundred and fifteen years that the Mayor of a Borough could feel that he had been elected without " undue influence ". The standing joke about Norwich, perhaps rather more than about most places, is that which records that a schoolboy, asked what Norwich was noted for, replied: " Bribery and corruption, Sir! "

Norwich has survived. Indeed, it had a proud moment during the Second World War when there were more men of American birth in its streets than natives. When one tried to explain to them something of the municipal structure, one might be met at the end by the puzzled query: " What's the Lord Mayor of Norwich got to give the boys? "

The answer today is, absolutely nothing. I am not certain if it was always believed. But it is true. The Lord Mayor can, at most, invite the citizens to a party, and very likely a tea-party at that. But the guests will not be his supporters, or those whose favour he desires. They will be a representative selection of the citizens who have elected him. Nay, the fact is they have arranged his election without threat, and without reward. It is well known that the political parties have agreed, these many years, to arrange that the Lord Mayor is chosen from one or other of the principal political parties alternately, and that the Sheriff who officiates with him is similarly chosen from the opposite party. The annual election is therefore a formal matter agreed and arranged beforehand, so that the principal offices in the City are held with no monopoly of influence by any one political party, in a balance of power.

It is a peculiarly English arrangement. I have sometimes said that it goes back to the very core of our being, to the time when our ancestors, voyaging in open boats, realised more than any other people in the world the awful equality of all being seasick together. Today, amid the tempests of political controversy, there is no dispute as to the regular order in which, as it were, watch succeeds watch, and efficient and acceptable government of Norwich is maintained.

V

ST. ANDREW'S AND THOSE WHO TAKE
THE VEIL

AMONG all the large family of Norwich streets, none strikes the visitor so strongly as those which seem to be overshadowed by another age. True, in most great English cities there are plenty of ecclesiastical buildings. London is full of old parish churches, though few of them are as old as the thirty-five parish churches of Norwich that survive out of the sixty it once held. Every village has some (usually old grey) place at which the inhabitants get themselves christened, married and buried and kept in touch with something other than mere getting and spending, one hopes. Many cities are dominated by some great Cathedral like Norwich, London (St. Paul's) or Westminster (the Abbey). York, Lincoln and Ely Cathedrals stand up against the skyline.

In Norwich, however, besides the Cathedral, there remain more than enough ancient sacred buildings. Learned authorities now count seven major monasteries within the fourteenth-century walls, as well as twenty lesser ones. Now, in any family the members who want to be supported while they lead what they feel to be a dedicated life are necessarily limited. That is what struck the general consciousness of Norwich about the end of the fifteenth century, if indeed it is not one of the major reasons for the Reformation. We have seen how the great Benedictine Monastery elbowed its way deliberately into Tombland. We shall see how a very different establishment, the Great Hospital, or what we should call Public Assistance for the Aged, grew up in the meadows between the Close and the river. That was not enough, not nearly enough. As time went on various bodies sprang up to carry the great burden of what we now call Welfare Work, which they felt to be a Christian duty and which, so they alleged, was not being done by the all-too-powerful Benedictine establishment and its " Hospital " in the meadows nearby. These new-comers are best known as the Black, Grey and White

Friars, or by their formal titles of Dominican, Franciscan and Carmelite. They all began with professions of poverty and austerity. They all became, in a few generations, immensely wealthy and powerful corporations. There were also the Augustinian Friars, who held very valuable river-side rights, Staithes or Quays at which toll could be levied in King Street. Against the western wall of the City was established the privately endowed College of St. Mary, with a Chantry attached, which owned a great tract of land, now a public park. And moreover, these were all "foreigners". The citizens and their Bailiffs had no jurisdiction within these high walls. Some portion at least of the wealth of all these establishments drained away every year to wherever their headquarters were. No wonder that there was no great popular movement to support them when they were, doubtless wrongly and avariciously, attacked.

Now, this is all very well, and may be dismissed as past history, best forgotten. Only it is difficult to forget it in Norwich. What happens to anyone who wants to attend, say, a concert, flower show, major exhibition or congress in that City? He (or she) is told: "It takes place in St. Andrew's Hall", and off they go to find this hall.

From Tombland, the western road leaves that tree-shaded, busy square, and passes between offices and shops, a great factory, and the church of St. Peter Hungate, largely built by the Paston family, a "redundant" church from which the resident population has receded and now an ecclesiastical museum. Opposite it is an important Congregational Chapel, then more shops and offices, and finally a wide-open space or "plain", as they call it in Norwich, running along the south wall of what is obviously a church building, not quite so big as the Cathedral, but comparable in size, though later in style. This is "St. Andrew's Hall" evidently, for its porch is full of large notice-boards, advertising every kind of public engagement, from revivalist assemblies, the celebrated Norwich Triennial Musical Festival, Chrysanthemum Show, or a political rally. Inside, what? A splendid nave with an immense west window, delicate shafting to support the roof, and its eastern arch, where one would expect to pass under a tower into a chancel, blocked by orchestra-seating reaching up

to a fine organ. If one penetrates under this one finds the
chancel, thus screened off, but equally fine in its dimensions
and style of the last phase, the perpendicular, of the church-
building of the Middle Ages. It is called " Blackfriars Hall ",
and the whole erection is, in fact, the great church of the Black
Friars, long secularised and adapted to the uses of the citizens.
This accounts for the double range of more than life-sized
portraits of bygone mayors and members of Parliament on its
walls. It is, in fact, Norwich's chief public hall, and few
cities indeed can have so fine a one. " St. Andrew's Hall " is
the great preaching nave in which the Brethren of St. Dominic
undertook to instruct the public. It will seat twelve hundred
people. " Blackfriars " is their presbytery, and is just that
much shorter, and without aisles. The cloister was in this case
north of the church, and parts of it are still visible. The
conventual buildings reached northward to the river and eastward to what is now called Elm Hill. Such was the result of
mendicancy. One has only to stand in that huge nave and
stare at its range of great windows, and its sheer cubic grandeur,
to feel how strong and contradictory are the currents which
govern the course of our human existence. This magnificence,
far more splendid than any hall the ducal and lordly aristocrats of Norwich and Norfolk possessed, is the result of austerity,
humility, sanctity. If not quite so big as the Cathedral, it is
far more sophisticated. There is none of the clumsy Norman
childishness about these pillars. They were designed, so the
latest expert opinion thinks, to give the utmost view of the
preacher. They were also economical. And how much more
the designers and builders of this church knew than those who
planned the dark and heavy Cathedral nave! Men had
learned to distribute weight, and to know what a stone wall
could stand in the way of wide openings to let in the light. Is
there something symbolical about the perpendicular style?
The light was let in. It is the last style of the Ages of Faith.
After that, men began to think. St. Andrew's Hall and its
adjoining Blackfriars Hall might be dismissed as interesting
because they are almost the only buildings of their kind in
Norwich which have survived. But once they did not stand
alone. Right across busy Prince of Wales Road where the
traffic lights alternate in front of the modern General Post

Office, there stood the equally enormous Franciscan church, 300 feet long and 80 feet broad, with its appropriate buildings, of which no trace remains, unless you count the fact that a by-street is called " Greyfriars ". And away in North Norwich, over the water, was the convent of the Carmelites, which has left some old walls, and its name to Whitefriars Bridge and Priory Yard.

We have already seen how the Augustine Canons had settled between King Street and the river, and how the College of St. Mary stood where the Assembly House stands today, and gave it its plan. But these were only the major religious establishments that had nothing to do with the parish churches. The numerous almshouses, the thirty-eight or so of little hermitages and anchorages tacked on to church walls, or tucked in beside city gates or larger monastic buildings, all provided a living for someone, who said prayers, sold pardons or benefits of one sort or another, or performed some desired service. Anyone whose hobby it is, can spend a delightful week in Norwich tracking down small sections of remaining flint walling, a pointed arch here, a piece of pavement there built into something else, sometimes commemorated by a tablet or by the name of the street or yard. One hopes that some of them did some good. It is clear from the long story of contention between them, the constant suppression of the smaller ones by the larger, the endless quarrels with the citizens about the rights they claimed of taxation, in one form or another, and the property they held, that they presented a major problem to the world of their day. Those that survived until the Reformation became, we know, the object of total and systematic suppression. The enormous mass of power and wealth they represented was violently re-distributed. Some of it founded our educational system. Some was captured and used by men no more scrupulous than those who had held high positions in the hierarchy of religious organisation of the Middle Ages. Wolsey is the best-known example of a churchman who made a career and a fortune. Others, doubtless, were almost saints and nearly martyrs.

But anyone who wants to know, can find in Norwich a good example of one of these ancient institutions which, either because it was effective, or because it was flexible, or by mere unaccountable happening that we call chance, survived the great upheaval and does in A.D. 1952 very much what it did in A.D. 1250; the clothes of its inmates, the style of its more recent buildings, the functions of its officers alone have changed. It is now called the " Great Hospital ", and stands, with the church of St. Helen, which it incorporates, lining the north side of Bishopgate, from the postern of the Close, for nearly half its length leading towards Bishop's Bridge.

Its long and curious history may be summarised. Anyone who goes to look at it will think for the moment that it is but another of the pre-Reformation churches of Norwich. And so it is, among other things. " A second glance," says the admirable modern history of it, " will reveal that chimneys rise from the ridge of the church and that liberties have been taken with some of its windows." Precisely! It may be that it was this very fact that has helped to preserve it. It was no aloof great power in the world of the thirteenth century. It was a church which opened its door to the victims of the unspeakable social conditions of those days. The " poor and decrepit ", the " infirm or ill ", were not merely welcomed: they were put to bed, between sheets, allowed a fire " to refresh themselves "—a rare addition to the spartan and rather naïve charity of the times. Something else about it lends it the particular character that will soon strike the discerning. It was founded by the Bishop himself, Walter de Suffield, no " Norman " stranger, but " a Norfolk man and typical of the medieval Lord Bishop at his best ", says the history. It was no offhand discarding of what so rich a man could well afford. "Whenever Walter de Suffield passed down Holme Street (Bishopgate) he would go in and give his blessing to the sick." At his death he left it money and land, silk bed coverlets, a Bible and a pipe of his best wine, a gilt cup and another cup " out of which the poor children drink ".

There seems to me to be something desperately appealing about the personal nature of this establishment. It was enlightened. It was self-supporting and independent. But I think its founder's frequent presence, and the use, after he had gone, of his very bed furniture, probably conveyed something to the half-witted, starving, maimed or bereaved wrecks of humanity who collapsed into its capacious accommodation, something far beyond mere health and respite. Here was a great Prince of the Church who cared for them as it is very unlikely they had ever been cared for before.

Of course, it was still an institution of the Middle Ages, if an unusual one. Its revenues were, in part, derived from the sale of Indulgences and such traffic. The eight chaplains which its increasing wealth enabled it to maintain were engaged in singing Masses for the souls of its benefactors. One of them left yet more property " to minister to the necessities of the poor priests who cannot celebrate divine services, being broken down with age, destitute of strength, and labouring under continual disease, flocking to the said Hospital for sustenance and hospitality ". But the fact remains that the care for all these was taken in the church building itself. It was not merely a place where things were said and sung. It was a place in which they were done. Later came the turn of that great fire-eating Bishop Despencer who summarily suppressed the labourers' revolt in A.D. 1318, and built the choir of the church, now the women's ward with its wonderful chestnut roof, upon 252 panels of which are painted an Imperial Eagle. This is thought to have been in honour of Anne of Bohemia, Queen of Richard II, when she came to visit the Hospital riding side-saddle, the first Queen, probably the first woman to do so.

So the place increased and prospered. It seems to have been able to avoid the local anti-clerical disturbances, as well as it did the dynastic disputes of the Kingdom. The depopulation of the country by the Black Death and the subsequent social revolution left it untouched. Presently the " infirmary hall ", to the west of the nave, was rebuilt, and the great square bell-tower at the end of its south aisle. Northward of this a Refectory, with the beginnings of separate accommodation for the Master, were added. This gave a chance that no medieval church-builder could resist, and into the angle thus formed was fitted a most charming little cloister, still intact. Then a chantry chapel was added to the south, with lovely lierne vaulting showing on the bosses or its intersection, carved and coloured renderings of the Coronation of the Virgin, the Nativity and cognate subjects. And so it has remained, down the ages, with additions, but little alteration. What one finds today, then, in the long, rambling building, with a stout tower

attached to its south-west corner, is three separate compart-
ments.   At the east is a normal church chancel which has been
turned, by being walled off from the rest of the church, into a
women's infirmary, now of two floors, with comfortable little
wooden snuggeries round the fire-places, and separate wooden
partitions of later date between the beds.   At the west end,
next to the tower, is a very similar arrangement for the men,
also walled off.   Between the two is the thus truncated portion
of the nave, rendered into a square church of three bays, with
the chantry chapel and south porch making the shape even
more peculiar, but, as it were, unintentionally admirable.   It
strikes one as unusually lofty in comparison with its width, as it
is, indeed.   But was that deliberate?   The effect is that the
worshippers in the pews sit facing the wall which fills the
chancel arch.   On this blank space is a large modern cartoon
depicting the history of the Hospital down the ages, in colours,
containing many portraits of well-known Norwich worthies who
have been Trustees, some within living memory.   Below it is
the pulpit.   The altar is in the chantry chapel, so that when the
congregation require to look at it, they have to turn half right.
I don't know if any devout Anglican feels that this matters.
The pews in the main body of the church retain their finely
carved poppy-heads.   In the chantry chapel is an elaborate
" strawberry-hill " Gothic pew erected apparently for the use
of the family of Ivory, the great Norwich " contractors ", as
we should call them, who added many splendid buildings to
Norwich in the reign of George II.

The ensemble, then, is unique, I fancy.   I doubt if there are
many thirteenth-century hospitals or hospices left anywhere,
and this church is an oddity even for such an unusual institution.   Is it any the worse for that?   The south porch contains
portions of the previous church, and in the wall near it, a
beautiful little squint with fine tracery, presumably to allow the
bellringer to see the elevation of the host and signalise it for the
benefit of those who could not attend the service.   But I doubt
if anyone is quite sure about this.

This composite building, with its odd-shaped church sandwiched in between its two main ward systems, its porch
enabling the public to enter from Bishopgate, its little cloister,
and portions of Master's house and offices, all remains much as

D

it was at the fateful day of the Reformation, except that I suspect it is better kept. For it is spotless. One could eat one's dinner off its floor or pews without a qualm.

The staff of the pre-Reformation hospital seems to have consisted of a " Master, eight chaplains, two clerks, seven poor scholars for choristers, eight poor bedridden people, thirteen poor people who daily dined and refreshed themselves at the fire, besides such poor strangers as pass by and have a free nights lodging "—at least as many as the beds would hold— " and as many poor chaplains of the diocese overworn by age or infirmity as the revenues would bear; also two sisters to wait on the poor ". Thus says the erudite modern history. We may picture, then, a complete, self-supporting welfare organisa- tion. It had its own pasture and vegetable garden, stretching away into the elbow of the river. It also had property else- where. It had its own swan-pit, indeed it has it still, and even sent one of its chaplains to minister to the wretched prisoners incarcerated in the cells of the Guildhall. It was, in fact, as near perfection as the Middle Ages could go, and the only criticism one can make is that it and all the then numerous little communities scattered about were based on promiscuous charitable instincts, and often created as a salve to the con- science of people who knew that their record was such that they were in grave doubt as to their fate hereafter. Such com- munities could not deal with the problem of disease and poverty, worklessness and glaring inequality on any broad national basis. If one managed, in dire need, to reach its door, one was cared for, as well as the master and his aides knew how. If one didn't, or if the beds were already full, and the dinner eaten, and the fire surrounded by those " refreshing themselves "— well, it was bad luck. Then along came Henry VIII, and we need not go into all the details of the total upset he made. He seized nearly all the revenues and property. His motive seems to have been no better than to placate the feelings of Norwich by making the Hospital what we should call a public poor law institution instead of a private one. That sums up the result that was visible when the smoke and dust cleared away, the bargaining bishops and recanting or renouncing politicians had shuffled through their performances. Part of the Hospital property went to endow the Grammar School of King Edward

VI. The establishment retained its general shape and became a public institution for the relief of the poor. Finally it was approved by Queen Elizabeth, after a somewhat flowery oration by the master, in Latin. Hence the inscription still to be seen on the tablet above the modern (1754) facing of the south porch in Bishopgate:

> King Henry the Eighth, of noble Fame,
> Bequeathed this City, this Commodious Place,
> With Lands and Rents he did endow the Same,
> To help decreped Age in Woful Case.
> Edward the Sixth, that Prince of Royal Stem,
> Perform'd his Fathers generous Bequest,
> Good Queen Elizabeth imitating them,
> Ample Endowments added to the Rest.
> Their pious Deeds we gratefully record,
> While Heaven them Crowns with glorious Reward.

My father, when pointing this out to visitors, used to say: " It's all lies; he only wanted to make himself big! " But do not let that slightly ungracious veracity detract from the nett eventual result. The Hospital remains today, improved out of all knowledge, but retaining its fine buildings and kindly intention. It is a wonder, for it has run the risk of every difficulty and disaster. Revolution and Civil War have surged around it. The strange theological quarrels of the seventeenth century have endangered its personnel. Charles I tried to capture its revenues. Its long succession of devoted masters had to deal with contumacious and riotous inmates. Some were fined, some dismissed. Those who were found " drinkinge at the howse of Susan Powle in St. Martin's at Pallace " were sent to the stocks, when they could not pay their fines. As the eighteenth century wore on, there was trouble, too, among the Trustees, mainly Aldermen, who formed the body deputed by the City Council to administer the Hospital. It became habitual to use the right of nomination to the Hospital as a means of securing votes. The Municipal Reform Act of 1835 did something to remove this scandal, and the subsequent minutes show the changes in diet and habit of a changing world.

Just before this the Hospital achieved what is one of its chief triumphs in organisation. " In 1826 twenty cottages were added so that old couples could live together under the care of the Hospital." These were to the north and east of the old main church building, and overcame the greatest and perpetual grievance against nearly all forms of " Poor Relief " : the cruel and unnatural, if hygienically necessary separation of old couples too infirm to look after themselves, to the men's and women's wards. The plan was extended to embrace a further quadrangle in the nineteenth century, and a thoroughly modern one, much better planned, in the twentieth. A fine new Hall was added, in memory of Henry Birkbeck, the Banker, for over twenty years chairman of the Board of Management.

There are few pleasanter places today than the lovely, well-kept gardens of the quadrangle, between the old church and the trees by the river, with the background of the spire of the Cathedral to the west and the picturesque cliff of Mousehold to the east.

This " religious ", therefore, among the streets of Norwich, is not a mere ghost of some former self, nor even a convert to secular uses, as St. Andrew's Hall may be said to be.

The Great Hospital in the meadow by the river makes a fine open centre to the City, whose busy traffic flows all round it, but never through it. The outward lineaments of the Middle Ages barely conceal the most enlightened care for old age. There can be no more charming figure than that of religious dedication standing to guard the elderly from the last inevitable human tragedy, the passing of the years.

Such is the member of the Norwich family who " took the veil ".

VI

KING STREET, THE WATERFRONT, OR HE
WOULD BE A SAILOR

THERE is no doubt as to which of the Norwich streets is most connected with the sea. In King Street you find the signs of the Ship and the Old Barge, the Ferry Inn and the Keel and Wherry. One of its by-streets, descending the steep slope to the west of it, is Mariners' Lane. Here is Waterman Yard and Swan Yard. For half its length, the long, straight street, leading due south from the old market-place on Tombland, into South Norfolk, runs parallel with the River Wensun. Here, at the continuous line of " staithes ", as they call a quay or landing-place in Norfolk, are tied up the craft, mainly registered in London or north-west Europe, that bring to Norwich all varieties of bulky, non-perishable goods. Mills and breweries, engineering and constructional works line the banks, which, like so many things in Norwich, have never become entirely sacrificed to ruthless commerce. A fine row of poplars decorates the eastern shore until, just beyond the great modern bridge that he who is now Duke of Windsor opened in 1923, there still stand the twin towers of flint that show how far the City wall came down, and dominated the stream.

I have no doubt in my own mind, although the matter is past all proof, for it happened in the Dark Ages, that this is where the pirates whom we call the Saxons landed after their adventurous voyage in their open boats. They did not come to attack Norwich, for it did not exist. They came, as I have told, to attack the Romano-British town of Venta Icenorum. To reach it they came up the Yare from Yar-mouth, and turned off from the Wensum up the smaller stream, which is still called Yare. (It is named, from the mouth up, by men who had no use for roads.) Venta Icenorum stood on its tiny tributary, the Tas. It was only after years of battering at that place, sometimes successfully, often not (for it withstood them, or got itself rebuilt in spite of them, for two hundred years, so archæologists say), that they settled where Norwich now stands, as I have related.

What can it have been like for those two centuries or so, seven generations perhaps, during which open boats, manned and generally rowed by people who could find no foothold—or was there not enough plunder in Europe, so that they took to the expedient of rowing, sailing perhaps, if they could, in fine weather, across the North Sea? Was it because they were themselves being driven out of the Elbe valley by stronger or fiercer people? Was Venta Icenorum, and were the other East Coast Roman colonial towns like it, so rich that they were a legend that could induce men to risk the voyage? Go and look at the North Sea in any month except July and August, and on many days even in those, and see if you can imagine it. From Calais and Boulogne, with the white cliffs in view, one can understand a bold heart daring the voyage. But the Saxons came, we are told, from Holstein or Friesia. They had to make a voyage that today takes a fine great turbine-driven ship six hours to make, and it can be rough. Either the threat behind them was very fierce, or the glamour of Roman civilisation was very attractive. But the continuity of it! Venta Icenorum was burned at least twice. The Roman walls you see today were built to protect it late in its history, and did it well; for historians think that these " Saxons " began to come round about A.D. 200 but did not settle—that is, abandon their boats and build themselves houses—without thought of going back whence they had come, until about A.D. 450. It took them as long as it has taken to make modern Canada and longer than to make New Zealand. They must have been wiped out over and over again. If they were moderately successful in plundering or partially plundering Venta Icenorum, they had then to take their booty back. How many ever managed it? Who made the process so long and hard? Was there some now-forgotten East Anglian King Arthur, who, remembering or having a tradition of what Roman armies had been, knew how to organise resistance, and quite late in the story, to build the massive walls, Roman fashion, with cement and rows of tiles for bonding, that we see today if we go to look at the village now called " Caistor ", but which actually contains the last traces of Venta Icenorum?

In the long run, the very long run, these Saxon pirates won. The Romano-British town was burnt out and destroyed. The obstinacy displayed on both sides makes it no wonder that the remote descendants of the mixed peoples, the East Coast fishermen of today, will go mine-sweeping for years at a stretch.

So there was no more plunder to be had and no one, presumably, to fight, and the great-great-grandsons of those who had first sailed up the Yare for rapine and murder, settled down. But not on the site of the town they had destroyed. Was it because of the blood on their hands, or because they wanted deeper water for their ships, or to be near the ford? Well, they settled where Norwich is today, and they must have landed at what we call King Street. That is a new name for it. Less than two hundred years ago it was called Conisford. What does that mean? " King's Ford." The latest information on the subject puts the ford at Trowse, where the smaller Yare is joined by the larger Wensum. It was not until the late eighteenth century that the name of " King Street " was adopted, and it may be that, until about that date, streets were known only by hearsay and bore no lettered directions. I have never discovered if " King Street " was considered to be a modernisation of " King's Ford ", or if it was adopted at the same time that what had been hitherto known as Redwell Street and Hungate became " Queen Street " and " Princes Street " respectively, out of a new feeling for the Royal Family. Anyhow, the name of Conisford has stuck to the ward for municipal elections, and anyone who looks down the length of King Street today will feel that there is something about it inseparable from the river and, eventually, the sea.

From the earliest times, the transport trade was valuable, and some of the first of the many quarrels the citizens had with various ecclesiastical bodies, which claimed the right to tax goods landed from craft, concerned the " staithes " of King Street where the Augustine Friars settled and the Abbot of St. Benets at Holme had, so he said, inherited or received certain properties.

There was an additional reason for the importance of King Street in the early life of Norwich. Its northern end abutted on Tombland, the market, and round the portion of it now running beside the G.P.O. and across Rose Lane was the first industrial district Norwich ever had, before, perhaps, North Wyk had developed north of Tombland and given its name to the whole settlement. The reason was that, as soon as the early inhabitants got beyond mere subsistence agriculture, the activities which could be called trades were nearly all concerned with wearing apparel. Food was produced from day to day. Building materials were wanted, but the most continuous making and selling, here or elsewhere, dealt with the wool and hides in which folk clothed and shod themselves and harnessed their mounts and pack-animals. Now, tanners and bleachers and fullers of some primitive sort need quantities of water, and seem to have found it in the small streams or " cockeys " which flowed, naturally enough, from the higher ground of the Ber Street ridge leading to the Castle. That is why the first church you find as you pass southwards along King Street is called St. Peter's Parmentergate. The parmenters were leather-dressers, if not " parchment "-makers. This, and the shipping facilities, made King Street an important thoroughfare, which contained many town houses of the landed aristocracy and continued to do so until the late eighteenth century. The façades of some can still be seen, though now broken up into offices and miscellaneous trade. One of the most remarkable is that now incorporated in one of the local breweries, which gained in Elizabethan times the name of the " Musick House " because it was used by the celebrated " Waits " of Norwich, the first orchestra or organised body of performers on instruments Norwich can have known. They were so good that the commanders of the great expedition against Cadiz took the Norwich Waits with them as their official band.

The vaults of the old place are far older, and indeed the earliest documents describe it as the dwelling of Isaac the Jew. It was in fact one of those semi-fortresses which the first people who dealt in coin and bullion built for the safety of their stock-in-trade. One would not be misusing the word much if one called it a very primitive " bank ". The sequel is well known. Edward I, at the insistence, it is to be feared, of the Church, indulged in the first great burst of anti-Semitism. Not that the worst of that ugly story is to be told in Norwich. The Ghetto, proper, adjoined the new Provision Market of the Normans, and there is some doubt if the horrible massacres that stain the records of so many English cities ever took place in Norwich.

The late Lord Mancroft had a theory that Norwich Jews were protected by the Prior of the Cathedral Monastery, because they were oculists and knew how to grind a lens. However that may be, there can be little doubt as to Isaac's strongly built house in King Street. It represents the very first beginnings of the financing of the overseas trade. As we know from the *Merchant of Venice*, voyages were long and uncertain, and the venture will often have been supported by the wealth of similar, if less romantic and vengeful characters than Shylock, placed at borrowers' disposal. Two sequels hang on the story of the old building. One is that when, in the twentieth century, archæologists began to busy themselves with the long and loaded history of Norwich, someone, poking about in the brewery premises, discovered the ancient vaulting under layers of plaster and aided materially in building up the long-forgotten story of the place. He (some humble employee) was rewarded, possibly with half a crown, or some such benevolence. Upon which, other members of the brewery staff procured rods and began poking about in little-known corners of the premises until, one fine morning, the then resident manager was astonished to see a length of steel suddenly emerge from the walls of one of his cupboards. It is recorded that, subsequently, archæological research was discouraged.

The other concerns that remarkable genius Nugent Monck, now known, the world over, as the creator of the Maddermarket Theatre. Before he moved into that building he gave the first performances of his " Norwich Players ", part Amateur Dramatic Society, part School of Drama, part Secret Society, here. It all sounds easy now that amateur dramatics have become fashionable. But they were not so in 1920, and it should be remembered that imposing programmes, including Gilbert Murray's translation of the *Hippolytus* of Euripides, Japanese " Noh " Plays, medieval Mysteries and a wide selection of Shakespeare, were played in the fine loft of the Musick House. There was barely room for a hundred and twenty seats, the stage was so constructed that the basket in which Falstaff had to be ensconced was brought in through the audience. The Norwich Players could not have gone on there, but the atmosphere of that medieval attic was ideal for the beginnings of such a venture.

Of course, no street such as King Street was could be complete without its quota of churches and monastic institutions. Where modern Prince of Wales Road cuts it was the great and flourishing community of the Franciscans, or Grey Friars, after whom a by-street is named. The fine stone wall just before the Musick House bears an inscription which tells that it was that of the Augustinian Friars whose property came into the hands of the rising Howard family, and Howard House, at the corner of Mountergate Street, was the garden house used by the junior members of the clan, Earls of Surrey. Of parish churches there used to be nearly a dozen, of which survive, beside St. Peter Parmentergate, that of St. Etheldred, or Etheldreda, daughter of Anna, first Christian King of East Anglia. The story is that the monks of Ely stole her body from the church-yard of East Dereham, where it lay. But they could not steal all her fame, and here is a dedication to her. A little apart from the busy roadway are all that remains of the church dedicated to Julian, or Juliana, the fourteenth-century mystic whose *Revelations of Divine Love* make her one of the earliest authoresses in the English tongue. The dignified, partially Norman building with her anchoress' cell attached was destroyed in 1942 by an air attack on Norwich. Near the walls is the site of another church, St. Peter de Southgate, demolished long ago.

That is what Conisford was like during the centuries from the time when the first boatloads of predatory ruffians beached or tied up the boats in which they had crossed the sea, and kept guard, sleeping in or around them, until with security and use the path they made became a rough track, between wooden houses in which such men settled for good. Thus their landing-place became in time part of a medieval walled town with a growing trade in derivative agricultural products, leather and woollens, with its dozen churches, not merely the three that remain and countless little shrines, chapels and anchorages. It must have ended at the walls (and these can still be seen), descended the precipitous bluff to the twin towers that guarded the stream, and so it remained until the last years of the eighteenth century, with a little rebuilding here and there, as it were a gradual alteration in styles of dress. But it was for centuries just a water-side place run by manual labour, and the signs of how it lived are still plain.

It is not until we look beyond the walls, and beyond the eighteenth century, that we begin to see what the mechanisation of handicraft and transport meant. The first great change was in the size and purpose of the craft that plied to and fro on that river. Men began to build bigger vessels, capable of carrying more for longer voyages. The importance of Yarmouth grew, its harbour, which had shifted backwards and forwards with the shifting sands of the beaches, seems to have been finally stabilised in its present channel in the middle of Elizabeth's reign. With the coming into use of the type of ship we roughly describe as a " galleon " it must have been necessary to tranship goods at Yarmouth, and the vessel employed was first a crude lugger with a square sail called a " keel ". Later, however, a more capacious and easily handled design called a " wherry " was borrowed, it is said from the Dutch, and lasted into the twentieth century. They are now extinct, but for at least a hundred years they were the characteristic craft of the Norfolk rivers, conveying immense quantities of non-perishable goods : coal and grain, lime and ballast, above all, timber, which was stacked several feet above the combings of their capacious holds. They ran to a length of 50 feet or so, by 16 feet beam, and drew 5 feet loaded. The heavy mast, forward, was swung in a " tabernacle " with a lead weight on its foot so that it could be lowered to negotiate the frequent bridges. From it depended the largest single sail in the world (for they were una-rigged), 500 square feet of tawny canvas. The hold ran from the mast back to the tiny cuddy under the tiller. When fresh painted, with brass wind-vane and pennon, they were a fine sight. Along each side of the hold ran a gangway, and it was along this narrow ledge, outside the hold and above the water, that the wherryman and his mate used to tramp, with their outer shoulder pressed against the butt of their 20-foot " quant ". This enormous edition of a punt-pole had a wooden, hatchet-shaped foot at the other end, which they planted against any firm object on the bank, and not often on the bed of the stream. The great bollards that can still be seen sunk in the bank at many places were for this purpose. Thus the wherry was independent of contrary winds in the winding reaches, and of no wind at all as the banks were increasingly built upon. They could negotiate bridges and carry loads.

Up to about 1910 they might be seen lying against the walls of Colmans' great mills at Carrow, discharging their load of grain, timber and such commodities. Steam-tug-drawn lighters superseded them. But something else happened to King Street, as the nineteenth century opened. There had been a chronic quarrel with Yarmouth down the ages as to the dues charged by that port for transhipment of goods inland. From about 1820 there came gradually into being a grandiose scheme for connecting the Waveney at Oulton with the sea at Lowestoft, and thus cutting out Yarmouth, by further connecting the Waveney with the Yare at Reedham. Thus sea-going ships could sail right up to Norwich from Lowestoft, and Yarmouth, short-circuited, would bitterly regret not making itself more accommodating. A bill was passed, capital and labour procured and the lock at Lowestoft and the " new cut " to Reedham were made, and are to be seen and used today. At the Norwich end, opposite the gates of King Street, a great harbour was to be dug in the marsh where Thorpe railway station was built later and named after the Duke of Clarence, subsequently William the Fourth. An inn sign, " The Clarence Harbour ", can be seen in Carrow Road. Alas for human plans! It never happened. For in the very decade in which these elaborate and costly preparations were made to create Norwich a port, steam began to replace sail, the tonnage of the average ship increased, and soon iron and steel made possible a size of ship that no Norfolk rivers with connecting canals could contain, not to mention allowing them to navigate. A few yachts did enter Lowestoft from the sea and penetrate to Norwich, before cheering crowds, while cannon fired and speeches were made at banquets. But the project was what we call a " flop ". True, it achieved something. That remarkable genius, Sir Morton Peto, took over the semi-derelict works, and modern Lowestoft harbour is largely his work. This also brought into play the fine yacht-basin in what had been the remote and little-used Oulton Broad. The " new cut " is still used by sea-going vessels of moderate size, and Norwich still receives bulk fuel at its Power Station and grain and timber at its mills by sea-going motor lighters, which have, however, to back out.

No, the future of the Carrow district was one which Sir

Morton Peto and other enthusiasts never foresaw. In the eighteen fifties, J. J. Colman, who had already inherited a village water-milling business, that had begun to deal with mustard and starch as well as flour, decided, like so many Victorians of his generation, to launch out. He and his partners bought some plots of land which were being discarded by the "Norfolk Railway", later the Great Eastern system, south of the river, just where it turns eastward from the gates of King Street, to join the Yare. In less than a quarter of a century he had added the wide grounds and ancient ruins of the nunnery of Carhoe or Carrow, had come to live in Carrow House, while his great smoke-stacks rose one behind the other, rivalling the Cathedral spire. The exit from King Street became a new district of Norwich, complete with schools and all the welfare institutions nowadays run by the Welfare State. His employees, soon numbering over a thousand and later two thousand, were the best paid and by far the best cared for in the city, while his name became world famous and his fortune rivalled his reputation as a member of Parliament for the County borough of Norwich. He sank the first artesian well, and installed the first electric light in Norfolk. That is how things turn out. The Reckitt–Colman mills remain to be seen.

King Street, then, has a nautical character, not too respectable to begin with, but acquiring status by going into trade. As it became useful, so it became honoured, and after many vicissitudes, its offspring became celebrated and rich. Today visitors come to photograph its old buildings, to keep appointments at its great mills and breweries. It has never lost a rather jaunty air, and it seems a natural coincidence that a broad stadium for professional football should now extend where it failed to become a fully equipped seaport.

VII

BER STREET, THE BUTCHERS' STREET, ALL BLOOD AND GUTS

I HAVE said that when one walks down a street in Norwich it is as though one kept step with a living person. So full of accumulated character are most of these highways that they seem to have acquired a human personality.

It is the fate of human beings to change. Often, when we are confronted by photographs of ourselves as we undoubtedly were, so few years ago, it seems to us—though it may be twenty, forty, or fifty years—that we can hardly credit that we are the same persons as the ones we see depicted. We do not much resent the giggles of our younger relatives at these revelations, because it appears plain to us that we are not that bumptious or sheepish young man, that scrawny or podgy girl the photographer saw and recorded on his negative, which cannot lie. We bear the same name, of course. But we have changed out of all probability.

Many a street in Norwich, for all its activity and prosperity, is so full of ancient buildings, its modern offices and industries are so often housed behind Georgian, or even Tudor frontages, that it looks, in patches anyhow, just as it always did. Those same leaded windows and gable ends, though they have modern plate glass on the ground floor, looked down on Elizabeth Tudor, or Horatio Nelson, sheltered Sir Thomas Browne or Amelia Opie from rain or sun.

Yet there are in Norwich, amid its family of streets, some members which have changed utterly, and as one walks them one says:

" No, this is not the place along which I used to go to school. It was not here that I saw the Prince of Wales (long before he was Edward VII) driving with Lord Suffield ! "

This incredulity about well-remembered fact belongs to the wide thoroughfare suggestively known as " Ber Street " since the earliest written records of Norwich. Those who do not know it as well as I will not find it easily, for one of the first things that ever happened to it, at least fifteen hundred years ago, was that whoever built the first mound, the mound on which the Castle stands today, did so in order to stop possible enemies using what is now Ber Street.

For it lies along the almost level summit of the long chalk ridge that forms the southward tip of the walled city. It must always have been a key strategic position, and I make a guess that that is what its name means. Ber = Hill = strong place = defended town. But I am no philologist, and offer this with diffidence. What is said by learned authority is that the track-way, paved, in the sense of being metalled, which led from Venta Icenorum, was designed by the Romans to cross the Wensum at the ford afterwards known as Conisford, and so perhaps to reach Caister by Yarmouth, though I believe this is in dispute. It may merely have led to Thorpe. Anyhow, the rammed earth that only the Romans knew how to make has been seen underneath the Castle Mound. Whatever local chief of some gang of outcasts it was who superseded the Romans, he had no use for the Roman track. He or his had left nothing but ashes and desolation at what had been Venta Icenorum. His one anxiety was lest someone used the track to march upon his sparse settlement on Tombland. When, centuries later, the Norman castle arose, the wall of its bailey or yard blocked Ber Street effectually and a church (St. John's, Timberhill) stood just outside the Castle jurisdiction and appears today to make the street almost a cul-de-sac. Its southern end is thought to have led to Hall Road, crossed the little Yare at Harford (? Yare-ford) bridge, and thus to Venta Icenorum, which we call Caistor St. Edmund. But in the thirteenth and fourteenth centuries this exit was given a gate in the city wall which makes it appear to lead down Bracondale to Trowse, where there may have been a ford (or subsequent bridge) leading out into south Norfolk. The effect was that the Ber Street you see today appears an enclosed space rather than a main traffic artery. The only clear evidence that it had been one lies in the fact that all early documents call it " street " and not " gate " (i.e. " gait "), which was the usual term for the unpaved casual tracks made by a water-borne people when they began to live on land. So Ber Street became a thoroughfare of the early settlement, but a curiously one-sided one. For while half a dozen steep lanes run from its eastern side down the precipitous bank to parallel Conisford-gate (modern King Street), that lines the river-bank, there are none on its western side.   Here the ground shelves less sharply, to a marshy hollow where the water collected in a pond known as " Jack's Pit ", the position of which can be traced at the intersection of modern Surrey Street by All Saints' Green.

This situation dominating the relatively high ridge that sheltered the infant settlement along the river accounts partly for the fact that an ancient trackway, once blocked and useless, continued to exist.   But there is another peculiarity about the street.   Why is it so wide?   It is still the widest street in Norwich save Prince of Wales Road.   Now, no one in pre-Norman days bothered about the width of a road.   Traffic, as we understand it, was unknown.   And why are there no lateral streets opening out on its western side?

When, in fact, you make the circuit from one end or the other of it, to find out what lies behind its unbroken western façade (save for one " loke " or lane not fit for wheeled traffic), you discover the odd fact that in a whole quarter of the city, from the backs of the houses in Ber Street to the backs of those in St. Stephens, there is not a building dating before A.D. 1800. There are wide gardens, a convent, a row of villas, private houses of Victorian date, and then the remains of the City walls, incorporated in Queen's Road.

Thereby hangs a tale.   The whole of this district on both sides of modern upper Surrey Street was once the parish of St. Winnold or Winnaloy, a Danish or Saxon saint whose " day " falls on the 3rd of March, and whose memory is perpetuated in the rhyme about the weather of the opening days of that reputedly boisterous month :

> First come David, and then come Chad,
> And then comes Winnold as if he were mad!

In the year 1348 came the Black Death.   I do not know if medical opinion has made up its mind as to what, exactly, this epidemic was, but its effects are clear enough in Norwich, in the Cathedral Cloisters, even.   Whole parishes were depopulated; it is said that a third of the population died.   It must have been far worse than the better-remembered Great

8. GEORGIAN HOUSES

9. THE GOVERNOR'S TOWER

10. THE BISHOP'S PALACE GATE
From a drawing by John Sell Cotman

Plague of 1666. The most striking thing is that several parish churches seem to have disappeared. There was, one supposes, no one to repair or use them, and they fell down. It is all the more remarkable in the Ages of Faith when one would have imagined that an all-powerful Church would have seen to it that its numerous functions continued, that the population was kept instructed in obedience, if in nothing else, and that the various sources of revenue did not dry up.

In this quarter of Norwich nothing happened. There was no population to be ministered to. The ground may seem to be covered now, in 1952, but I remember it in 1900, when it was full of orchards and gardens, from All Saints' Green to St. Catherine's Plain and the walls, save for the recently built " Carlton Terrace ". Such were the medieval times. A whole section of a large (by the standards of the fourteenth century) and flourishing town like Norwich could become completely vacant, and remain so for centuries.

Ber Street thus became an adjunct to the Cattle Market, which, as the centuries passed, became too large to be accommodated on Tombland, and shifted into the Castle " Bailey ". Now, the peculiarity of medieval markets renders the term obscure to the modern motoring mind. To the medieval view, a market was not a traffic centre. It was the reverse. It was a place in which saleable property was safe from disturbance. To the heads of the municipality this was an advantage. It rendered easy taxation and examination for a rudimentary standardisation. Of the various markets of Norwich, none of them lies on a main traffic artery save Tombland. The Bailey of the Castle, taken over gradually for the Cattle Market, was an enclosure, not a crossways. Anyone who saw cattle being driven up for sale by road, as they still were up to 1914, will understand the importance of Ber Street. Every Saturday morning and at the great Christmas and Easter Fairs and at Michaelmas it served as what we should call a " parking " place for drove after drove of frightened, fidgeting, lowing beasts, rounded up and kept together by drovers and dogs, until a place could be found for them in the open iron-fenced pens in the Cattle Market adjoining. The drovers were of two almost racially divided tribes. One was composed of ragged, vociferous, and usually not too sober Irish

E

who had accompanied the young beasts from the bog on which they had been born. These tatter-tails were said to spend not more than two or three nights in bed most weeks of the year, and they certainly looked as if they spent those in their clothes, their bed a spread of straw in some loft. How and where they fed, what their names were, the years they lived, I never discovered, or whether they had any other life. They are unthinkable in the present age of registration, national health insurance, and comparative sobriety. Later in the day they would be seen clustering round the dealers and auctioneers, who must have known them by sight and exercised some rudimentary control over them. Should some intending purchaser hesitate they would bunch round, crying: " Make it a dale! " If in fact a " deal " transpired they would fling up their battered, square-topped hats and sticks and give three cheers. They were paid by some mysterious system in which "Luck money" played a part.

The other tribe were the poor nondescripts who in the early years of the twentieth century still existed in that Norwich of low wages and uncertain employment in which " bullock-wopping " and the odd shillings that resulted were a recognised perquisite, if not a means of livelihood eked out with parish charities, private charities, running errands and general hopelessness and helplessness. The dogs ranged from the skilled Norfolk sheep-dog to any mongrel that would snap inoffensively but sufficiently effectively to keep beasts, particularly sheep, together. It was quite usual for some frantic creature to run amok and end up, if not in a china shop, in any other shop with an open door, and frequently in the little patch of garden that remained to the Bank House in comparatively select Bank Street adjoining. That is why so many Norwich front doors and garden doors had waist-high iron gates that could be closed on Saturdays. They are gone now. Careless organisation? Not altogether. There were elements in Norwich population in those days, less than fifty years ago, quite willing, if not anxious to drive off any odd animal up one of the maze of yards with which Ber Street was surrounded, and in which its population teemed like ants, from which it never emerged.

Ber Street, then, acted as a sort of vestibule, if such a term can be understood, to the Cattle Market, in which there were then no properly built auction-rooms. The selling was done in the open, come fair, come foul, by sheer lung-power, and it was in Ber Street, increasingly as cattle began to arrive by rail after about 1850, that the sheer mass of all that flesh destined to be butcher-meat and horn and hoof and hide, was roughly sifted. It was the only street in which such dislocation, complete suppression rather, of all traffic could be tolerated.

The slowly moving mass was further constricted by the parking all along both sides of the roadway of the carriers' waggons and private gigs of all those thousands who drove up by road, some from the neighbourhood of Lynn, Brandon, or Lowestoft. They all had a horse of some sort to stable. They all needed bread-and-cheese and beer. It is not wonderful, then, that, even in Norwich, which visitors described as composed of " every corner a church, every other house a pub ", Ber Street had, as late as 1929, when the great shift of the population was well under way, twenty-two public-houses, not mere beer counters, but each with a yard containing some kind of stabling. There were still then a dozen butchers and allied trades, not counting handy people who " did a bit on the side ", as we say nowadays. The biggest single shop was that which sold every description of the then distinctive agricultural workers' wardrobes: black felt hats with a pointed crown and brim turned down before and up behind, corduroys, silk scarves for Sunday. Smocks had gone out, I expect the early agricultural machinery had rendered them dangerous. It was a street of a fierce local patriotism. On most weekdays, to tread its wide pavements (for it had never become constricted in width) in middle-class clothes was to invite remark if not insult.

"Where do you live? " a witness was asked at the Court.

"Ber Street. What's wrong with that? " came the reply.

On Saturday, however, any sartorial distinction would not be noticed, if it existed, for there was added to the difficulty for the office-worker of forcing one's way through the herds of animals, that of the reeking manure that encrusted one's footgear. On Sundays the place was hushed. One could almost hear the headache resulting from Saturday night's debauch pulsing up all those crowded yards. On Monday morning there would be the pathetic little queue at the pawnbrokers'.

But it had its festivals. At fair time it was invaded by

gipsy crowds, the men with earrings and canary or crimson neck-cloths, the women with jet-black ringlets, bold eyes, and that princessly walk that comes from carrying a basket of saleable wares on the head or hip. The police wisely held aloof, standing guard—in couples, not singly—at either end, to contain the rowdy element. I would not suggest that the women were promiscuous. " Hallo, me old darlin' ! " was probably the greeting for an admirer so regular as to be a consort. The men had old scores to settle, and settled them, sometimes in gangs, sometimes singly, with fists, or with sticks. The tail end of a fine pugilistic tradition had descended from the great Jem Mace with his reach of seven feet (so it is said) and a coloured man known as " Pongo " Plum represented the less sportsmanlike side of it. His career ended when he challenged the great Slavin, who was visiting Norwich. Slavin would not meet such a character, but contemptuously sent his " puncher ", an ex-guardsman. Plum made an awful mess of his face, but the practised bruiser came back time after time above the heart, until Plum sagged and fell. It was, of course, the end of his career.

Such was the Ber Street I remember. I suppose that the nature of its life kept rents low. Anyhow, it was here, during the nineteenth century, that a colony of Italian emigrants established themselves. Coming from their overcrowded, poverty-stricken land, I suppose Ber Street seemed to them paved with gold. The men, small, dark and simian, found some sort of work. The women, their abundant hair bound with richly coloured scarves, trundled piano-organs, with a baby slung across the shafts, into the better residential districts, and turned the crank-handle. It used to be great fun to take them a penny and be rewarded with a brilliant flash of teeth, a gracious smile, and a muttered " Tank you! " For, scanty as their rags might be, and penurious their lot, those women had magnificent headpieces, each one worth copying upon a bronze medallion.

I lost sight of Ber Street in 1914, and for years my feet trod other ways. It must have been twenty years before I had leisure to look at it attentively. I was astonished by the change. It was not a single or sudden revolution. There were at least three main causes. One was the beginning of the Welfare

State. Another was that a fortunate person such as I was had looked forward to returning to the state of things I remembered in 1914. Not so the average inhabitant of Ber Street. They had no intention of returning to those unlighted, undrained and unpaved yards in which they had existed, often in single rooms, with a fine view of the common privy and single tap that served them. And the City Council was determined that they shouldn't. So big areas became vacant, demolition orders, and the lowered value of property no one wanted, caused the collapse or the pulling down of rookeries, the abandonment of little shops. The third cause was the new motor traffic. It demanded wide parking places and warehouses for goods brought by road in bulk. Yet another was the policy, now half a century old, of reducing the number of small public-houses. Nor were they required. Country people no longer drove 40 miles, to put up at Norwich for the market. They came by car, and went home to tea. (Tea? The Ber Street I remember used to fill itself with draught stout. The little pot-bellied horses took their people home, drunk or sober.) Court and yard gave place to big dumb buildings, closed at night. The failing horse trade no longer brought the gipsies. The Italians, grown miraculously rich, opened restaurants. The cry of " hokey-pokey, penny a lump " was heard no more. Ices were sold in cornets. The population that had lived by " bullock-wopping " supplemented by parish charities became insured and regulated, the charities devoted to education. The police no longer stood guard in pairs lest the flood of rascality brim over and flood the city. The noisome churchyards were tidied up and planted with flowers. Pongo Plum became a dim memory. He would not have been permitted to exist in the nineteen-thirties. Houses of resort were closed because they were no longer tolerated, and levelled to the ground because they were verminous. Great ranges of new flats, with steel frames and concrete galleries, made a garden-city background to replace the old one that would not have looked strange in a cartoon by Rowlandson. The little old shop that sold corduroys was bought up by a great store and equipped with a restaurant and lift, and more plate glass than the whole street had once possessed. Most remarkable of all was the trans-formation of the chief activity of the street. The crowds of

Irish cattle no longer came by rail to Trowse, nor were there half-civilised, half-tipsy, ragged creatures to herd them on to the market. They came by car—or at least by transporter—to be sold in adequately built auction rooms. If, today, some returning wanderer were to allude to " Blood & Guts Street " he would be met with a stare of blank incredulity.

It is an old fairy story, that of the bad boy of the family, forgiven for his good humour, smiled at for his incongruous picturesque speech and appearance, made use of for all the rough, dirty, disagreeable jobs that no one else wanted. He was cheap when he was sober, funny when he was drunk; anyhow he had always been there, and that used to be a good reason for his continued existence.

It is so no longer. Fairy tales come true; Jack, the cheerful rogue who broke his mother's heart with his improvidence, has sown his beans, and climbed his beanstalk. At the top he found a giant, whose name may have been poverty, hopelessness and helplessness. The giant has been slain and the proceeds are Jack's. He calls it the Welfare State. It has rendered Ber Street unrecognisable.

VIII

COLEGATE, FISHERGATE, AND THOSE WHO MADE THEMSELVES USEFUL

INQUISITIVE people sometimes say:
" Yes, we've heard all about the Cathedral and the Castle, the Market and the means of transport. But what have Norwich people *done* all these centuries? Cathedrals and Castles can stand in very small towns, or the latter in none at all but the open countryside; markets can happen wherever people have something to buy and sell, and transport goes where people want it to go. What did the people in Norwich do? "

It is a very reasonable question. Here, in these streets, for well over a thousand years, some say nearer fifteen hundred, people have lived out their lives, managed to get themselves housed and fed and clothed, and these old streets can tell you all about it. Especially they can tell you about the main bulk of the people of such a place as Norwich who were not reverend or noble, nor wealthy from commerce, nor able to move about much. No, the majority of the population must always have been women, spending most of their waking hours watching a kettle boil, in some sort of interior, minding a child playing on the doorstep, going a few yards to fetch water or fuel, cooking the raw food brought into the house, mending and making endlessly, and finally having, if only from sheer exhaustion, some leisure, some time when they folded their hands in their laps, told stories or sang or listened to those who could, played infantile games or danced, or watched such activities going on, nursed the sick, gave alarm at the threat of flood or fire, and closed the eyes of the dying. What can we make out of them, the vital stuff of human society, any society or gathering together of folk into tribes, villages and finally towns? They are what gave the character to the place in which they lived. The ecclesiastics and lords had their fine fanes or palaces, and left their names upon a gateway or a street to be remembered. Yet meanwhile, all the unremembered must have eaten at least

once, and probably three times a day, and found some shelter
for their heads and cover for their bodies, and it is only during
the last fifty years (or generally less) that they have had houses
and heat and light provided for them, and not fashioned by
their own hands, not to mention the medical attention, education and protection (including protection from old age), transport and relaxation that are given them now by the community
of which they are a part.

How did it all start?

Well, we know something, and these old streets, alive with
the human pulses beating, human voices speaking, steps
echoing, shadows flitting, can tell us much more. We know
that when the events recounted in the New Testament were
taking place, there was no such place as Norwich. The river
wound, probably in several streams, not one, through wide,
semi-submersible marshes, amid clumps of oak and alder, rush
and reed; when it came against a hard lump of gravel or chalk
left behind by the glaciers of what was even then an enormously
long time ago, it just changed direction, flooding through the
softer ooze. Someone, at some time or other, called it " Wensum ", or so learned people spell the sounds which the Romans
made into their name for it, when they began to write histories
of their soldiers and colonists in this remote corner of their
empire. The suggestion, I believe the latest, is that there may
have been a Romanised aboriginal town of sorts, two and a
half miles away at " Caistor ", where perhaps the spectacular
and semi-fabulous Boadicea rode about in a solid-wheeled
chariot, and ruled over a half-animal population. The
Romans did away with her, and built, or local people built in
imitation of what they thought was the Roman fashion, streets
of houses with glass in the windows, better central heating than
much of Norwich had recently, drains, possibly statues at the
street corners. It must have looked very queer in that landscape. For where Norwich now is, was nothing. At most here
and there a kind of human pigstye, in which, on a circular or
oval floor of cobbles, beneath a kind of umbrella of thatch, the
" ancient Britons " existed in a state of life so animal as to be
barely distinguishable from that of the beasts they kept. Such
people scratched the ground and planted barley, and odd little
objects which may have been weights by which they wove some

kind of shirt, or weights by which they sank fishing-lines in the
river, show some attempt at covering themselves and filling
their bellies. Their huts were few and far between, but
presently the Romans made amid them a trackway of rammed
earth, all along what is now Ber Street, and descending perhaps
to a ford where Fye Bridge now stands. It is fascinating to
wonder what the " Britons " thought if they saw, from time to
time, a small squad of soldiers marching, or a train of pack-
horses moving along towards a considerable seaport place, now
(1952) being dug and measured, at the other " Caister ", just
north of Yarmouth. One of the confusing things about the
whole picture is the habit of the Middle Ages of labelling as
" Caister " or " Caistor " any place with traces or traditions of
the Romans. It now seems unlikely that there were ever
many permanent military Roman formations anywhere near
until, late in their age, the Romans built what is now " Burgh
Castle " overlooking the Waveney. That is really all we know.
One or two hovels beside a trackway that had been made by
far more civilised people is all there can have been, on the
ground now filled by what was to be Norwich.

So it was, for centuries, while boatloads of pirates and " displaced persons " attacked the romanised town at " Caistor "
and at long last burnt and plundered it so there was little or
nothing left. Then, having no longer anything to fear, these
gangs of rapscallions thought one day (and we shall never know
which day, or exactly why) that it was not worth while to
voyage back whence they had come. They beached their
boats and built themselves huts. But not to any large extent at
Caistor. They stopped, sensibly enough, on the larger river,
the Wensum, nearby, just where the lowest ford made a crossing
possible, and where at the same time their sea-going ships could
ride with no difficulty. Here grew up little groups of single-
room, timber-and-mud huts, with perhaps a hole in the wall for
window and one in the thatch for chimney. It is doubtful
if they had names for the tracks they made in the firmer ground
from one to the other. The only names that have come down
to us belong to a later, fiercer, better-armed set of pirates:
the " Danes " of history. It is in their tongue that the street-
names Colegate, Fishergate, Pottergate, Wassailgate, Parmentergate, Finkelgate were coined, and were still so called

when the first maps were made in the middle of the eighteenth century.

What can the people have been like who made these first settlements with such an eye for position, or such energy, that the burg was worth attacking and plundering in 865, when the Danes certainly came to do so? The first, and earlier settlers had come by boat. Did they bring their womenfolk, or did they marry the women they found about the place and whose male folk could be done away with? Anyhow, settle they did, and there is a very good model in Norwich Castle, made by a recent Assistant Curator, which shows the single-room dwellings, standing detached, along the tracks that were to become the streets of the town. One certainly followed modern Bishopgate, though no one knows if it led to some sort of ford or bridge, or merely out into the grazing-fields where the kine were. Holm Street, leading to the Cow Holm, was its first name. And it seems natural enough that there should be a track running along the northern bank of the river, where Fishergate and Colegate form an almost continuous line. My guess is that the ford, or rude crossing by some sort of a plank bridge, where Fye Bridge stands today, made, at certain states of the tide, some small difficulty in taking the larger boats any farther upstream. So the fish was landed from sea-going craft that had come up from Yarmouth, where we find the name Fishergate. These boats may have been larger, since they went to sea, but I am not certain of this, for when we come to times with any written record, we find that fish often meant shellfish. Whelks, in fact.

West of the first bridge or ford was Colegate, where baskets of charcoal were unloaded. The boats which brought this may have been smaller, for they did not have to go to sea. The charcoal was made in the wood anywhere not too far from the river. For there was no other means of carrying it, save packhorse, which could only take perhaps two baskets at a time. (I say "baskets". The first record of charcoal I know was when the Prior of the Cathedral bought it in "trays", as his account-keeper called them. That was in the fourteenth century.) Anyhow, we now begin to get a dim domestic picture. Here were fish to eat, and charcoal to make a more lasting fire than that of sticks. Where did the sticks come from? Once again it is guesswork, but one supposes that what is now Mousehold Heath was always wild and free to the citizens of North Norwich. In South Norwich there was a common between what are now the Ipswich and the Newmarket roads where they leave the City. It is now called Town Close Estate, and the rents from the houses built on it go to make the income of the City Charities. But it seems always to have been waste land. Here, then, or on Mousehold, the surplus members of the family, the old granny and the young children, gathered an apronful of sticks, and made a blaze in their earth oven, and raked it out, and pushed in their little loaves of barley meal. Or so it seems. I don't know, and I doubt if anyone knows much. But the look of a few remains of very early houses in Norwich, laid bare by bombing, and the written police-court records (of much later date, of course—fourteenth century), give us a glimpse of what the domestic life of Norwich may have been for centuries. There was a mint, and coins were issued by A.D. 900, so that Norwich was no mere crude waterside settlement, already by that date. The name " Old Mint Yard " was lately to be seen in Fishergate, though I think this referred to the minting of halfpence in the eighteenth century. However, there was a man called Minter in A.D. 1300. They seem to have had to queue for their food even then. There was a black market, and many a man and some women were fined for buying up corn, etc., before it reached Norwich, and putting up the price when they sold it retail. These police-court records say that a dirty dog called Alan de Catton found eight drowned sheep and sold them for good meat. Robert Sheepseye had a net and fished in the river, which was poaching, apparently. A tanner, a linen-draper, a farrier, a painter all lived in Conisford in the year 1288 and traded there, not too honestly. So one could get small jobs done to one's house or horse, a pair of shoes or a shift. The linen must have been real flax. Geese and fowl were stolen.

The ale-wives were a perpetual source of trouble. They were always selling beer on the sly, and bad beer at that. One, Gervys, fripperer, and Walter Hee had fullers' blocks on which they worked up old clothes in a fradulent manner. There was a baker's shop.

So much for Conisford. Now let us look elsewhere. Along

Pottergate came the earthenware from some kiln outside the city, apparently to the west, where the Earlham Road now runs. Nearby, in St. Peter's, lived Peter the mustard man.

They had water. Hugh de Caistor had a bucket and cord. We know, because there is a record that they were stolen. Had he a well, or was that only for the nobles and the wealthy? Did he dip his bucket in the river or a foul pit? Richard Coleman lived in St. Gregory's. Was he the charcoal merchant? There was a fearful row because " the cooks and pastry makers warm up pasties and meat on the second or third day ". It may sound innocent, but you cannot warm up food on pewter platters.

There was a basket-maker in St. George's, Tombland. They were a quarrelsome set in St. Clement's. Alice, wife of Roger Wrong, drew blood of Matilda Littlecope. How real that neighbours' quarrel sounds, across nearly seven centuries! The names are not imaginary. They were real enough to be entered on some form of summons.

The neighbourhood of Wymer—the long, narrow ward that bordered the southern bank of the river—was no more salubrious. William the skinner had thrown the bodies of dead cats into the Lothmere (one of the numerous " pits " or ponds that still abounded in the half-built-up City), " whereby the air is poisoned ". He must have been an unpleasant neighbour.

However, there was a mitten-maker whom one would be glad to know, in the bitter Norwich winter. Over in Conisford, again, there was trouble because the wife of John Boatman sold beer " by the single pot ", and three pots do not make one gallon. Yet they got their beer, even if it were short measure. Sometimes perhaps it wasn't, for in the ward of Over the Water a chaplain of Norman's Spital (one of the score or so of small welfare establishments where the bailiff's authority was unwelcome, if not illegal) " beat the serjeants and broke their wands ". He made a rough house and appears to have had his fine excused. Perhaps the serjeants didn't want to go and collect it. He was not the only such character. William of Denham killed Alice of Causton's cat. As for the price of candles, it was wicked. And there was tallow in the wax! One would hardly have thought people were so particular, in the days of Edward the First.

There was constant trouble with people who raised the Hue and Cry for no justifiable reason, to the public scandal. They could be reported and fined. But what must have been the constant stream of gossip, tale-telling and recrimination, in those muddy lanes, blocked by the refuse of the untidy and rendered dangerous by the mounting-blocks by which the infirm (or the merely selfish) got astride of their mounts, and by the flapping of the unmended shutters of the parsimonious. Apples and pears were stolen from the gardens, too!

There were also peculiar means of creating annoyance and extorting money. The ecclesiastical courts, which were quite independent of the authority of the bailiffs, took care of what may be broadly called " morals " and fined people for divers irregularities. This became, as time rolled on, a valuable source of income, and the less scrupulous clergy sent out touters, to bring small delinquents to their courts instead of the bailiffs' court at the Tollhouse. That, however, the bailiffs would not stand. Naturally they had trouble enough anyhow; but that sort of thing threatened their very existence.

Of course, what little we know about all this daily life is admittedly thirteenth century. But can the average happening to the inhabitant of Norwich have been any easier in the earlier centuries. Was the King's Governor in the Castle likely to be any gentler than the Bailiffs? Earlier still, what can have been the risks and discomforts, not to say disasters, under government by the Danish " Army " (or band of marauding foreigners from overseas) when it sheltered in Ber Street in A.D. 865? And as for the year 1004, we know that Sweyn burnt and pillaged and massacred. Naturally a wooden-built, straggling, overgrown village was easier to rebuild than our more elaborately planned towns were after the Second World War. But I am trying to picture the daily life of the housewives and tradesmen and their children. For they persisted. That is the remarkable thing. The great Lords and Churchmen came and went, with their professional armed retainers, who, one suspects, argued very little and paid not at all, and took what they wanted, and forced the average householder to do what they, the intruders, said. Yet Norwich did not succumb as the Romano-British town, Venta Icenorum, or " Caistor St. Edmund " on our maps, succumbed, after about two hundred years of repeated, if not continuous attack. No, Norwich absorbed the Danes, who presently became converted to Christianity and brought their own saints, Olaf and Vedast, to give names to churches, alongside the Saxon Edmund and Etheldreda and Cuthbert. After Sweyn's great stroke of revenge in A.D. 1004, it took only sixty years for Norwich to be so prosperous and important that the Cathedral Church was built here, and not at Dunwich or Thetford or Elmham, and whole parishes had to be done away with to make room for it, and scores of houses obliterated to make room for the Castle.

Norwich absorbed the " Frenchmen ", as they called the Normans, and all that is left of them and their " Conquest " is the fact that a French saint like Giles had a church in that quarter of the town. People had money to spend; several of them spent it so unwisely that they were haled before the Bailiffs as " tipplers ". By A.D. 1350 we find statements about fresh-water fish, so that Fishergate must have been busy. So were the churches, that were all rebuilt, until there was hardly a trace of the old crude partly timber buildings of earlier times. Religious services grew more elaborate. Westlegate (as it is now spelt) was the street where the makers of fine white bread for ceremonial occasions dwelt and traded. In Parmentergate the whit-tawers or leather dressers made parchment, perhaps, but some say leather riding-breeches, of better stuff than tanned hides. But Finkelgate is a mystery. What went on there, who Finkel was or why the street should be named after him, I have never discovered.

So we draw on to (comparatively) modern times. The rows of houses became continuous, if often elbowed out by ecclesiastical and conventual establishments. The walls were built, the place took shape. At what date some citizens were wealthy and enterprising enough to have their houses built of stone, we cannot tell. We can see what are left today. There used to be eight flint-faced houses left from the pre-brick Norwich, probably the fifteenth century. There are still six. If anyone wants to know how well Norwich survived massacre and conquest, lepers and the Black Death, there is Bacon's magnificent house in Colegate, all flint faced, with his merchant's mark over the door in signs, but legible enough no doubt to the men of that day. Yet another can be seen in

St. Clement's Church Alley. The finest of all is the Bridewell, as it came to be called, where William Appleyard, the first Mayor under the new Charter, lived in A.D. 1404. The wonderful sharpness and accuracy of the jointing remain to be seen after five hundred years. There are three other flint-built houses but only portions of them remain. After that, brick came gradually into use. But the task of keeping order in the new Guildhall was much the same as it had always been in the old Tolbooth. It may have been worse. Men became more ambitious and better armed. No wonder the Tudors were " strong " monarchs.

In 1554, Mary's reign, John Sturgen was fined 3s. 4d. for suffering men's sarvants (the writer is plainly Norwich born, that is how he pronounced it) to spend their money in his house " to ye great hynderaunce of ther maysters and to the evil example of others ".

" Thomas Glene for delyvering his stuffs to poore folke, to be wroughte by a waighte a great deale above ye standard deceyving ye poore subjects." He was in fact a sweater, and had to pay 12d.

In 1636 is the first presentment for not paving streets and " not attending church ". Norwich was growing particular. The system lingered on until at least 1802, when a printed form was used to embody this thousand-year-old inspection of nuisances, minor delinquency and human frailty. I quote these records only because they are all we have. They are negative. All government must be. It consists in telling people what they mustn't do. That is why all high-spirited countries like England hate and avoid it as far as is possible. But I hope that, by reflection from this negative, we can obtain some positive idea of how people lived, all those centuries, in the very streets in which we walk today. True there were no numbers to the houses until 1840, no names even to the streets until the Danes began to call them Colegate, and so forth. I cannot be certain at what exact spot in King Street (Conisford) lived Agnes " le book bynder ", who was " not in tithing " in the middle of the thirteenth century. But it is certain that she did live there somewhere, and had to take the responsibility for her dead or missing husband and help to carry on the faintly civilised tradition by which Norwich has survived. The great names of men and Acts of Parliament that adorn the history book are names only. The more splendid buildings remain, to shelter others than their builders. But in between them, all these centuries, there have been those rows of little unglazed bars and workshops, with some sort of dwelling behind in which the real Norwich has existed.

11. THE BARKING DICKY, WESTLEGATE
From a drawing by A. H. Mottram

12. THE LAZAR HOUSE

From a drawing by A. H. Mottram

IX

'MID PLEASURES AND PALACES, IN SURREY STREET AND ELSEWHERE

I HAVE tried to take the reader into the humbler dwellings that lined the old streets of Norwich, to see how all the smaller people subsisted. I called them " those who make themselves useful ", and I visited nothing larger than the house of a man substantial enough to be Mayor like Appleyard or a merchant like Bacon.

Yet there were from the earliest days houses in Norwich—I mean houses, domestic dwellings, not Castle or convents—which were large and commodious and of some pretension as to their architecture. It is not straining the meaning of the word much to call them " palaces ". In fact, their owners called them that, so surely I may. That is why, as one strays along the old streets of Norwich, one finds Palace Street, Duke's Palace Inn, Old Palace Road, Palace Yard, all referring to different palaces, and there were others that have disappeared and left no name.

Next in order to these are a number of houses so large in plan, so splendid in their appointments, that one cannot ignore them without leaving a deceptive gap between the Castle and the Cathedral on the one hand and on the other the little single-room cottages in which many of the population existed until my lifetime.

The first dwelling to deserve the name of Palace in Norwich still wields a ghostly influence strong enough to determine the southern limit of Tombland. We know little enough about it, save the traces of stone vaulting below ground, which may have supported a building largely of wood. The site is covered by numbers 26–29 Tombland, solid Georgian buildings a thousand years younger than the " Palace " of the Earl, the Saxon ruler of Norwich. What kind of a place can it have been? Can one, by a herculean effort of the imagination, abolish all the buildings now surrounding Tombland? It will be a pity, for the Erpingham and the Ethelbert Gates, the church of St.

Georges, Tombland and many of the dwellings and offices range from the superb (Erpingham Gate) to the comely. Yet that is what one must do if one wants to try to see the Earl's or EORL'S palace, that looked northward across a Tombland at least double the width, from west to east, of the present square. It must always have had a slight slope towards the river which encloses it (at a distance of some hundreds of yards) on the north and east. As he looked out from his front door, when he set out hunting, what did the Eorl see? A score or two of timber-framed, thatch-covered, mud- or clay-lump-walled bothies. Perhaps the Scottish butt-and-ben gives some idea of their plan and elevation (though north of the Tweed they are usually of stone) standing, quite irregularly, round a trampled space, slippery with pig manure and stinking of rotten fish. If he looked left (west), it is probable that the track which is now King Street led into it here, from south Norfolk. There was no church of St. George, but somewhere near the present churchyard another track may have come in from the west or mid-Norfolk side. Opposite to him, almost certainly a paved—that is, rammed earth—track descended to a ford where Fye Bridge arches the river today. It is hard to guess what he can have seen to his right. No Cathedral, of course. Perhaps some branch of the paved track the Romans had made leading along what is now Palace Street, to the Manor House of the chieftain who owned (that is, held probably from him, or from his superior, Earl Godwin) the adjoining manor of Thorpe. This is thought to have been on the site of the present Bishop's Palace, and there may have been some crossing of the river again, at what is now Whitefriars Bridge. Other people will tell you that a paved track ran under the present Cathedral, along Bishopgate (then Holm Street) either to the grazing facilities of the marsh, or possibly to some other crossing of the river. But it is all very vague, and probably then did not amount to much more than miry paths amid watery meadows, intersected by dykes. In the background were the orange gravel, green or grey grass, sulphur-yellow furze and purple heather of Mousehold Heath. But on his extreme right, on the site of No. 7 The Close, was the church of St. Mary in the Marsh. Crude stone walls, perhaps little windows with a pointed top of two tiles leaning together and held up by a small pillar. You can see just such a one in St. Mary Coslany church today.

I wonder what the Eorl thought about. The Saxons defeat one's imagination, because they left so little that feeds that part of one. Lethargic but persistent (their conquest of our island was a miracle of slow determination, if you can picture a miracle taking centuries to perform), sentimental, in a hopeless pagan way, then Christian in a primitive fashion, with gross-bearded married priests. What is it that renders them so mysterious? Was it their unknown history in Europe : the climate wetter then perhaps than now which they endured; their habit? One has a vision of long days spent cattle-raising and hunting. An evening before blazing logs in some rude barn of a Hall. A gargantuan meal of pork and seagull, floating on rivers and rivers of muddy ale, sour cider and a sharp brew of honey. Tall, fat(?) women with yellow hair, great dogs lying about in the rushes, a minstrel chanting lugubriously to the sound of the harp, and very soon . . . snores. Torpor. That is what the Saxon's history impresses on one's mind. They could conquer an island, at length, but they were helpless against quicker-witted (better-armed?) Danes, and inclined to buy them off as much as to fight them. Alfred the Great must have been a very exceptional Saxon. Gurth the swineherd was the average. The Normans, one suspects, found them exasperating, and dealt with them brutally, efficiently, summarily, as they thought. But after a century or so the Saxons engulfed them. In an old place like Norwich, the outward signs, the sharp lines of Castle and Cathedral are Norman. But the temper is still very Saxon. Listen to the conversation in the Cattle Market any Saturday.

As I have said, these Saxons organised enough trade to demand a proper coinage, and the Mint of Norwich circulated the coins of Athelstan. They were not poor, then! they were brave, if quarrelsome. But there clings to everything we know about them the feeling of something heavy and slow. It would not surprise me if the Eorl's palace were built of whole tree-trunks, but the buildings shown in reproductions of the Bayeux " Tapestry ", which is now thought to have been worked little later than the Norman Conquest, if they are not romanticised to glorify the new masters of England, lead one to think that

by that date, anyhow, the Saxons were using a good deal of
stone. We know what happened next. For over a century at
least the outward shape of Norwich was distinctively Norman.
The " Eorl " was replaced by a new chief with new functions,
who lived in a stone keep, still standing, and not in some rude
" Palace " on Tombland.

When the English nation emerged, and some of its wealthier
citizens at least began to build themselves fine houses on a scale
that approached what we may call " palaces ", we get some
hint of what they were like from " Stranger's Hall ", which
stands on the north side of the spot in the main western highway
called nowadays " Charing Cross ", which was in fact the
Shearers' Cross, a crucifix in the roadway, presumably, at or
near which the shearers or cloth-dressers may have met to
decide matters of policy of their Guild, prices, etc. Just here
the roadway divides, the southern arm becoming St. Benedict's
Street, leading to St. Benedict's Gates, the northern Westwick
Street, to Heigham or " Hell " Gates postern. The spot is
still about the centre of the walled city, and what we call
" Strangers' Hall ", and know as a fine " Folk Museum " of
domestic articles, furniture, clothes, games and vehicles, stands
upon " the fourteenth-century crypt or strong room, built of
stone for the storage of valuables. This formed the base of the
timber-built house of Roger Herdegrey, Burgess in Parliament
in 1358 and Bailiff of the city of Norwich in 1360."

So says authority. This, then, is the state of life such a man
had attained on those dates. He had a stone strong-room below ground, a timber house above.

What one sees today, used as a very lively and up to date
Museum, as far removed as possible from the " mausoleum "
type of museum, is an accumulation of three or four houses built
in different centuries on the same spot. The name " Strangers' Hall " is a mystery; the place had nothing to do with the
" strangers " or foreign immigrants into Norwich down the
ages, and nothing to do with the L'Estrange family. It would
be impertinent of me to talk about the present excellent museum,
which is so well described by its custodians and their literature.
I am trying to recreate the life of these old Norwich streets, and
not to tell the long, well-documented story of how, after Herdegrey, Nicholas Sotherton (I think the ex-mayor who rode hell for

leather to London to tell the Privy Council about Kett's Rebellion) built round the Courtyard about 1539, and how Francis Cock, grocer and mayor, inserted the splendid staircase and other parts in 1627, or how two lovely eighteenth-century rooms were added at the back, as anyone can see, until in 1904 Leonard Bolingbroke bought it, repaired and furnished it, and gave it to his native city.

My interest in the place here and now is because it shows how these Bailiffs and Mayors lived and what our modern housing owes them.

What was such a house like? Entering by a fine door (the carriage entrance is separate) one comes into a little courtyard. (There are similar ones in Suckling's House, east of St. Andrew's Church, and in Appleyard's House, now the Bridewell, nearby.) All wealthy and comfortable people had an interior yard, which came to be called a " courtyard ", where the life of the big house could go on, without annoying and sometimes threatening interference from the unpoliced streets, with their crowds of beggars, foreign invaders or political mobs. All such houses could stand a short siege. From this one mounts some stairs and enters the main Hall, now called Banqueting Hall.

This is the eternal nucleus of all dwellings. It is a much-improved and enlarged edition of the first house man ever built, when he gave up his cave or his tent and began to erect a permanent shelter with a roof. I do not know how early he improved on the roughly circular hut with a central post like a tent, that we know Boadicea's poorer tribesmen used, and made four walls, with an entrance in one of them and a roughly central hearth, with a hole in the roof for smoke. Nor do I know who first made a hole in one wall to obtain some light other than that which came in from the doorway (as it became when a door was substituted for a hanging over the entry).

It is, however, easy to see how far men had got by sometime after A.D. 1350, when Herdegrey's wooden house was replaced by one of stone and brick. All the primitive functions of the first house can be traced in the great Hall here, and we can see how far they had developed. Here are the four walls, and the fine high roof. It is just what Oxford and Cambridge College Halls were, and some are little altered today. From the door, a set of " screens " has been arranged to keep out weather and to shut off the kitchen smells. There is no sign of a fireplace as yet. Perhaps they wore their outdoor clothes; the merchant and mayor certainly wore a gown for at least half the year. Perhaps they warmed themselves in the kitchen, as the monks did in their " warming room ". Perhaps they had a pan of charcoal. But already the centre of the floor is filled not by a rough hearth with a fire smoking through the roof, but by a long table, at which, we know, the master sat at the " head " (farthest from the door), his wife and family and guests round him. Somewhere in the middle of the table was a great salt-cellar, and below that came the scriveners (clerks) and foremen who lodged under the roof, then as many apprentices and workpeople as " lived in " and worked in the garrets and cellars, and at the far end of the table, near the screens, servants, beggars, the staff and the recipients of the charity of the day fought the dogs among the rushes for what was passed down to them.

The window has developed into a magnificent " solar " or sun-alcove, a glazed bay where the women sat, to catch what sunshine there was (not much in Norwich between November and May). It looked out into a garden enclosed in high walls. There it was: the dwelling complete in one apartment, but surely by that time some lean-to where the kitchens now stand had been added? The " butt " had acquired a " ben ". Later again the staircase was put in, and gradually the walls were honeycombed with the doors you see leading off into newly added bedrooms, attics, domestic offices, nurseries, workshops, stables, cellars, as the master and all his community (for it was more than a family in such a place) became tired of huddling together in the straw, as they had in the earlier " great hall " in the keep of the Castle, with only hangings or partitions to divide, or some little box of a chamber in the walls for privacy and toilet. Yet, diminished and adjusted, the faint ghost of the " Hall " is still with us. Even the flats and many of the houses in the newest housing estates have what is significantly called a " front " or " entrance " hall, for access to the various rooms, from the front door. (Compare the terms in other tongues: entrée, couloir or stoep, or close.)

I know of few places which show the development so clearly as " Strangers' Hall ". The gradual disappearance of the courtyard can be traced in the original Norwich Union Insurance Building in Surrey Street and the Artillery Barracks in All Saints' Green, where it has become a mere drive, or paved area before and around the step of the front door.

Now I must justify my use of the word " Palaces ". While simple citizens were becoming rich on the flourishing and expanding trade of Norwich and serving their City as Bailiff or Mayor, the great crisis of English history was approaching, sweeping, as it were, on the crest of a wave, new people, not mere Herdegreys or Sothertons, but the powerful Howard family, into prestige and prominence, opulence and tragedy. They took over and rebuilt or re-edified old monastic buildings such as St. Leonard's Priory on the slope of Mousehold. They also built others. One of their minor palaces was from my infancy until 1901, when it was destroyed, the large and prospering school of my foster-aunts. To me it was all that and something more. Much of it, still handsome and stately after three hundred and fifty years, was a paradise. For its builders it had sinister results, however.

" Thomas Howard, 3rd Duke of Norfolk," says the learned Mr. E. A. Kent, F.S.A., writing in the *Journal of the Norfolk and Norwich Archæological Society*, " was at one time a favourite of King Henry VIII, who made him his Earl Marshal. . . . He had had two nieces, Anne Boleyn and Catherine Howard; both had become Queens, and both had been beheaded . . . the Duke's son, the brilliant and headstrong Earl of Surrey, was said to have been particularly involved in an attempt to seize control, as soon as the King, who was then approaching his last illness, should die. This seemed to the King very like treason, and he ordered the arrest of both the son and the father, and a trial to determine the issues. In the Record Office can be seen the Charges against the pair in the hand-writing of Chancellor Wriothesley and underlined by the King in a tremulous hand. They commenced with questions by what authority the Royal arms had been borne by the accused in the first quartering of the coat of arms; and as to the meaning of a statement made by Surrey, that if the King should die who should have rule of the Prince (afterwards Edward VI) but his (i.e. Surrey's) father, or himself."

Bad enough, but there was worse. Mr. Kent discovered that

the powerful, ambitious Duke had built his son the splendid house, parts of which I remember, changing the very name of the street to " Surrey Street ", and had incorporated in a window of stained glass his arms, quartering those of Prince Edward ! Mr. Kent sums up : ". . . both were found guilty of high treason and sentenced to death. Surrey was beheaded on Tower Hill on 19th January 1547, while the Duke's execution was fixed for the 29th January; he, however, had the luck to escape, for the King's death took place the very day before, and the Council of State did not like to begin a new reign with the shedding of blood. Had Chancellor Wriothesley seen the glass roundels in Surrey House, they would have seemed to him to offer a strong confirmation of the alleged intention of the Duke and his son to control the Kingdom."

The magnificent old house is gone these fifty years, and if the ghosts of the unhappy Anne Boleyn (please pronounce it Bullen) and Catherine Howard, and their cousin, the poet Earl, ever haunted, headless, the rooms where I played as a boy, I never saw them or heard their moans. I was happy there, and so were two generations of school-girls. I only mention all this to show what sort of people had some of the greater houses of Norwich. Surrey House was a good example of the expansion of the old simple hall. One entered its courtyard, in which a coach and four could have turned, and many must have done, under an archway from the street. It was cobbled, and the wings of the house retained many of the lattice windows, and a roof of wonderful madder-pink tiles. The main *corps de loges* had been rebuilt in George III's reign, but retained the stone floors and kitchens of an earlier day. Behind was a wide garden with a dozen of the biggest and most prolific apple-trees I ever knew and a fig-tree some thirty or forty feet wide. Gateway, courtyard, main building, garden, with offices and stables in the wings either side of the gate. That was the plan. That was what the brilliant if overweening Henry Howard, Earl of Surrey, left behind when he lost his head on Tower Hill.

It was by no means the only Howard House in Norwich. Mr. Kent also quotes Thomas Baskerville the topographer's account of what he saw in Norwich in 1681 : " Taking a boat for pleasure to view the city by water, the boatman brought us to a fair garden belonging to the Duke of Norfolk, having handsome stairs leading to the water, by which we ascended into the garden and saw a good bowling green and many fine walks; the gardener now keeping good liquors and fruits to entertain such as come to see it."

This was the property which had been the Austin Friars' in King Street, and is now the yard of Morgan's Brewery Company. The fine old flint wall still lines the street, and the house at the corner of King Street and " Mountergate " is still called Howard House. It was in fact the " garden house " of the pleasaunce, and had in the Duke's day an uninterrupted view across the river and marshes to the wooded hills of Thorpe. But such was the insatiable appetite of these noblemen that neither St. Leonard's Priory nor Surrey House nor this delightful garden by the river could satisfy them or their descendants, for Baskerville continues (in Mr. Kent's quotation) :

" . . . we rowed under 5 or 6 bridges, and then landed at the Duke of Norfolk's Palace, a sumptuous new-built house not yet finished within, but seated in a dung-hole place, though it has cost the Duke already 30 thousand pounds on building . . . for it hath but little room for gardens and is pent upon all sides both on this and the other side the river, with tradesmen's and dyers houses, who foul the water by their constant washing and cleaning their cloth, whereas had it been built adjoining to the aforesaid garden, it had stood in a delicate place."

Today, anyone who leaves the Provision Market by Dove Street, which breaks its northern side just east of the Guildhall, will pass, in a hundred yards or so, the church of St. John Maddermarket and its churchyard, and come to the traffic lights. Ahead, Duke Street leads on northwards to Duke's Palace Bridge, and on the right is Duke's Palace Inn, the last poor remnant of the most magnificent of all the great Howard Houses in Norwich, despite what Baskerville remarks, so truly, about its sordid site. The road one treads, Duke Street, was in fact the entry of the splendid palace that extended many yards, east and west and down to the river.

There had been at least two successive buildings here: an older one, in which Queen Elizabeth was entertained in A.D. 1572, and a new one, built in 1672, in which Charles II was received and banqueted with, if possible, more extravagant luxury. Tread softly, then, as you pass down Duke Street, where the lorries grind up the hill and cyclists swarm, for you are treading in the footsteps of royalty. Where these jostling pavements run, the pikemen in Howard livery held back the cheering crowds and fine riding-horses were halted, champing, while their exalted riders dismounted to enter the banqueting hall. Some of the stone had come from the Abbey of St. Benets at Holme, which the Howards had acquired out of the Reformation. Charles and his Queen were thus entertained:

"All the house throughout was noblie and richlie furnished with bedds, hangings, & ye apurtenances for lodging. The old Tennis court turn'd into a kitchen and ye Duke's Bowling Alley (which as yu know is one thirty foote wyde & one hundred & ninety foote long) made into fine seurall rooms for eateninge; where after their majesties roome being most sumptuously adorn'd with all things necessary, & parted from ye rest, the other foure do likewise help to shew the greatnesse of his heart who made this noble preparation & entertaynment."

All gone away into thin air, the stone and brick and timber partitions (by which the "roome" for the royal guests was "parted from ye reste") as completely as the huzzas that greeted them, and the viands and wines they swallowed. Thirty-six years later some sort of dispute arose about the "Duke's servants"—i.e. players—who included Thomas Doggett, who gave the Badge the Watermen of the Thames compete for. Allowed to set up stage plays, "a shew of comedies", on condition of behaving themselves civilly, they were forbidden the City by the Mayor, who, it is said, feared a Jacobite demonstration. Others say that Thomas, the eighth Duke, found the place useless, its foundations weakened by the river, and gave orders for its entire destruction. Anyhow, it is gone, all but a window or two in the Duke's Palace Inn. The Duke made £2000 " of the stuff ", and may have thought himself well out of it.

And even now we have not done with the irony that pursues all earthly things. We might say that the pride and pomp of the great ducal house were bound to collapse from its very weight and costliness. We cannot say that about another palace in Norwich. When Herbert de Losinga was commissioned to build Norwich Cathedral he was given the old, rough manor-house of Thorpe, which stood in the meadow by the Wensum, but on the Norwich side of it. As the centuries passed there

grew up, on the primitive stone foundations of this " keep ",
a house worthy of the long succession of the Princes of the
Church who reigned there, and finally one of them, Bishop
Alnwyck, enclosed the whole in a wall with the great gateway
that overshadows St. Martin's-at-Palace Plain. Here one may
peep in, unobtrusively, and see a lovely garden with forest
trees and wide lawns stretching to the north wall of the Cathedral itself. Flung about by changing fashion of the centuries
are ruins of chapels and halls, and mere traces of former
additional buildings to the present Palace, and very lovely
and peaceful and appropriate it all is, with the mellow chimes
marking the quarter hours, and the birds flitting across the
grass. Yet anyone who knows must have a qualm. For in
this holy place have been enacted scenes of violence far more
wholesale and nearly as complete as ever overtook the ambitions
of the Howards.

In the Commonwealth years the Bishop was the learned and
pious Dr. Hall, and what the rude Parliamentary soldiers did
he summed up later in a tearful and searching account which he
called with reason " Hard Measure ". Thus it runs : " What
clattering of glasses, what beating down of walls, what tearing
down of monuments, what pulling down of seats, and wresting
out of irons and brass from the windows, and graves; what
defacing of arms, what demolishing of curious stonework, that
had not any representation in the world, but the cost of the
founder, and the skill of the mason." They melted the lead
off his roof, but worst of all, they made a bonfire of his books.

The poor, inoffensive old man retired to what one supposes
he considered a " garden house ". It can still be seen, by
following Westwick Street and quitting the City by what was
Hell Gates and following Old Palace Road. It is called the
Dolphin Inn, and had a very beautiful flint-and-stone " flush-
work " front of two bays, and its lovely situation on the bank
of the Wensum in what was open country must have consoled
the victim of such violence. He was buried in the village
church of St. Bartholomew. It was left for Hitler's bombers in
1942 to destroy his grave and severely damage his country
" palace ".

So the Bishop's last memorials suffered much the same fate as
those of the ambitious and not very scrupulous noblemen.

Some will say cynically that it just shows! But I do not. Silly violence of the acquisitive or the destructive kind is still silly violence. It is not the design of Providence but the lack of balance and reflection in human beings. It will not get better until we have better people, and the old streets of Norwich are full of pointed " morals " all the more effective for being unspoken.

X

THE WAY UNDER THE WALL

THERE is one of the old streets of Norwich that you will not readily meet. Its, or shall I say his, origin is so forgotten, his use so completely superseded that he may be ignored; were it not that he is, in all, one of the longest continuous thoroughfares of the City and can tell us more about its character than many other members of the family, perhaps no one would seek him. My father's friend, old John Fitch the antiquary, wrote an account of " The Gates of Norwich " illustrated by steel engravings, which gives such facts as are known.

No one seems to know when the first bank and ditch with perhaps a wooden palisade was erected all round Norwich, making it, formally at least, an enclosed or fortified place. When, eventually, this was replaced by a wall of flint, this was said to be " over 2 miles long, 20 feet high and 5 feet thick ". The remainder of the circumference was sufficiently marked and defended by the river, which formed the only limit in the whole of the eastern side and for a portion of the north-west.

Immediately within the wall and following its course there came to be necessarily a passage, and it survives to this day, under different names, betokening its various uses. The latest and most intelligent historians point out that the wall was by no means planned solely as a measure of defence. Indeed it was noticeably inefficient as such. Hugh Bigod and his Flemings made little of whatever fortification there was in 1174, burnt and pillaged, slew or held to ransom some of the citizens. Nearly a century later the disinherited Barons under Sir John Davyvill broke in and behaved with great violence. Kett's men got round or over the wall. Yet, we read, its presence " established the area controlled by the citizens " and " gave them a means of supervision over traders coming into the city to sell their wares ". In fact, it gave Norwich shape. The actual stone fabric took about eighty years to erect, and was only finished by the determination (and generosity) of one Richard Spynk, who has now a street named after him in the wide and pleasant Mile Cross housing estate. It had twelve gates (some traces of where they stood can be seen), forty towers and one thousand six hundred and thirty battlements, or so it is said in early " directories " by those who may have seen it intact. There it was, and for some five centuries Norwich looked like the picturesque " walled town " that might have figured in any romance. On any alarm, the City musters would man it, cleaning out the ditch and repairing the masonry they so neglected between emergencies, close the great wooden gates across the main means of ingress, and look out from the towers that flanked these, and the smaller towers ranged from place to place between. To this day, the position of the wall, and the considerable remains that exist, govern the direction taken by traffic.

Let us now make a closer acquaintance with the " way under the wall ", as it is called in all the earlier maps. The best place to start is on the River Wensum, at the southern tip of the old kernel of the city, close against J. & J. Colman's great works. Here, beside the gate that ends King Street, ancient Conisford, can still be seen a good deal of the twin " Boom " towers that stood on either bank of the river, which could be thus closed against traffic by a chain or boom from one to the other. They are now overshadowed by high industrial buildings and the shipping along the quays. Yet there can be no mistaking what they were or for what purpose. One of these was made the residence of a man whose duty it was to prevent the passage of any vessel that had not paid the City toll " or to oppose force, if necessary, to disloyal persons approaching ". There was a small tower across the adjacent street also, under which the Conisford gates opened. It was demolished in 1794.

Then, leaving the river and King Street, to follow westward the " way under the wall ", we come across one of those incidents that make Norwich, in spite of its hundred thousand souls and key industries, seem like a big village, and result in its being known for centuries as " the City of Gardens ". What we find here, once we quit the busy quays and thoroughfare and try to mount the steep escarpment of the chalk bluff to the west, is some hundred of yards of wild woodland, sandwiched between crowded residential streets and factories known all over the world. It is a scramble to mount beside the wall, here mostly as intact as it ever was, and we do better to leave it for a few yards and make the ascent by the one-way street called Carrow Hill, a piece of mid-Victorian welfare work, planned to occupy the unemployed of the eighteen-sixties.

As we come panting to the top, there above stands the largest and most spectacular of all the towers of the enceinte. In some accounts it is called " The Great Black Tower " because it was faced with black flint, in others the " Governor's Tower ", from its being supposed to have been the residence of the military commander during the time of a siege. Norwich was never besieged in that sense, and so far as we know, any military commander it had in its various emergencies stuck to the Castle. However, as a piece of picturesque medieval building the tower is impressive enough, far greater in girth than the great smoke-stacks that now rival it in the landscape, and higher than the huge silos of the big mills on the river below. It was struck by lightning in 1833 and the wooden interior fittings burnt out. Adjoining it, in the private grounds that open on to pleasant Bracondale, is a fine section of the wall, which shows its construction and loop-holing, and how wooden (?) staging enabled the guard to see over the parapet. Then we lose it altogether, save for one ruined bastion, which serves to show where stood the gates of Ber Street. But pause a moment and glance at this record of the survey of the walls made in A.D. 1386. Apparently wardens were appointed for each section. Thus, " John Danyell, Walter Danyell, John Occle, The Wardens of the Black Tower, to make the said tower and the roof of the same in good and sufficient repair, likewise the wall on each side of the Tower, inside and outside, with casting and pinning, as may be required, to the middle space, and to make the staging ".

That was how it was done, and a complicated system of assessment upon residence and " murage " tax upon trade entering from outside provided the cost.

" In 1625 and 1636 the Black Tower was made a prison for unruly, infected persons." They stood no nonsense in the time of the Stuarts.

Ber Street Gates had a portcullis between two towers. Evidently these were commodious, for the commissary of military stores at Woolwich for housing ordnance stores in the Napoleonic Wars.

From Ber Street north westward we lose the wall again and the " way " under it, although I daresay pieces of flint rubble can be found built into the backs of many of the houses between Ber Street and Finkelgate, and along Queen's Road. I am not going to scramble through all the back gardens, to the justifiable annoyance of the peaceful inhabitants. Especially as in a few hundred yards Queen's Road is cut by All Saints' Green, and where today we see the Lame Dog public-house was Iron Doors, later Brazen Doors, a small or postern gate, not large enough to admit carriages. On 19 August 1726 the Tonnage Commissioners ordered that " Mr. Henry High, in the repairing of Brazen doors, take care to make the inward door wide enough for a horse with pads to go through ". This looks as if there were an inner and outer door, and for centuries these are spoken of as being made of metal. Presumably they could cast a whole door of metal for a small dimension, but the larger two-leaved doors of the more important gates had to be built of wood. However, a few weeks after the entry quoted above, Mr. Benning the carpenter and Mr. Freeman the stonemason were ordered to " forthwith go about the widening of Brazen Doors ", " enough for a coach or cart to pass through, provided St. Stephen's parish will undertake to maintain the road ", " that there be but one pair of gates on the outside and that be 8 ft. and a half high to the foot of the arch, and 8½ ft. wide ". So there one gets the dimensions.

Although a modest member of the company of the Gates of Norwich, this one, like that of Ber Street, had the City Arms, in plaster, and painted, upon its masonry on the outer face. It must have been a pleasant byway. Look at the great Georgian houses, just within where it stood, one now a restaurant, the other the Headquarters of local Artillery formations. But with what ease and elegance did these Aldermen live in such buildings, that bear the stamp of Bretingham, one of the foremost builders of Georgian Norwich.

Now, by dodging behind the houses in Queen's Road, we find here, running north-west, the real " Way under the Wall ", called in this section Bull Lane. Therein lies the whole later history of the walls, and indeed of Norwich itself. For in the year 1556, of all unlikely people ever to do such a service for a place like Norwich, Philip of Spain and Mary Tudor his wife granted a charter authorising an enlargement of the City. They gave it the whole peninsula from the ridge between Earlham and Hellesdon where the Yare and the Wensum come within a mile of each other, to the junction of those rivers at Carrow enclosing Mousehold Heath, and the whole valley to Thorpe on the east, and thus brought 8,000 acres within its jurisdiction (as much as Birmingham had when this century opened). The walls ceased to mean much, except in an emergency. If you had a savage bull, the place to keep it was in an enclosure next the strong, old and now otherwise useless wall. Here are pieces of it, and in some cases half a tower, built into the back of dwellings, until, under the shade of the trees in the nearby gardens, one comes out in busy St. Stephen's Street, next the traffic lights.

The St. Stephen's Gate stood on the rising ground just where these lights wink red and green with a flash of yellow between. It was an imposing double-towered portal, and a presentment of it can be seen on the wall of a neighbouring inn, where the enterprising brewers have had it modelled in a plaster panel, depicting citizens working and children playing before it, and the flag (quartering old France) fluttering from the pole on one tower. The shapes of the Castle keep and the Cathedral spire are visible above its battlements. This portrayal shows how the Age of Chivalry looked after its portals, and how the Age of Industry can make a romantic picture of how it was done.

" At an Assembly held on Friday before Michaelmas in the first year of Richard III it was agreed that one Robert Godard, a hermit, should have his dwelling over the Gate of Needham (as St. Stephens was then called) and the custody of the ditches of the City, so far as they extend for the Aldermanry of St. Stephens, paying 6s. 8d. yearly, and that he should repair the chamber and the soller (solar?) over it occupied by him."

So that is how hermits lived! I have often wondered. He must have been a man of substance. And his was not an isolated case. Apparently it was a tradition, for in 1435 and 1483 hermits were buried here who had occupied the gate. They had disappeared by the eighteenth century, for on 7

G

August 1754 it was " ordered that a proper person be employed to scrape the silth off the road without St. Stephen's Gate, so far as it is paved, and to keep the same pavement clean by constantly sweeping it, and to have a room provided and glazed for his habitation there, and to have such other allowance for his pains and services therein as William Crowe Esq. shall think he deserves ". (This was, I think, the Alderman of the " small " ward or subdivision. But how sanitary-minded we were becoming!) Alas, it all came to an end. On 27 October 1792 the *Norfolk Chronicle* observed : " On Monday last the ruthless hands of men began to execute the sentence of demolition passed upon the venerable Gates of this City; Brazen Doors have met their fate, St. Stephens follows next." Presumably it had to be, though York and Lincoln among other Cathedral cities have managed to preserve theirs.

From St. Stephen's or Needham Gates, the Way under the Wall becomes wider and more imposing than anywhere else in its long extent. It is called Coburg Street now, which, so far as I can find out, dates it about the time of Albert, Prince Consort, and the little mid-Victorian houses which can here be seen, built right on to the wall, using its masonry for their structure. Some of them have been cleared away and left the old gaunt ribs exposed to view, the rough arches which, as on Carrow Hill, seem to have carried a parapet. Was it of wood, was it temporary? Here and there can be traced a tower, a battlement or a loophole. From Coburg Street one emerges into the public gardens called Chapel Field, a triangle of 8½ acres, running along the wall, with its apex pointing towards Bethel Street. It was the pasture attached to the College of St. Mary (now the Assembly House), and when one considers how it must have appeared, a good strip of open country within the fortified enclosure, one understands why medieval towns could stand a siege. The food was inside their walls. The Victorian Drill Hall, built by public subscription for the Volunteers, adjoins the Gates of St. Giles' Street, and incorporates the last tower of the wall before one arrives at that portal. The Volunteers of 1859 not only built their own Drill Hall, but bought their own rifles and uniform. There's enthusiasm for you. My father drilled with a muzzle-loading Enfield rifle. He used to say, of the target practice : " If there was a particular zing after a shot, you knew the fool had forgotten to remove his ramrod!" Imagine thirty inches of steel whizzing down the range! Fortunately they did not practise here, but had a musketry field on Mousehold.

St. Giles' Gates were not spectacular, enclosed in a single tower, with the City Arms upon it. The street within was imposing, but without, the road led to Hingham and Watton only. Frequent repairs were necessary. On 7 July 1756 the Tonnage Books say: " Ordered that the walls of St. Giles' Gates be painted and the battlements repaired, and a ringe of lead put round the top of the roof, to protect the same from the wet ".

Beyond St. Giles' the wall pitches steeply down the north-western escarpment, to the upper reach of the Wensum, where it enters the City. The Way under the Wall is called Wellington Lane, evidently since Waterloo, but at its lower northern end, after passing Pottergate it becomes Duck Lane. What a picture that conjures up! The old wall, long disused as fortification, and no longer very important as a boundary, served to provide the duck-keepers of the city with a convenient place in which, with hurdles and brushwood fencing, they could keep ducks.

There is no gate to the long street called Pottergate (i.e. Potters' gait or track). From its name one feels it must be a very ancient track, named by the Scandinavian or second wave of invaders, like Colegate, Fishergate, Parmentergate (which we have corrupted to Mountergate), Finkelgate and Westlegate. It must have been stopped up when the walls were built, for it has a continuation outside them which loses itself in Earlham Road. Its eastern or inner end joins London Street and appears to lead, via Queen's Street, to Tombland, comprehensibly enough, since this was the market. Yet it points to the Ethelbert Gate of the Close. A queer, lost, forgotten by-way, that must once have had its importance.

At the foot of the hill, St. Benedict's Gates spanned the street, which became, outside them, the road to East Dereham, relatively important as the western highway to mid Norfolk. Until in 1942 the bombing of Norwich destroyed it, there was a good piece of the lintel of the gate, and an iron pin on which it swung, still standing.

It was near this that an entry in the Norwich Court book

shows that " Thomas, the Dean of Norwich [what we should call Rural Dean] had made a purpressure on the ditch, for which he was amerced 2/- and John de Martham, chaplain, was amerced 12*d*. for undermining the ditches of the City and carrying away clay and sand or gravel ". It is the old story, what was everybody's was nobody's and one could help oneself. But if the vigilant City fathers caught one at it, one was fined. And quite right too. The old records are full of such entries; just as folk nowadays pilfer the towels and spoons and glasses of the railways, so in earlier days they pilfered gravel and ballast from the City wall, or rather, the bank and ditch upon which it stood. It was a cheap way of obtaining material, but sometimes turned out costly.

If we owe Hitler a grudge for destroying what small remains there were of the masonry surrounding St. Benedict's Gates, we can thank him that the same stick of bombs destroyed some ramshackle cottages built upon the last level stretch of wall, that extended hence to the small postern, called Hell Gate, or Heigham Gate, that covered what is now the crossroads by the beforetime L.M.S. railway station on the river bank. This portion of wall can now be seen, and from the crossroads, the gate having left no trace, the way is open to the pleasant riverside suburb of Heigham. Beyond this postern the wall disappears altogether, the river forming the boundary and defence, until, some two hundred yards upstream, the masonry can be seen around the first gate north of the river on the opposite bank. Anciently St. Martin's at Coslany (Cossa's island, they tell me), or more familiarly Oak Street, this thoroughfare joined the road to Aylsham and north Norfolk that issues from the next, or St. Augustine's Gate.

You may well ask what the little postern on the west bank had about it that it should be called " Hell " Gate. Old accounts of Norwich say it was " from the low dismal appearance of the street which communicated with it " and that it was " a mean building and never a passage of much traffic ". The same qualities beset Brazen Doors on the other side of the city, but it was never spoken of in such terms. Nor was Heigham Gate always so mistreated. At an Assembly on St. Matthew's day, in the fifth year of Henry III, on some question relating to the way leading from it to the river, it was called " Blake Gate ", which, so commentators say, meant Black Gate, but by Sunday, next after the Feast of the Exaltation of the Holy Cross, in the sixteenth year of Richard II, it was described as Port Inferni, and a little later as Helle Yate. Of course, it was the most low-lying of all the Gates of Norwich, and gave upon what was, at least in early days, a river bank so swampy and unapproachable, that the citizens felt quite safe in leaving it open for some furlong or so, and resuming the wall on the higher ground east of the river. Is Hell a mere corruption of holl or hole, Norfolk dialect for a ditch? Did it simply mean, down-in-the-dumps gate? Or was lower Westwick Street one of the several Turpis Vicus or Bad Streets found on the old maps, streets of turpitude, if you like. No one seems to know. I should have said that at least parts of Lower Westwick were no worse than Ber Street, or others, though it is noticeable how the prestige of all the streets of Norwich declined the further one receded from the Provision Market and centre of civic administration. This is very traceable in the lists of the medieval musters of militia, or Home Guard. Parishes or subwards, like St. Peter's and St. Stephen's, provided a number of fully armed men, and many less well armed. The remoter parts near the gates had a difficulty in making up their quota.

So there the matter rests. The name had been dropped by mid-eighteenth century, when this postern was rebuilt.

Well, let us cross the river and pick up what little we can trace of where St. Martin's Gate stood. Here, in 1622, Mr. Thurston, the city surveyor, had to attend the " Committee " " with his instruments, to inform them touching ye ascent towards Pokethorp ". Or, as we should say, to take the levels, eastwards. Some small portions of the wall are in the houses and gardens lining Baker's Road. Here in 1637 was " a dwelling under the walls wherein Margaret Gilson, widow, searcher of ye infected poor, then dwelt, was granted to her to hold during the pleasure of the Court, and not otherwise, because it was intended that that House should continue for ye only dwelling of such a searcher when need shall be ". One may wonder how often the " infected poor " did not need " searching ".

St. Augustine's Gates stood where the traffic lights are, and gave access from a busy prosperous street, always full of industry, to the Aylsham and north Norfolk road. From thence the wall ran along what is now Magpie Road, after a well-known inn sign.

" The city wall from hence to Magdalen Gate is partly built upon from the within side," says Blyth's account of 1842, " and the towers converted into cottages." Some fragments can be seen. The name of this gate used to be " Fyebrigge Gate " because the thoroughfare is the main northerly outlet from Tombland, whence the main road to north Norfolk via North Walsham and Wroxham crossed the river by the bridge of that name, and earlier by a ford. Magdalen Street is so called because at some distance outside its gate, on the Wroxham road, adjoining Mousehold Heath, stood the Lepers' Chapel, now a branch Public Library. The gate itself was called sometimes the Lepers' Gate. There is no mistaking where it stood, from the sudden widening of the narrow street, and the cross roads with their traffic lights. East of it one can still pick up what was the Way under the Wall, here called Bull Close, for the same reason as Bull Lane on the other side of the City. In the second and third year of Philip and Mary this portion " is fallen into a soden and presente decay . . . Mr. Fuller, Mr. Furnour, etc. with the Chamberlains ben appointed to have Rewle and Oversighte for repayring of ye same by their discretion . . . the hooll ward shall be taxed by ye alderman . . . according to the old Ordynaunces ". That presumably kept it up. Portions of a tower can be seen near the junction with Silver Road. Beyond was " Barre Gates " or Pockthorpe Gates, and then a short length of wall and a tower on the river bank—" the King's River ", as it was called in Richard III's day.

Hence the deep, slow-flowing Wensum, " navigable for keels of sixty tons ", says King's map of 1766, " the distance to Yarmouth is 32 miles ", takes over the duties of the wall, under the sharp ledge of Mousehold Heath, that shortly turns it from an easterly to a southerly course. On the City side the ground is still open meadow, belonging to the Great Hospital, reaching to the Cathedral Close and containing the fine brick-built Cow Tower, which is in fact the tax-collecting post from which the Prior's servants collected toll from vessels. About half-way to King Street Gate and the Boom towers (where the wall recommences and we began our peregrination), and due east of the Cathedral, is Bishop's Bridge, more correctly Prior's Bridge, which gave separate outlet from the Close and the Hospital beside it, without going through the City. Some of its stones may date from the original structure, at some time uncertain after the Conquest and the building of the Cathedral. In 1393 it was put in charge of the City for maintenance. In Edward III's time a City Trumpeter lived in the tower which used to span the fabric, where the bays jut out over the piers, " except in the time of war ". Then, one supposes, trumpeters were busy away from home. The roadway must always have been narrow, and in 1791 the tower was so ruinous as to cause danger.

Is that all? Not quite. The long, mysterious, nearly obliterated personality of the walls of Norwich has one further expression. A little south of Bishop's Bridge is Pull's Ferry, the most photographed of all the ancient comely houses of Norwich. It is the only water-gate, for anciently it spanned a dyke that ran right up to the back of the houses now surrounding the Lower Close Square, once the farmyard of the Convent. It is also the best preserved, for it has been re-edified in these nineteen-fifties, and now holds the office of an architect, and in the old gate house itself, Girl Guides. The view from the opposite bank of the river, now a busy thoroughfare, of this old relic of the Wall of Norwich, with the Cathedral in the background, is so striking that it needs no words of mine.

XI

ST. MICHAEL IN THE GARDEN

As one tries to get a view of Norwich as a whole, what does one see? Go up on to the path that makes the circuit of the Castle Mound. Go up, if you have breath, by the cork-screw stair of one hundred and twenty steps in the angle of the Keep on to the battlements. Look out from the balcony of the City Hall, or from the tower of any one of the parish churches—there are still over a score of towers to choose from—and look around. What is the prevailing impression of a city of over one hundred thousand souls in 1952?

The answer, astonishingly enough, is—Trees!

Not for nothing was Norwich called the City of Gardens. In any month from September to Christmas you walk in fallen leaves in most Norwich streets. In any month from New Year to April you will see the dragon-green or silver trunks and the fine lacework of twigs shining with moisture or delicately out-lined with frost. From Easter onwards there are leaves and flowers at nearly every street corner. Nor are these mere flowering shrubs. There are more trees of forest size within the City boundary, even within the area of the old walls them-selves, than in the average equivalent of the open fields outside. I make no comparison with planted coverts, of course, but the point is important, as I shall show. This is a permanent characteristic of Norwich. It has always been so. How do I know? Because the history of the churches is well enough known. They are among the oldest and most permanent of the features of the streets. Many of them have pre-Conquest dedications to saints who are associated with Scandinavia or the coast between the Rhine and Elbe mouths. And two of them are associated with trees, St. Michael-at-Thorn and St. Martin-at-Oak. The former is called St. Michael ad Spinam in early Latin documents. The latter apparently always had an oak-tree in the churchyard, in the branches of which was a holy image of the Virgin. All the other churchyards had trees in them, as most of them have today. That accounts for the embowered appearance of Norwich, for, excluding the Cathedral Close, there are over thirty churches left, nearly all with a clump of trees; only a few have mere bushes. If you come in from Cromer, you will find busy Magdalen Street's row of shop-fronts broken by St. Saviour's and St. Clement's greenery. Old disused St. Simon and Jude is nearly hidden by trees, and St. George Tombland is surrounded by them. If you go out by plain, business-like Ber Street, St. Michael-at-Thorn spreads its pink petals or rusty leaves over the pavement, and St. John Sepulchre has a regular grove.

Now try the other dimension, west to east. If you come in from west or south-west Norfolk, St. Giles' has an unusual border to its churchyard, of standard wistaria. St. Peter Mancroft has an avenue leading to its north porch. Or, on the other western thoroughfare, St. Gregory has a knot of graceful birches and St. Andrew a splendid wild cherry. St. John Maddermarket has a regular bouquet. St. Miles Coslany has limes and St. Mary Coslany also. Palace Street does not need arguing. St. Martin's-at-Palace church stands at the gate of a gentleman's park; he happens to be the Lord Bishop of Norwich, but the view from his windows might be miles in the country. Old narrow King Street is another example. The trees of St. John Timberhill and All Saints' jut improbably between the houses. This is the basis of this characteristic of the streets of Norwich, but anyone may reply:

" Of course. There is great legal difficulty building on a churchyard. Consequently the churchyards of Norwich have retained their trees. They are rather numerous and that gives the place an air."

Yes, but these churchyards are only the main features in the green look of Norwich, the focal points, as it were, around which the foliage, so unusual in a city of its size, is gathered. But these trees in public places such as the churchyards, parish meeting-places and dumps, are not all. There were trees in the very streets. The oldest, most celebrated must have been that which stood only a little west of the house in which the Pastons lived and where some of the Paston letters may have been written. The street is still called Elm Hill, retains its cobbles and ancient house-fronts, and is perhaps the most pictured and photographed of all the streets in Norwich. This result was not achieved without considerable pressure on the City Council, but the project has justified itself, as anyone can see by the type of business and professional occupier now using the repaired but structurally ancient houses lining it. The elm that now justifies its name is the third I can remember, but the street was so called when the first maps that can be dignified by such a name were made, about A.D. 1760. Old Kirkpatrick, the City Chamberlain who made such prolonged researches into the streets of his borough, found that it was first called so in the days of Elizabeth, and ever since then it does not seem to have been without its elm-tree. Who replaced them as the successive elms died? For the elm is not the tree to which we attribute the utmost longevity. There you have it, the curious continuity of habit that makes the streets of Norwich so human. Incidentally the fact throws a queer side-light on a little realised piece of English history. The older name of the street was Houndgate, which seems to have been derived from the fact that it runs out eastward into what is now Wensum Street, opposite the spot at which the Bishop of Plantagenet times had the kennels for his hounds. This may well be believed, for from what we know of the Bishops of those days, such as Despencer the warrior, and others, they were quite likely to have kept a pack of hounds, if not several. When, however, we come on to a different type of ecclesiastic, gentle and scholarly, immersed in theological speculation and historical research, such as Matthew Parker and Joseph Hall, it is equally easy to believe that they did not hunt, and the kennels became an inn (the Maid's Head Hotel stands more or less on the site today), and the street was known by its elm-tree.

It is not the only one so known. In stately St. Giles' Street, where the splendid Georgian house-fronts of the Aldermen of the eighteenth century follow one another with hardly a break, there leads off just north of the churchyard, Willow Lane, which has quite another celebrity today. Here is a little, typical Norwich house, completely enclosed in a high wall, so that you would pass it by had not the princely loyalty of the late Lord Mancroft, a Norwich man by birth, caused a plaque to be affixed to the property he bought and gave to his native City. The inscription tells you that this was the house in which the queer, wayward George Borrow passed what may well have been the happiest and most tranquil—if tranquillity meant much to such a man—days of his life with his old mother, a Parfrement of East Dereham. This lane has been called after the willows that grew in it, or rather, I imagine, in the hedge of the neighbouring churchyard, since the days of King Henry VIII. They have been supplanted by a row of houses that are not older than Georgian, but the name sticks, and has stuck all these centuries.

These are streets along which one can drive anything up to the size of a modern lorry, and the names they have borne so long derive from trees of forest size, standing along them, in the midst of the City. But the green texture of Norwich that is so noticeable from a distance arises in part from smaller growths. Down what is mistakenly sign-posted as " Pitt " Street, as if it were named in commemoration of William Pitt, lies Cherry Lane. It runs along what was five centuries ago the churchyard of St. Olaf, the martyr King of Norway. The church was demolished or allowed to fall into disrepair and carted away. It may be that the Black Death depopulated the parish, or it may have been some one of the innumerable squabbles between the various ecclesiastical bodies of the Ages of Faith. Anyhow, St. Olaf's went, centuries before the Reformation, which is generally credited with the demolition of churches. Not only that, but the name became corrupted out of all semblance into St. Tooley, just as it is in a similar instance in London. One may well ask, " What gets into people? By what queer contortion is a famous name so transmogrified? " I know that it is often foolishly spelt " Olave " and that a good many innocent folk, in Norfolk at least, think it is another way of writing " Olive ", which they pronounce " Olave ". But that does not account for " Tooley ".

Well, it's done. The church is gone, the name is forgotten. In its place was a noisome pool that became in the course of centuries a general rubbish-dump or " pit ", on the principle that what is public property does not matter. It was filled up, but it had been there so long that the street was labelled Pit Street. A later and politer generation, wishing to forget the smell connected with it, converted it to " Pitt " Street.

All very nice. But I wonder what happens when, from one century to another, St. Olaf descends from his honourable place amid the stars dedicated to martyrs to visit the various dedications to him on earth. Does he mind when he finds that his street now bears the name of a later eighteenth-century statesman? Or is he pleased that cherry-trees grew along his churchyard wall and that fragrant name has stuck in spite of all the vicissitudes of history, and the oafish forgetfulness of human beings?

Let us not leave Pitt Street without catching another pleasant whiff that should come to anyone with imagination. The lane that leads from St. Mary Coslany to St. Miles Coslany is Rosemary Lane, and the wonderful old house, Pykerell's House, that rears its fifteenth-century roof beam alongside, used to be the Rosemary Tavern. What happened? Did the curate of St. Mary's say to the curate of St. Miles, " Let us have rosemary along the walk from my cure of souls to your cure of souls "? I do hope he did and was met by a handsome rejoinder.

So one might go on, up and down these old streets by Flower in Hand Yard, and even Flower Pot Yard. There were no less than three signs of the " Vine ", and while one or other of them might be disposed of as a mere fancy, it is not so easy to dis-believe in The Vineyard, in Magdalen Street. We know, I think, that the climate used to be milder, and wine was made as far north as the Suffolk border. The actual stubbs of vine-roots, I am told, have been dug up at Ditchingham and Bury St. Edmunds. Scientists say our globe does not spin evenly, but gyrates like a football that has received only a glancing kick. Thus the poles are displaced, and in fifteen thousand years the polar ice-cap will come as low as Newcastle unless, of course, some counter oscillation modifies the process. This tilting of the earth as it spins has shifted the limit of viniculture. Any-how, here are these allusions to the Vine and the Vineyard, and no less than four signs of the Grape, in a City in which that fruit no longer ripens without the aid of glass.

I have been sticking to the streets to show how early the citizens formed the habit of planting and maintaining trees, shrubs and plants, in their busy thoroughfares, and how it has lingered down the centuries. There lies, of course, behind it a further factor common to all old towns, but perhaps preserved more completely in Norwich than in many of them. Nowhere that I know of do you see, besides greenery at every street corner, a glimpse of green behind the houses, broadening out from private gardens, which are still to be found behind houses adjoining the Provision Market, to public lands, as one approaches the walls.

This often-overlooked feature of medieval towns accounts for the enormous length of the sieges they were capable of sustaining. The dairy stuff was within the walls. When some potentate or legislative body set about building a city wall, they did not merely include houses and paved streets. That would have been an impossible task for the successors of the original settlers in any Saxon burgh, and certainly in Norwich. They were obliged to include broad fields, trees, and even, in some cases, arable. (The enlargement of the confines of Norwich by Mary Tudor and Philip of Spain enclosed some thousand acres of ploughland. But that new Tudor Norwich never stood a siege.) Of course much of it is gone. Yet it is astonishing how much remains.

King Street is not a fair case, for nearly half its eastern side backs on to the river. The opposite bank, now densely appropriated by structural engineering, transport and sport, carries a splendid line of willows, 30 feet high. The sharply rising ground between King Street and Ber Street has been largely built up, but as one approaches the wall, here intact, one finds some hundreds of yards of dense coppice. Between Ber Street and the walls, as we have seen, lay a parish which seems to have been depopulated by the Black Death and abandoned. Even the nineteenth century failed to obliterate the open ground and forest trees still standing in the garden of the Convent of Notre Dame and in the large enclosure called St. Catherine's Close. The Earl of Surrey's garden has been only partly obliterated, and that again brings us to within less than a hundred yards of the Provision Market. Following the wall westwards, the case needs no arguing, for here, behind a long stretch of wall pretty well intact and sandwiched between it, a great modern factory, and the professional quarter adjoining the City Hall, is " Chapel Field ", now a public park. Its 8½ acres have a queer history. Once the pasture of the great College of St. Mary in the Fields (it was within the walls) it became the Butts at which the compulsory Archery of the

Elizabethan age was practised. When fire-arms replaced the bow, another use was found. It was made the Plague Pit for the hurried mass burials of 1666. The Plague disappeared, we know, and the City Fathers were left with one burial-ground too many. They deemed the City churchyards ample for the purpose, as may be gauged by the fact that many of them stand several feet above the roadway, which certainly has not sunk. Most roadways accumulate height, naturally. The church-yards outstripped them by sheer density of human material shovelled into them. The " parish pump ", source of all public supply, generally stood at the corner of the churchyard. That of the parish of St. John Maddermarket may yet be seen *in situ*. The first public analyst of Norwich declared that the water the citizens used was " pure essence of churchyard ". So the City Council turned Chapel Field into a reservoir. A glance at its shelving border will show how it was accommodated to that purpose.

Time rolled on. The City grew and the demand for water intensified. Finally the beginnings of a modern water supply were installed elsewhere and Chapel Field was turned into the handsome and well-planted public park, bordered by wide, high avenues. Anyone who believes in ghosts would meet a queer company there any All Hallows' Eve. Chantry priests, rich and proud; Elizabethan bowyers and fletchers, tough and hearty; the first water engineers. Today a light-hearted crowd dances to the strains of a military band. In 1914, those who were to form the armies of the Somme and Passchendaele drilled there, and in 1940 some of the survivors, older but just as devoted, formed the first musters of the Home Guard.

From " St. Giles' Broad Street ", as it is called in the older directories, and well it deserves that distinction, for it is archi-tecturally the handsomest street in Norwich, northwards to the river below, there is no public open ground, though there are many churchyard trees and private gardens, and one public garden in old obscure Pottergate, a children's playground. This was from a very early date a closely-built-up area, just as the " morning-room " of the typical Victorian middle-class home would be filled with odd jobs, women sewing, tradesmen repairing, making and painting. There is no church here and no gates, and yet a certain number of big trees contrive to lift their topmost boughs among the roofs. Not until we come down to Westwick, running along the river bank at the foot of the steep slope, can we emerge to the open air of the water-side, now disfigured by the traces of some of the most savage bombing in Norwich. But from what I have said, there need be no despair. The station of the line that connects Norwich with mid-Norfolk and Lynn and Leicester has been rebuilt, and already the bushes are reclothing the banks of the stream that was so pretty when John Crome painted it, and there still is, a little further up, where stands the damaged front of the Dolphin Inn (Bishop Hall's Palace, giving its name to Old Palace Road), an ideal country house, or river-side villa for the grandee of the seventeenth century. Opposite this, Heigham Hall has a miniature private park that helps the green vista. But I am straying beyond the walls. It is the green in the old streets that I want to capture, and there is not far to go. The bridges here—and there are three in 300 yards—bring the wanderer's steps back to St. Martin-at-Oak.

You have been here before. It is one of the noteworthy members of the family. Just behind it stands someone else, as it were: a member of the family who does not wish to be seen, someone with downcast eyes, who thinks a lot, but does not speak unless moved by the spirit.

What am I talking about? You will never know unless you leave well-used and historic St. Martin-at-Oak and dodge down Jenkin's Lane, a corridor between the houses so narrow that it is uncomfortable for more than one abreast. It leads out into what was one of the largest of the open green spaces of Norwich, and is still of considerable extent and bordered by trees of 30 to 40 feet in height. What does it contain, that it should be so secret?

The answer is before you. The ruin of good red brick at the corner of the narrow lane is the original Quaker Meeting of Norwich, hence perhaps its obscure position. Over the wall is their burial-ground, with, I believe, for Quakers, an unusual array of tombstones on which may be read the names of the Gurneys, Birkbecks and others of the founders of what is today Barclays great Bank, and their friend, Amelia Opie. That is all very well for the eighteenth century, and accounts for the obscurity of the place, before the small and despised sect came to contain most of the wealthy, learned and distinguished, and built itself a more central place in Goat Lane, just west of the Guildhall.

But why was this corner always so green? Once more, as so often in Norwich, no one really knows. On the earliest maps, in the earliest deeds, it is called Gildencroft, and once filled the whole space between the walls and St. Martin-at-Oak Lane, and between St. Augustine's Street and Pitt Street on the east, and Oak Street on the west. Moreover, St. George's Street, anciently called Gildengate, seemed to lead to it from the Guildhall. So an easy explanation was found. This was the ground where the Guilds paraded, marching along Gildengate from the Guildhall. Too easy, in fact, for the Guilds had little or nothing to do with the Guildhall or Gildencroft. It must have been some ten to twelve acres in extent, and parts of it were an early recreation ground. Jousts and archery went on there. A little bothy on it was called Tabor's Folly, and is thought to have held the players on tabor and tucket, to which tune youths and maidens danced. The dangerous type of street football, known as Camping, had its place.

So say some, whose testimony has been laboriously gathered up by the late E. A. Kent, F.S.A. He also found that the abusive Thomas Nashe, Elizabethan pamphleteer and " columnist " as we should call him, said it was the Gypping or Gilding croft where herrings were cured, better, it was alleged, here than at Yarmouth. One need not believe Nashe, who was, like all his kind, more anxious to miscall his opponents than to record fact, but his immediate successors were sufficiently impressed to spell the name of the place as he altered it on the maps of the period. So there it is. You can take your choice. All that concerns me is that here, within the walls, were some acres, now only two or three, of green grass and tall trees.

Is that all? Not a bit. The main internal pasture of Norwich, as you see it from Mousehold, stretches from the gates of the Close, includes the garden or rather park of the Bishop's Palace, and fills the whole north-eastern elbow the river makes below the escarpment of Mousehold Heath. The Close and the " Hospital Meadows ", as they are best called, for they abut upon the ancient Hospital of St. Giles, just outside the Close wall, make up altogether another ten to twelve acres of greenery and tall trees. Finally, the " Castle Ditches " that surround the mound cover 3½ acres, and the Cattle Market, that surrounds the eastern and southern sides of them, is also planted with avenues, among which are almost the only plane-trees in Norwich.

That is why, in these days of frenzied rebuilding, the general air of Norwich, from any high or central viewpoint, is rather that of a big village. In spite of unique industries of world-wide fame, from mustard to canaries, great financial institutions, and centuries of compressed City life, the old place still has air. Its family, as I have called its streets, are in the garden, and always have been.

H

XII

ST. MARTIN'S PART IN THE GREAT QUARREL
(KETT'S REBELLION)

ST. MARTIN owes his chief renown to a great act of Christian charity, when he divided his cloak with a beggar. But the appropriateness of naming one of the older Norwich streets after him did not appear until that crisis in the affairs of our island known as the Reformation. St. Martin was a soldier, and this parish, one of two in Norwich with churches dedicated to him, was the scene in A.D. 1549 of the most savage and protracted fighting that has ever taken place in Norwich. This is the more remarkable since Norwich missed the Wars of the Roses, and the Parliamentary Wars two hundred years later.

The life of this member of the Norwich family is therefore human enough, and runs on similar pattern to that of many a life of the elderly man of the nineteen fifties. How many of us were humble but relatively safe, useful but peaceful enough members of the kingdom of Edward VII and George V, until, in 1914, our century-long peace was rudely shattered. Since then we have been through sufficient physical risk and turmoil for our lifetime. And now, if my prophecy is of any worth, we may very likely die in our beds, after all.

That is exactly what happened to the street we know as Palace Street, which contains the bulk of the parish of St. Martin " at Palace ", as it is called because the formidable wall of the Palace of the Bishops of Norwich, continuing that of the Close, confronts the whole length of the street with its impressive bulk. War is a fitful fever. It can alter and destroy, but it cannot last. What it spares returns to peace, and only occasionally is there some mark on the stones, some scar on face or limb, to show what violence shook human existence briefly. The street owes its existence to those years of strong-fisted " pacification " that succeeded the Norman Conquest. Some say that the Roman track which ran all along the ridge of Ber Street and descended, under the Castle mound to Tombland, continued under the Cathedral and is to be seen continuing in Bishopgate. Others say it turned north to Fye-bridge. I shall not pretend to decide. It is, however, clear that once the Normans had planked down their great Cathedral where it stands, they had stopped up whatever way led east-ward from the old Saxon market-place, and it seems likely that Palace Street then came into existence as the way to White-friars Bridge, and later to Bishop's Bridge, and so to Thorpe, Yarmouth and East Norfolk generally. The very latest opinion seems to think that some means of crossing the river existed on the site of these bridges, soon after the Conquest, at least. That is how Palace Street came into existence, and as the place prospered a church was built which seems to have been called " St. Martin-on-the-Hill ", for " hill " in Norfolk means any-thing a foot or two higher than the submersible marsh. Rebuilt on this site, the present church dominates one of the many " plains " or open spaces of Norwich, backing on to " Quay-side ", the higher of the landing-places on the river-bank. It remains today a useful parking place adjoining Tombland, which, despite the Normans, has never ceased to be the main road junction of Norwich. Presumably the little " plain " was also an appropriate approach to the impressive gateway of the Bishop's Palace, that still overlooks and lends character to it. Apart from that it is an unpretentious part of Norwich, and for centuries no one foresaw that the fate of the City and possibly of the country would be contested there, rather than round the Castle or the newer municipal centre that had grown up round the Provision Market and its Guildhall.

The crucial date for Palace Street was the year 1549, and the battle fought in it was the first phase of what has come down to us as " Kett's Rebellion ". For a long time it was fashionable to write about the English Reformation as though it were a dispute between the Pope and Henry VIII, with local reper-cussions between the Church and the population. But we may now reasonably ask ourselves if the general structure of English society in, say, the year 1500, or the year 1400 even, could have continued indefinitely. Had Henry VIII never lived, is it likely that this island would have continued to be organised in sparsely populated manors, held under Feudal tenure and worked by peasants on a subsistence basis? We shall never know, but we may think that there were causes for the complete change in outlook that took place between 1500 and 1700, which had little to do with Henry VIII. One thing is plain. The open-field strips began to be enclosed by a new sort of man who wanted to keep sheep in hitherto unprecedented numbers. This, combined with the aftermath of the French Wars and the Wars of the Roses, and increased by the suppression of so many religious houses, wrung the economy of the Middle Ages all out of shape. Men began to move about, the old land-owning classes, ecclesiastical or secular, lost control, a long process of painful readjustment began to take place.

Amid all this vague disturbance emerges the figure of Robert Kett. Attempts have lately been made to show him as a democratic hero, attempting to protect the " rights " of the " poor ". Some of us wonder if the poor were conscious of any rights at that date, still more may wonder if an industrialist (he was a tanner) and landowner of that time was deeply concerned in the principles of the French Revolution which happened years later. What we know for certain is that Robert Kett was engaged in a quarrel with another landowner, Flowerdew, apparently as to which of them should enclose some land. It came to a head in Wymondham market-place on 7 July, a hot day, when there may have been a good deal of drink flowing. At the end of it Kett found himself leading a crowd estimated (for what the accounts of those days were worth) at several thousands, on Norwich, in order to right the public wrongs. What these were felt to be we shall see, but some of us may have a suspicion that a good many of the crowd were out for what they could get. Kett himself started with a purely private grievance. To understand the situation thus created we have to remember that there was then no police force and no standing army save hired companies of professional soldiers. The sentiment regarding authority had been crumbling for a century. The men in the crowd who followed Kett, or rather perhaps pushed him in front of them, were all members of the local " musters " of that date, a sort of Home Guard left over from the Feudal system, except of course a possibly large number of mere scallywags of the sort Falstaff, Nym, Pistol and the rest fairly represented. In either case they had rudimentary side-arms and were used to them. The more stable elements did not see why, if land was going to be enclosed, they should not benefit in the general scramble they had seen going on all their lives. The less stable elements were out for loot; Norwich was rich.

What sort of order they marched in, how much control Kett or anyone else had over them, is a question to which we have only the vaguest answer. He seems to have halted at a tree on the roadside near the village of Hethersett, still surrounded by a railing and marked by a notice on a tablet: " Kett's Oak ". What for? Did he hold an inspection and marshal his forces there? His brother William, a butcher, is spoken of as his lieutenant. Small bodies of like-minded people made some attempt to capture Lynn and Yarmouth, and, failing, joined his forces sooner or later and probably in driblets. We come to one accepted date. On 10 July his " army "—said to number twenty thousand, but who counted them?—reached the hamlet of Bowthorpe, a mile west of the City. Here the High Sheriff of Norfolk, Sir Edward Windham, rode up and proclaimed the party rebels, " and only 'scaped by his horsemanship being better than his rhetorik ". Apparently the gates of the City had been closed and the walls manned, for on demanding passage and refreshment, Kett's force was refused and marched round the north-western face of the defences, by Hellesdon and Drayton bridges and by one which they made themselves, thus crossing the Yare and the Wensum. This brought them to the open, heather-covered ledge of Mousehold, now a public park that overlooks the City from the north-east. Kett set up his headquarters at the " Oak of Reformation ", which stood on the site of the present water-tower. But partly owing to the denial of the City, and partly perhaps from sheer wantonness, much damage had already been done. Enclosures had been broken down in all directions, and large numbers of sheep and deer seized and slaughtered. Men must eat, and the sort of men that Kett led were not going hungry. It is difficult now to disentangle the disjointed and partial contemporary accounts, but it looks as if the major gentry had been rounded up and made prisoners in the Earl of Surrey's house that occupied the ruins of St. Leonard's Priory near by. These included Thomas Codde or Cod, the Mayor, who may have gone out to negotiate. There seem to have been several debates and interviews. Some sort of a petition,

containing many rather reasonable demands for reform of the
Church, the system of land tenure, and the weights and
measures, mixed up with prohibition of keeping rabbits and
pigeons (which probably damaged the crops), was formulated
and sent to the King. The curate of St. Martin's-at-Palace,
Matthew Parker, afterwards Archbishop of Canterbury, seems
to have gone out to preach to them. The rebels are also said
to have attended service in the City churches, which argues
some degree of " infiltration ".

So passed a week or so of futile and deteriorating exchanges.
During this, a prominent citizen, Sotherton, got to London, and
may have carried with him the original, or a copy of the
" petition ". The King (or the Privy Council speaking for
him) gave some indication that the spirit of the demands
would be met, and the York Herald came down to Norwich
and made a speech to the embattled crowd. He seems to have
spoken severely about their iniquities, but held out the hope of
pardon. Kett appears to have overruled the more moderate
of his followers who were willing to lay down their arms, on
the grounds that pardon was for evil-doers, whereas those with
him were innocent men only asking for their rights. The
facts of the case are complicated by a story that a boy in the
crowd made a rude gesture at the herald, one of whose
attendants shot him dead. That may have rendered negotia-
tion impossible. It sounds just the sort of thing that might
have happened. Rude and completely fearless Norfolk boys
would do much the same in any heated political meeting today.
They would not nowadays be shot for it, but the effect on any
possible negotiations can be imagined. After that, fighting
seems to have broken out, though I have never been able to
convince myself that there had not already been skirmishes.

The whole affair was reported years later in a compilation by
one Nevill called *The Norfolk Fury*. On this Blomfield, the
local historian, and everyone else since, has based some account
of the affair, but it seldom makes sense. The probabilities can
be estimated by anyone who climbs or takes a bus up to the
ledge of Mousehold Heath and looks down on Norwich, from
the water-tower, from the site of which Kett looked down.
Houses now impede the view, but a few score yards north,
where the modern Britannia Infantry Barracks stand, the

problems of attack and defence become plain.   Norwich had a
respectable wall running along the skyline from the tower
still visible among the trees of Bracondale above the river, on
the left (or south) right round to the north-west, where the wall
met the river again at what is now the ex-L.M.S. railway.
Here water made the defence for about 200 yards, and the wall
then continued all round to Barr Gate, by the eighteenth-
century Nelson Barracks, at our feet.   Thence, below us, along
to the river at Bracondale, there was no wall, but mostly open
meadows.   No doubt, when the wall was built, two hundred
years before Kett's time, the river-banks had been so marshy
and cut up by little dykes that no wall was needed.   But Kett's
men seem to have swum the river at their ease, thus turning the
fortified Bishop's Bridge, leading into Bishopgate, that encircles
the Cathedral Close.   However, once over, they still had to
contend with a long façade of large, substantial buildings, houses
in King Street, then the walls of the Greyfriars, then the even
more unscaleable wall of the Close.   The one place at which
they could pierce this second line of defence was precisely where
Bishopgate led into St. Martin's-at-Palace " Plain ".   Once
there, they had only a few yards to go to arrive at Tombland,
the main road junction.   Furthermore, from St. Martin's they
outflanked Whitefriars Bridge and took the whole of the
northern section of the wall in the rear, thus solving their
military problem.

This, according to the accounts, they did twice.   The first
time they had only to deal with the City " muster " or Home
Guard and apparently reached Tombland, where Augustine
Steward, the deputy Mayor, acting in the absence of the imprisoned Mayor, seems to have organised defence lines that held
them.   There is a lot of vague talk about an artillery duel,
though where Kett obtained his guns is not stated.   It is said,
however, that whoever commanded in the City, with incredible folly moved forward what artillery the City had, from
the neighbourhood of the Castle, where it was safe and might
have guaranteed at least half the built-up area, to a position in
advance of Bishop's Bridge, under Kett's nose.   He promptly
captured it.   There is no making out if this is the source of
Kett's guns, or if he had obtained others.

At last we come to the arrival of the Marquis of Northampton, from London, with troops said to amount to one thousand four hundred men, composed of fully armoured knights, a body of Italian mercenaries and others unspecified. He pitched his camp about 1 August in the Provision Market, and proceeded to push Kett's people back, evidently with great difficulty, for they captured the chief of the Italians and hanged him in full view of the City, fighting magnificently, dragging the arrows from their wounds to supply their own ill-provided archers, and crawling with severed limbs into the *mêlée* to do what damage they could. It is reasonable to suppose the City inside the walls was approximately clear, though one has a suspicion that the attackers had many friends within the defences and that gates were surreptitiously opened, or other means of ingress found.

Anyhow, on 8 August (over a month after the operations started from Wymondham market-place) they attacked again. They seem not to have relinquished Barr Gate and to have refused another offer of pardon. Once more the key position was St. Martin's-at-Palace. Here Northampton apparently sent his armoured knights to bring back his artillery, which had been outflanked. Anyone can descend from Mousehold, and follow Bishopgate and see how likely this was. The main evidence is a tablet on the wall of a house opposite the Bishop's Palace Gate (the Close walls appear to have been quite unscaleable). It states that Lord Sheffield was killed on that spot. More detailed accounts say his horse had come down over some entrenchments, and he was here battered to death by " one of them whose name was Fulke ", who " basely murdered him with a club, although he had discovered himself and had offered the villain a large reward to save his life ".

The immediate effect of the fall of this nobleman, described as " the King's Lieutenant ", of thirty-five others who were buried in the adjoining churchyard, and of six other knights buried at St. Simon and St. Jude beyond Tombland, seems to have been a panic. Indeed, it became enshrined in legend. When I was a boy there was no such tablet, but only a paving-stone in the sidewalk with a gigantic S on it. Yet all the semi-literate inhabitants of the alleys and yards that then surrounded the spot knew what the S meant.

This probably decided the battle. One cannot understand

why no attempt was made to sally from the Close by the Bishop's Palace gate or the numerous posterns. In fact one suspects that Northampton was an inept commander. He was soon in flight. Norwich was given over to pillage and arson, for several weeks. But here the extemporary organisation of Kett broke down. He had appointed " governors " to many of the Norfolk Hundreds, but does not seem to have been capable of taking over the more complicated City administration. Perhaps the rowdy elements were beyond his control.

The Privy Council, now thoroughly alarmed, as well they might be, forthwith detached the Earl of Warwick (later Duke of Northumberland) with an army destined for an expedition into Scotland which included a body of Swiss arquebusiers. About 23 August he arrived at the City, and cleared it, street by street, largely by gunfire, to which the rebels had no answer. Even so, much of his baggage was misdirected and captured, and there were several days of confused fighting. At length, the City recaptured, the Royal Army issued from St. Martin's Gate, and prepared to attack the rebel camp from the north. Either from ignorance or helplessness, Kett failed to hold his men. They fired their camp and came down from their comparatively strong position to what is known as " Dussens Dale ", the lower part of Mousehold near the walls. In spite of initial successes, they were outgunned and then charged by the heavy cavalry and cut to pieces. Kett fled and was captured, and the usual barbarous repressive slaughter was carried out, while his " army " melted away. Robert Kett was hanged from the battlements of Norwich Castle, and his brother from Wymondham steeple.

So today, as one strays down the quiet backwater of Palace Street, and halts to admire the fine Georgian houses surrounding the " plain ", including one that was inhabited for years by John Sell Cotman, and reads the inscription on the tablet about Lord Sheffield, one has the impression of some elderly, grey-haired figure about whom lingers a legend of prolonged and purposeful violence. Can this quiet place ever have reeked of blood and black powder, and resounded to the shrieks of the wounded, the shouts of the victors, the clatter of steel-clad horsemen and their heavy steeds, flung to earth and done to death, between the strong walls and the burning houses? Well, it did. It may look peaceful today, but for nearly two months in 1549 Norfolk men defeated one professional army and gave another all it could do. Within a generation, most of the reforms demanded in the " Petition " were granted, and the courage and steadfastness so misdirected were turned to the making of the great Elizabethan era. All those independent spirits did not pass in vain.

" What did you do in the Great War, Daddy? " One of the recruiting posters of the First World War put the question into the mouths of the children of those who did not volunteer. Kett's men could have answered. But the answer, as it has come down to us, is confused as the fighting was, or as the motives that caused it. Something happened on those old stones that people living near have never forgotten.

XIII

THE STRANGERS, JEW, NETHERLANDER AND WALLOON

FAMILIES are not what they were in size. But it is still possible to enter some hospitable house, thinking to meet the family, parents and children one has known some time. Then, in the group of people round the tea-table, someone says: " Do you know our cousin . . . have you met our friend . . .? " and one is face to face with a stranger, admitted for some good reason to the intimacies of that house.

So it is in Norwich. There is English history and to spare, even pre-English history. Then suddenly one comes on something different: on traces of people who entered into the life of the place, who became Norwich born, but who will always retain some sign of their other origin. They are the " Strangers ", to use the term by which they are described in the municipal records, when they had to be legislated for. In such a place as Norwich, created out of invasion on invasion, whose growth has been marked by brute force, one has to distinguish. There are two main qualities that mark out the Strangers from the Invaders. These latter cease after 1066. They took Norwich by force, and it absorbed them until their origins were forgotten. The Strangers, on the other hand, came about A.D. 1100, no one quite knows, and continued to come, because they were, more or less, welcome. Why? Because they served a purpose, and later because they were fugitives from tyranny and persecution and Norwich gave them shelter, a fact of which all trueborn Norwichers are inordinately proud. We are not so ready to admit that they did us good, improved our finance and our textile trade, and added a rich contribution to the achievement of Norwich in the Arts and Sciences, in that gradual substitution of the work of the head for the work of limbs, which is one measure of advancing civilisation.

Then, at length, they disappeared. In some cases the slow halting improvement in the conditions in the countries of their origin permitted them to return and resume their own

nationality. In many instances they had grown rich and prosperous during what was to them, after all, exile in England,
however welcome a refuge it may have been at first. In yet
other family histories we find the Stranger settling down, inter-
marrying with local people, his name becoming merged by the
marriage of his daughters with local citizens or adjusted so that
it became English, as his sons forgot whence they had been
brought.

The three main strains of Strangers that influenced the
streets of Norwich, changing their character, giving rise to new
buildings or adapting existing ones, are the Jews, the " Dutch "
and the " French ".

Like everything else in Norwich, the history of the influence
these peoples brought to bear on its streets, and thus on its
general character, is complicated by mistakes and incompre-
hension. The story is long and intricate and often extra-
ordinary. The general effect on Norwich is good. None of
these people brought poverty or low standards of life. The
Jews came for the reasons that have led them to migrate into so
many countries. The Flemings, or first wave from the Low
Countries, came to reorganise the growing textile trade. The
true " Dutch " (though that is a very misleading term, they
themselves preferred " Netherlander ") came as religious and
political refugees. The " French " were French or Walloon-
dialect-speaking Belgians. Finally, at the time of the revoca-
tion of the Edict of Nantes, there came from France proper,
French Huguenot refugees, in some ways the most distinguished
of all. Traces remain of all these various people who arrived
in Norwich between about A.D. 1350 and about 1685.

The earliest and most permanent of all these elements that go
to make the character of Norwich streets is of course the Hebrew
one. Half-way down King Street stands a lofty building of
some architectural pretensions. Two large windows of the
time of James I light its first floor, raised above the street on a
blind but plainly substantial basement. It is now built into
the premises of Young's Brewery, whose surveyor's office
occupies some of its best rooms. Its name in the directory of
the nineteen-fifties is " The Musick House ", and nothing could
be more typical of the fascination of the streets of Norwich.
For that name does not indicate its latest, or even its nineteenth-

century use and quality. The story is so long and complicated that it might be the story of some guest one encountered at a party with whom one might not unreasonably begin a conversation like this :

" Good afternoon. You are taking part in the performance this afternoon, I see."

" No ! "

" Oh, I beg your pardon. I thought you were in fancy dress."

" These things. No. They are my ancestor's. But they are more becoming and much better quality than any one can buy today."

" Of course they are. It's just the fashion that has altered. For the worse, I think."

" I don't bother much with fashion. I've seen too many ! "

" Quite. I rather think I misunderstood our host when he introduced us. I gathered you were a musician. . . ."

" That's the name I have inherited. But actually I am in business."

" I hope you prosper."

" Oh, yes, thank you. I'm on the professional side now. I used to be in the Retail Trade."

" Songs and pianoforte pieces ? "

" No. Beer."

" Ah ; humble but popular ! "

" Rather a come-down. I had been accustomed to the clergy, the landed gentry and the higher branches of the law. I was glad to get back to a responsible position."

" Forgive me. You say Get back."

" That is how I started life. Banking ! "

" Really. Yet you stick to your inherited concert name."

" It's as good as many another."

" What was your ancestor's instrument ? "

" It was one of the Waits."

" The olde Yule-tide Waits."

" They may be nowadays. But the Norwich Waits of those days were nationally famous. Rather like the London Symphony Orchestra ! "

" You don't say ! "

" I certainly do. And then, latterly I have had to do with Mr. Nugent Monck, which almost justifies my title."

" Of course. What a story ! "

Yes, it is a story. It begins in the basement of the old place. It is only a few years ago that research showed the cellars used by the brewery to be of inordinate size, strength and antiquity. The vaulting would have been no discredit to the crypt of a cathedral. By endless perusal and collation of deeds, and research tedious to recount here, it was gradually made out that the northern gable of the present building, and a larger extent below ground, was the strong house of Isaac the Jew, a financier who came to work with the Normans. The position of those invaders was much that of a trading corporation which wants to exploit some large new concession and has to look round for capital. This the Jews could provide in precious metal. Indeed, what else could they do, being debarred by the Church from all skilled trade and agriculture. Few strains of medieval life are more thoroughly disgraceful than its chronic anti-Semitism. The Jews were wanted. They were needed. They were employed. They were hated because they were successful. Finally they were massacred, robbed and exiled.

The story is by no means so bad in Norwich as elsewhere. At the Musick House it has been discovered, by the mason's marks on some of the stonework, that the builder employed was probably the one at work on the Cathedral Priory. Only the church and the Jews could afford stone houses. What Isaac's Hall may have been like can be well seen by comparison with Moyses Hall at Bury St. Edmunds. (I have said elsewhere that the late Lord Mancroft, one of the most distinguished sons of Norwich of Jewish religion, always thought that the Prior protected the Jews because they were oculists. They knew how to grind a lens.) Isaac was allowed to live outside the Jewry and was plainly a privileged person. It is not certain if he was one of the Hebrew Congregation that sought sanctuary in the Castle from the outbreak of anti-Semitic rioting of the thirteenth century. Anyhow, he and his disappeared. The old house passed from hand to hand. Henry III gave it to Sir William de Valoines. Its subsequent owners and in some cases occupiers were Ralf de Earlham, Richard of Norwich, Alan de Frestone Archdeacon of Norfolk, Constantine de Mortimer, Sir James de Audeley, Sir William Benhall, Lady Katherine Felbrigge,

Sir William Yelverton, Recorder of Norwich. A distinguished company. Plainly it was a town house of county gentry. But there was more to come. The Pastons had it, and then the great Sir Edward Coke, Recorder of Norwich and Lord Chief Justice, " among his 99 other and larger places situate all over England ", Mr. E. A Kent, F.S.A., says. Like all Paston property, it went into Chancery with the collapse of the fortunes of that family, and re-emerges as belonging to Thomas Coke of Holkham. From him it went to Alderman Knight Gobbett, under whom it seems to have been the home of the Norwich Waits, the famous band of musicians (they played among other instruments, recorders, and we are told " Five Recorders are a whole noise ", which sounds as if it must be true !). Thus it acquired the name " The Musick House ". It descended to the wine and carrying trade, as the gentry began to forsake Norwich, and came to the present careful and responsible owners in 1863. Coke seems to have built the southern (second) gable under which are those splendid windows, on the site of the Norman porch. In 1919 the Norwich Players were allowed to rent the top floor, which had been inserted in Issac's original hall, and here Nugent Monck began the world-famous part of his career, and this floor, over the modern offices, still houses the Musick House Guild.

That is what can happen in Norwich to the strong room of a Jewish banker of the twelfth century. If the explanation has been lengthy, I can only say that the present building, which would excite the remark of any photographer or artist, does not, without all the history, explain itself as being what I have described, or what it is commonly called. Isaac the Jew would be surprised. So would the Pastons, some of whom seem to have lived in it for nearly a century.

There are other marks left by the Jewish people on the streets of Norwich. Those who were not friends of the Prior had to live in The Jewry, which was situated in what is now Greens' extensive outfitting establishment in the Gentlemen's Walk. On the opposite side of the road, the Haymarket Cinema covers what was Abraham's Hall. In these cases, however, the mutation of the centuries has obliterated any obvious trace. Not so behind the queer-shaped little doorway on the western arm of St. George's Tombland church alley. This opened into what had plainly been at one time, probably after the re-entry of the Jews under the Commonwealth, a synagogue. Can you see the gaberdined and bearded figures, with shawl and slippers, gliding in there, not especially wanting to be seen. They shared with the Quakers a portion of the old Gildencroft for their burial-ground, being also unblessed, according to the medieval Church, so that they could not use the parish church-yards. We have got over those superstitions by the time we come to the nineteenth century, when the Jews built themselves a synagogue in what is still Synagogue Street, between " Mountergate " and St. Anne's Lane. It is still to be seen, and it is ironic that its remains occupy part of the site of the Austin Friars' Priory. Badly bombed in 1942, the congrega-tion built themselves a fine modern synagogue, just outside St. Giles' Gates, opposite the Roman Catholic Church of St. John.

The opening service was most impressive. I sat wearing my hat, on the men's side. I did not see many praying-shawls. Where a Christian place of worship would have the altar hung a fine, heavy curtain of dark blue velvet embroidered indis-criminately with lions, five-point stars and other emblems. From behind this came a very fine-looking priest (I believe a cantor from London) in the proper vestments, carrying what looked at first sight like a very elaborate bagpipe, but turned out to be the Roll of the law on its silver-headed rollers. The congregation stood, and a friendly worshipper found the place for me in a book printed in Hebrew and English on opposite pages. I joined in what seemed to be responses, and found I was singing, or rather intoning, part of the Psalms. It came to an end, the priest re-entered the Holy Place behind the curtain and restored the Roll to its place, and we non-participants drifted out. There was a police guard outside, which made me wonder, since I have met little anti-Semitism in Norwich.

Thus was the Jewish Community in the 1950's confirmed in its place in Norwich streets after its wanderings during the centuries.

The settlement of citizens of the Low Countries certainly began after the marriage of Edward III, but they do not seem to have left any distinct and separate trace of themselves as a Community. This comes with the later settlement of Eliza-

13. THE PROVISION MARKET AND ST. PETER'S MANCROFT

14. PRINCE'S STREET

beth's reign, when it is said 330 Flemings and Walloons were invited "and that their total number including women and children soon amounted to 5,000 ". It is clear, however, from the contemporary accounts that by the barbarity of Alva's campaign in the Netherlands many had already been driven from their homes and settled in London and Sandwich. Their numbers rapidly increased, and there seem to have been disputes between the Northerners or " Dutch " and the more southerly, called indifferently " French " or " Walloons ", as to which owned the patent for " bombazines " and " white works ". They were eventually granted the use of the choir of the long-secularised church built by the Black or Dominican Friars, which now forms the principal public hall of Norwich, the nave being known as St. Andrew's Hall and the choir as Blackfriar's Hall. Here, under the modern boarding of the floor of the latter portion, are the tombstones of the settlers, largely from Amsterdam, who for the best part of a century formed a compact, wealthy and highly civilised section of the population of Norwich. There can be no mistake about the character and language of this congregation by the time James I had been succeeded by his son. For on the wall built by the Friars generations earlier there still remains a fine bronze plaque, several feet in extent, framed in stone and bearing this touching and polyglot inscription:

Epithaphmin

Joannis Elison

Circter XXXVI Annos Ecclesiæ Nordovico-Belgicœ

Pastoris Fidelissimi

Nati XI Aprilis MDLXXXI, Denati XIX Augusti Anno MDCXXXIX

Cuius adorandum docuit Facundia Christum,
Et pia dexteritas pandit ad astra Viam,
Hic jacet exanimis; tacet eheu mellita Sonora
Linguaq; sed post hac non habitura parem.

Den waerden Elison, wiens heijlge leer en leven
Soo quamen over een en maeckten paden even,
Leijdt hier in't Stof outzielt, wiens Hemels-vloeijend stem
Nu swijght: en sijns gelijck en komt ergeen na hem.

That worthy Elison, whose holy life and preaching
Did equally advance with both his Dutch Flock teaching,
Lies here in dust dissolved, whose loud sweete voice no moore
In this Church Sounds, but now sings in that heavnly Chore.

I

Hier Rust'l Eerwaard geheent ons Vaders Elison
Die door Godts woord ons Ziel doorstraalde als de Zon
Bevroore aarde doed; Endeed weer als herleven,
Ons gansch bevroore Ziel; Hij leyden ons tenleven
Steeds door hem Zelfs betracht, daar hij is voorgegaan
Hij leerden onsten heijl on bij Godt wel te staan
Hij hreech zijn avond hier enwacht een blijde morgen
Hij wrocht zijn Xalicheijd in't leven vol Van Zorgen

Franc de Bruijnne	Impensis IOANNIS Filij	Door Leendert Sijmonsz
scripsit	natu maximi mercatoris	gesneeden
	Amstel odamensis	

One does not need to be fluent in all the three languages
involved to perceive that when, after over a quarter of a
century of ministry, the faithful pastor of the " North Belgians' "
" loud sweete voice " sounded no more in that church, but in
the " heavnly Chore ", his son, a merchant of Amsterdam,
had this very handsome memorial written by Franc de Bruijnne
and cut by Leendert Sijmonsz. For by then they had won their
battle, Alva and all he represented had collapsed. The pastor
himself had been " home ", as he probably called it, in 1634,
and there in Amsterdam he and his wife, Maijken or Mary,
were painted by Rembrandt. Photographs of this pair of
handsome portraits now hang below the fine plaque, and no
words of mine are needed to call attention to the substantial
dignity and spiritual elevation of mind depicted on these
countenances. Disbelieve Rembrandt if you can. And remember that these two people lived in Norwich, walked these
streets, and entered " Blackfriars " Hall, which was their
assigned church, every Sunday morning for at least a quarter of
a century. This is the most vivid evidence I can produce of a
certain element in the streets of Norwich. The Strangers
contributed that, in return for the shelter afforded them against
tyranny. I think Norwich was repaid, not merely by those
handsome people. It was a " Dutchman ", Solempne, who
founded the first printing-press in Norwich. The founder of
the Norwich School of silversmiths was Petersen; I do not
know if that name betokens Dutch origin. But I, as a boy,
heard the last sermon preached in Dutch in Norwich, about
A.D. 1900. Since then, religious exercises in the language of
the Netherlands have been confined to the church in Austin
Friars. But the names linger in Norwich—Dover (Donneart),

De Hague, De Light and others. It may seem shadowy today, but what shall we seem in 2050?

The French-speaking Strangers were allotted the ancient parish church of St. Mary the Less in Queen Street. In origin the same, generally speaking, as the other parish churches of Norwich, it is additionally remarkable today for the fact that it shows how, in the Middle Ages, as the density of old cities increased, such a building became incorporated in the surrounding lay buildings. Shops and other premises touch its walls on three sides, while the tower, at the west end, has one buttress protruding into what was the drawing-room of a City house and is now the office of Norwich Consolidated Charities (thereby hangs a tale, but not one to be told just here).

The effect is that the church is entered by its south porch down a short, cavernous alley between dwellings. On a dusky evening it is not hard to imagine the little troop of families making their way under the lamp supported on an arch bracket of iron, with all that *farouche méfiance* (as they would have called it) which is characteristic of French-speaking people in particular, and refugees in general. Father and mother I am sure herded the younger members of the household under their wing, casting scornful looks at anyone not of their special community, and ready with tongue or sidearms to defend themselves against unfriendly citizens or interfering officials, just as they had defended themselves in the towns of their birth. Nearly all townspeople, I will wager, skilled weavers and professional people, strong of character and lofty of spirit, they had declined to be dragooned into religious observances which they had ceased to believe, by Alva, in case of the earlier immigrants, or by their own anointed king, Louis XVI, after A.D. 1685. Martineaus and Colombines, Barbés and Lacohees, Beaumonts and Beauvisages, Kalieres and Lefevers and Mounsears, their names are to be found on many a handsome mortuary inscription. Moreover, they had an apprenticing charity, which maintains its activities today, and is connected with the French Huguenot Hospital of London (now established at Horsham). I sit on its board and solemnly ask boys and girls if they have any French ancestry to give them preference. Occasionally one of the above is claimed as ancestor. In the main, of course, they have become assimilated to the local population, leaving a memory, indeed a historical record, of doctors and divines, philosophers and technicians. James and Harriet Martineau are both national figures whom we owe to French-speaking Strangers of Norwich.

Historians have to be wary people. Centuries hence it will be noted that in 1940 Norwich had a very active branch of the Free French, or Resistance Movement, which collected funds to the tune of some hundreds of pounds to send French arms to recapture France. In 1946 Norwich was exchanging official visits with its " sister town " of Leeuwarden. There is direct connection with the migration of centuries earlier, of course, but there remains the fact that Norwich streets are places in which you may always meet, from century to century, organised bodies of Strangers, sheltering amid the native born. Norwich is like that.

XIV

ST. STEPHEN'S. AN ACQUAINTANCE WITH
ROYALTY

WHENEVER a new monarch ascends the throne, on which
some forty have sat since the Conquest, the old gables in
many a Norwich street must glow with a sense of renewal.
They have seen so many. I do not think so much of the earlier
visits, by kings in armour who more than once came to take away
the liberties of Norwich for one misdemeanour or another. Nor,
in fact, are there many houses, or even churches, old as
much of Norwich is, that saw Plantagenet, York or Lancaster
kings.

It is when we come to the new England, the Protestant,
mercantile Britain of today, in which Royalty plays a part
unequalled save in some north-western European countries,
that we can easily find streets which contain bricks and mortar,
timber and stone, before which a Royal procession has passed,
which have resounded to the loyal hurrahs, and worn the
garlands and devices by which happy subjects show their
pleasure.

Two " Progresses " stand out, highly coloured and noisy,
centring round two of the most sharply outlined figures among
all the great gallery of English kings and queens. One is the
visit of Elizabeth, the other that of Charles II. A contrast in
every way, yet how unutterably English! A Queen, with
every quality a woman and a sovereign can need, exaggerated
until she becomes a great Renaissance Princess; a King, half
French and half Scots, who had spent half a lifetime in armed
camps and garrisons, in defeat and flight, and then came back
to conduct a policy so mortally dangerous that he would hardly
have succeeded in pursuing it under any other cloak than that
of outrageous frivolity degenerating into ornamental black-
guardism. " Good Queen Bess ", who scared her subjects out of
their wits, and the " Merry Monarch ", who would have been
shameful if he had not been ribald.

Those were the only two that Norwich streets knew between

Henry VII in 1497 and Edward VII in 1909. The street most particularly associated with both these Royal Progresses was St. Stephen's Street, into which the road from London, either by Newmarket or by Ipswich, must naturally lead. It is rather tragic that the bombing of Norwich in 1942 destroyed several fine old gabled houses which may well have looked down upon both these occasions. There are, however, a few roof-ridges and windows the shape of which shows clearly enough to what times they belong. Apart from the actual fabric by which it is surrounded, St. Stephen's Street is the same narrow alley that it always was. As to widening it, a protracted argument has raged, begun in the nineteen-thirties, about apportioning the money to be granted by the Ministry dealing with such matters, and the width to which such widening is to be carried. Plainly, to make an adequate modern roadway means depriving property-holders on the south-eastern side of their entire sites, while on the other difficulties of tenure and contour operate. The argument still goes on, and is based, as anyone can see by a glance at the map, on the fact that St. Stephen's never was a main thoroughfare. Norwich people never set much store by going to London. The roadway which emerges from St. Stephen's Gates and leads thither is not called London Road. It is called Newmarket Road in its westerly branch, and Ipswich Road on its easterly. The main roads to Norwich from the places to which Norwich thought it important to go cross on Tombland, half a mile away on the other side of the Castle Mound. This fact had a decisive effect upon what actually happened in St. Stephen's on these two occasions nearly a century apart. When Norwich can no longer ignore London, the traffic problem these twenty years has been of a gravity that has caused St. Stephen's to be a one-way street. In spite of sustained efforts, no solution is yet in sight. These facts, however, did not worry the capricious and formidable woman who came riding along the muddy or sandy track, the "road" to St. Stephen's Gates, on Saturday 16 August 1578. That, I fancy, was the foremost quality that won the citizens' enthusiasm. They had not seen a Queen riding side-saddle before them since the consort of Richard II had done so nearly two hundred years earlier.

There she was, a real ruler, erect on her horse; and what a

weight of responsibility did she not carry on those magnificently draped shoulders! For if, on the one hand, she was
no mere consort, as Anne of Bohemia had been, so equally she
was no constitutional monarch such as those who succeeded
her. It has been said that she was her own Prime Minister
and Cabinet, and her endowment of intellect and courage,
classical learning and bargaining shrewdness was nearly equal
to the sum total of that which could be claimed by many
a government since her day.

Yet more than all those impressive personal qualities was the
fact that, to the Norwich of her time, she represented a strong
and settled government. All those who stood to greet her who
were middle-aged could remember something so much more
threatening than her implacable decisiveness. True, if one
were unwise or unscrupulous, one might lose the head from
one's shoulders. But that was better than some protector's ambitions or the painful fanaticism of her tragic elder sister.

The Queen came journeying from Suffolk and had been
lavishly entertained at the Earl of Surrey's, I think it must have
been at Kenninghall Palace, where, so little time before, her
sister had sought refuge from the threat of Wyatt's rebellion.
So, all the way from the City boundary at Harford Bridges,
where, on her way from Braconash, she crossed the Yare, she
was accompanied " by the Mayor and Corporation, attended
by the principal inhabitants most sumptuously apparelled.
Here the Mayor," says the account, " after having addressed
her Majesty in an handsome speech, presented her with the
City Sword accompanied with a covered cup of silver gilt,
containing one hundred pounds in gold. The procession
then set forward, the Mayor carrying a mace or sceptre which
he bore before the Queen. The Procession entered by St.
Stephen's Gates which, in order that all things should be
appropriate and fitting for so illustrious a visitor, were duly
adorned. A new portcullis was made, the building was placed
in thorough repair, and so were the walls at this point. Moreover the gates were beautiful within and without. On the outside was a large escutcheon of her Majesty's arms, with a falcon
as her badge. On another shield was the cross of St. George,
and on a third the arms of the City. Beneath the Queen's
coat appeared this motto ' God and the Queen we serve '. On

the inner or City side of the Gates appeared the red rose, then the red and white roses united and for a second time the arms of the Queen. Beneath all were the following lines:

> Division kindled strife;
> Blest union quenched the flame;
> Then sprang our noble Phœnix deare
> The peerless Prince of fame.

Here the waits of the City, habited in their clothing, stood ready with their music. At the close of a song of welcome, Elizabeth passed forward after other displays, to lodgings in the Bishop's Palace." Her rest was interrupted by the presentation of many loyal addresses.

There was a good deal in all this that is not described by the contemporary chroniclers, because it was too well known and dangerous to mention. This " Progress " was no mere flare-up of antique chivalry and the delight of a beery crowd in a public ceremony and the sight of that almost unearthly being, a Royal Princess. One quality that gave a sharp edge to the emotions expressed by all that medieval hyperbole and parade was admiration for Elizabeth's sheer physical courage. Daughter of a mother judicially murdered by her father, she had been imprisoned and threatened from birth, by a continuous succession of revolts within the Kingdom and plans for invasion from without. Any conspirator in the uncontrolled crowd that jammed St. Stephen's Street could have shot her, and if he had escaped, might have been richly rewarded. Yet she rode down through the narrow street, an ideal spot for an ambush, flaunting her isolation (which meant no consort and no heir). On her way thither she had imprisoned two of her hosts, immediately after accepting their hospitality, for she possessed a good share of her father's brutal truculence. The heraldic roses on the stonework were no mere ornament. They meant that the prosperous trading classes at least hoped they had seen the last of the Wars of the Roses and the ambitions of heavily armed noblemen. This new Protestant class was in the ascendant in a place like Norwich, and it is true that anyone who had attacked her that morning would probably have been lynched on the spot. Yet that was no guarantee of her personal safety. There was probably genuine admiration, as always in England, for anyone who took such risks as she did, and a hurried assiduity to gain her favour before she took a dislike to some civic bigwig, and vented her displeasure on all and sundry.

From the Bishop's Palace on the following Tuesday she went to Costessey Park to hunt, passing through St. Benedict's Gates, and here another " concert " or tableau awaited her, accompanied by an address in which Cupid, Modesty and Chastity bore especial, if incongruous parts. She managed to keep her face straight. One cannot help wondering how, apart from enjoying the irony of being credited with virtues she must have despised, her thin veneer of patience sustained the task of listening to so many perfervid orations. It may well be that she shrewdly concluded that while they were soft-sawdering her at such length, they were not muttering treason amongst themselves.

On the Wednesday she went up to Mount Surrey, the palace of another victim of her father's, where the gasometer now stands on the edge of Mousehold Heath. This meant crossing the Wensum by the Prior's (erroneously called Bishop's) Bridge. Inevitably " Stephen Limbert, the master of the Grammar School, delivered an oration, which so pleased Her Majesty that she said it was the best she had heard, and gave him her hand to kiss, and afterward sent back to inquire his name ". He may well have been more flattered than scared, for she was at least as good a Latinist as he and appreciated the use of classical tongues as one of the elegancies of life. She had a full share of those, to us, incomprehensible contradictions of Renaissance Princes, an exquisite sensibility combined with a callous disregard of other people's attachment to their lives. At the magnificent banquet here offered her the French Ambassador was among the guests. She must have forgotten the massacre of St. Bartholomew. On the Friday she left by St. Benedict's Gates, " all the approaches thereto being hung with rich cloths, pictures, garlands, and a thousand other devices ". At the gates themselves a stage was erected covered with cloth of gold and crimson velvet. And she nearly heard yet another address before passing on to Sir Roger Wodehouse's at Kimberley. This, however, was cancelled on account of the lateness of the hour. Either from thankfulness for this mercy, or from some prompting of her tortuous and secret policy, or possibly from one of those gleams of graciousness that relieved her somewhat bleak behaviour, she seems to have been really touched. She knighted a dozen local worthies, Knyvetts and Bacons, William Paston, Richard Shelton, two Wodehouses, Gawdy of Gawdy Hall, and Robert Wood the Mayor. She was heard to say, " I have laid up in my breast such goodwill as I shall never forget Norwich ". Then, waving her riding-whip, and with water in her eyes, she said " Farewell, Norwich ".

So she went. She would have been surprised, perhaps, to learn that the hospitable Hall at Kimberley, for which she was bound, would give its name, because its owner was Queen Victoria's first " Colonial Secretary ", to townships on the other side of the earth, one of which would be delivered from a siege by a larger British army than she can ever have dreamt of, and which she would have thought madly expensive. She seems to have visited Blickling, but no one tells us if she saw her mother's ghost which haunts that splendid, if rebuilt house. Behind her, in Norwich, she must have left a heartfelt sigh of relief. She left something else. In her train were hangers-on infected by the Plague, whatever it might have been. In spite of stringent measures, cleanliness in slaughter-houses, relief of sufferers and segregation of the infected, also the appointment of an official to enumerate the deaths, something like a quarter of the population died, if the official figures are to be trusted.

Thoughtful people who push their way up busy St. Stephen's, still too narrow for three lines of traffic, may try to recall that August day, and the stench of the verminous crowd, the noise, the blunt, crude emotions. It is hard to suppress a shiver when one sees how easily the release of a trigger or bowstring, or the mere dropping of a big stone from the second floor of any of the houses, might have altered the course of English history, and perhaps that of the world. The following entries appear in the City accounts:

Rewards given by the City of Norwich to the officers and servants of the Queen's Retynewe in this her Progresse Ano. 1578 according to the usall custom :

Item, to the Clarke of the Market of the Queens Household, for his Rewarde	xl!
Item, to one that brought the City Sword from Hartford Bridge to Erlsham Bridge	xl!
To the Groomes of the Chamber	xx!
To the Yeomen Weutores	xx!

To the Portones		xx.s
To the officeres of the Spycerie		xx.s
To the Sejants at Armes		xl.s
To the V ordenary messangeres		xl.s
To the Yeoman of the Mall		xx.s
To the Yeoman of the flagones		xxvi.s viii.d
To the Marsheall		xxvi.s viii.d
To the Footemen	iii	vi.s viii.d
To the Trumpetores		iii.s iii.d
To the harbingeres		xxvi.s viii.d
To the Sorvayor of the Waye		xx.s
To the officiores of the butterye		xx.s
To the cooks and boylores		xx.s
To the muscyones of the Vials		xx.s
To the Black Guarde		xx.s
To the officiores of the Sellor		xx.s
To the viii musytiones that follow the Tente		xx.s
To the muscyones cornets		xx.s
To the Harrolds at Armes		xx.s Total

xxxvi.s
vi.s
viii.d

Such was Elizabeth's visit to Norwich.

Ninety-three years later, on Thursday, 28 September 1671, the great-great-great-grandson of her father's sister—or her great-great-great-grand-nephew, if you like—Charles II, followed in her footsteps. It would be more exact to say that he sent his long-suffering little Portuguese Queen by coach, along the same route as Elizabeth had used, while he, who had been enjoying uproarious banquets of herrings, among other viands, with his brother James and young Monmouth at Yarmouth, came riding by St. Olaves and Haddiscoe, and crossed the City boundary at Trowse Bridge. Thence his party rode up Bracondale, then really a dale of bracken and heather, with splendid woods that remain to this day. For some reason not explained, they skirted the City wall and entered by St. Stephen's Gates. Did he intend to join the Queen and accompany her into the City? Between them they made a thorough mess of it. The civic party of welcome was drenched while waiting at Trowse, and then had to be split, in order to show the Queen some courtesy. This detachment was late. The royal coach was already over Cringleford Bridge, and the Recorder had to make his speech to her Majesty on Eaton Hill. Meanwhile Charles and his following had entered the walls, received a purse of two hundred guineas, and gone forward to the Duke of Norfolk's Palace, where Norwich Central Public

Library stands.   So the citizens had two successive spectacles. First of all, about half-past four, they saw their " merry ", plucky, but rather caddish monarch surrounded by a hundred young citizens, all mounted, most of the City fathers and assorted Howards, of whom a number of families seem to have survived the mass executions of the Tudors and the Parliamentary Wars.   This cavalcade passed down " a lane all the way of liverymen (being about 200) and the city regiment (of about 700 persons), the vast number of Dukes, Earls, Lords and young nobility of both sexes and persons of quality ". There seems to have been a noisy enthusiasm " vast confusion and crowds of people of all sorts offered to press into the Duke's Palace to see so noble a sight as Norwich was never before honoured with : for indeed, half the people in Norfolk and Suffolk had got together within the City, and scarce room left for horse and man to stir about ".

So that is what it was like on that showery September day, getting dusk, as the palace gates finally closed against the mob of sight-seers.   These old beams and arches, such as are left in St. Stephen's, glimmered back at the dark, Franco-Scottish face of the King, who probably bore himself with distinction.   Next him will have been the spoiled and pretty Monmouth, who inherited his father's ability to win popularity in spite of his obvious shortcomings rather than because of his virtues.   I wonder what his mother thought, and where she was.   They say Charles did love her.   Buckingham was there, and the Duke of York, I do not know if his illness had yet turned him into " dismal Jimmy ".   He had real ability, and might in happier circumstances have been a great sea-lord.   Or did the Catholic fanaticism he dare not show outwardly, but which was to complete his downfall, already contort that pallid face?   Better be a frank cynic like the King ; English people will always applaud that.   No one seems to have shouted, " Charles, where's your wife? " as they did to his successor George, one hundred and fifty years later, in London.

Later, when it must have been getting dark, the remainder of the procession brought her in her lumbering great coach.   I wonder what she thought of St. Stephen's, and if any of the rowdy crowd had stayed to cheer her !   For if they would not stand her religion, they had a respect for the uncomplaining woman who was, after all, the King's real wife, and had never had a sporting chance against the mob of weak limpets, cheeky trollops and greedy hags that trailed behind the King. There is no mention of how many of them got into the overcrowded Duke's Palace, but the two royal processions and the ducal one of Norfolk's jammed in somehow and had their dinner, as we know, in the converted bowling alley, where the show-rooms of the Eastern Electricity Board now are. So Charles and she were ostensibly man and wife for that night.

He seems to have pulled himself together next day and was at his best, and his best seems to have been quite charming. He " touched " people for the " King's Evil " and evidently had that gift of making fools believe anything. He took wine with the Bishop, climbed on to the leads of the Guildhall to wave to the cheering multitude, just as his successor, our Elizabeth, did from the steps of the City Hall in 1951. Then he went with some difficulty, which we can understand if we try to picture his coach forcing its way down what is now Dove Street, to the " New Hall " (St. Andrew's Hall), where he had the sense and tact, so characteristic of him and so valuable, to knight splendid old Thomas Browne, who had stood up for him at a time when nothing seemed to be more lost than the Stuart cause. His Queen was there, and he took her with him to Blickling to dine with the Hobarts, then sent her back to the Duke's for the night, while he went on to the ruinously magnificent banquet Sir Robert Paston gave him at Oxnead.

A gentleman called Corie who was Recorder paid her this tribute: " How infinitely gracious Her Majesty was to allow our City, being pleased to condescend so far as to let all sorts of people (of what degree soever) to kiss her hand, even as she passed along the gallery, with a most admirable and saintly charity and patience so as our whole inhabitants within and without doors ring and sing of nothing else but her praises con-tinual prayers and tears being offered up for her temporal and eternal blessings, by us who all conclude that if there be a saint on earth it must undoubtedly be Her Majesty, since no eye alive did ever see or ear hear of so much goodness, charity, humility, sweetness and virtue of all kinds to meet in one earthly creature as are now lodged in Her Majesty's saintlike breast ". So apparently she had her admirers. It must have been her influence which caused the remarkable fact that of all the mass of silver and gold plate that lay open to opportunity, none was stolen, and a valuable pearl necklace dropped in the crowd was restored to its owner.

So they parted again, Charles to pass on to that visit which was to bring about the ruin of the Pastons in about fifty years, and Catherine to her life of dignified Christian charity and observance of duty.

Let us make what we can of St. Stephen's scarred façades and gaping holes today. It has had its royal moments, and when, in the long patience of God, we contrive to have a fitting entry from the London road to the heart of Norwich, its characteristic, medieval narrowness and shadow will disappear, and it will be harder than it is today to be sure of its close acquaintance with Royalty.

XV

THE GOOSE & GRIDIRON, AND SIR THOMAS BROWNE

THOSE who have been sufficiently interested to read thus far will not have failed to notice the immense variety of the streets of Norwich, one of the qualities which help to build up their resemblance to human beings. I am now coming to the younger members of what I have called " the family ", and they present the same characteristics as younger members of large families often do. They have had better education and opportunity, they are probably lighter-hearted than their elder brothers and sisters, who have been sobered if not stunted by sharing the overwhelming responsibilities inherent in a large family. Before I pass on to these relatively carefree youngsters, I want to sum up some of the qualities of the elders and see what they amounted to.

Why? it may well be asked. The past is the past, let it bury its dead. By all means; but let us make sure what is dead.

Here we are on the brink of controversy. Lately when a distinguished exhibition of the life and works of Francis Blomefield, the local historian, was held in Norwich, a well-known Labour Alderman, as Chairman of the Public Libraries Committee, in whose premises it was held, opened it with some such words as : " We are to examine the works of one who can show us how we got where we are. I have usually been more interested in studying where we go next from where we are! " There is a statement of a point of view. My own, which the reader is not obliged to share, is that one cannot discover where one is to go next without knowing whence one came. " A man's past," said Galsworthy, " that's what he is." To me, then, an attempt to see whither one is going without knowing whence one came, is like asking a fish to swim without a tail, an aeroplane to move without propulsion, a tree to grow without roots. True, there are animals that swim without tails. Exactly. They drift. There are 'planes that move without spitting anything out behind. Precisely, they are gliders. There are vegetable growths with no roots. We call them fungi.

On the occasion of the Blomefield Exhibition I refrained from pointing this out to the Chairman: I did not suggest to him that he was drifting or gliding or covering with green mould his general view of life. His is a point of view. Mine is another. I am quite sure that the traffic of Norwich is what it is because of something that was deliberately done in the eleventh century; that St. Peter Mancroft churchyard and the private gardens of Surrey Street are what they are because of things that happened in the fourteenth century; that the Bethel Hospital stands where it does on account of an explosion in the seventeenth. I am quite sure that the modern air and rail traffic of Norwich, the look and speech of its citizens, its character in 1952, are what they are, not by deliberate choice, or according to any theory, but by virtue of completely irrelevant happenings, some a long while ago. I believe, in fact, in the apparent irrelevance of human history. I am willing to attribute some part of it to a will which is certainly not merely human, which may be graphically described as superhuman, or " Providence ", as our fathers would have called it, so short a time ago. We need not stop to argue the scope of " Providence ". It is enough for me that it had considerable scope in Norwich, and I want to gather up a few of its manifestations before I come on to the beginnings of mechanisation, organisation—the streets of the Welfare State, in fact. Some of the older streets have a deeply marked significant character, by sheer irrelevance, or Providence, whichever you like.

Let us follow, for instance, what happened to either of those monarchs whose " Progresses " across England led them to St. Stephen's Gates, into Norwich. The roads that lead from Newmarket and Ipswich meet some three hundred yards outside the Gates. Both today are magnificent highways. The Newmarket Road has an avenue of eighty elm-trees of a hundred years growth and forest size. The Ipswich Road, a trifle less formal, is tree embowered.

But once they enter the Gates they are channelled in one of the narrow, darkest streets that have survived in Norwich. Moreover, it leads nowhere. Intensive bombing in 1942 has

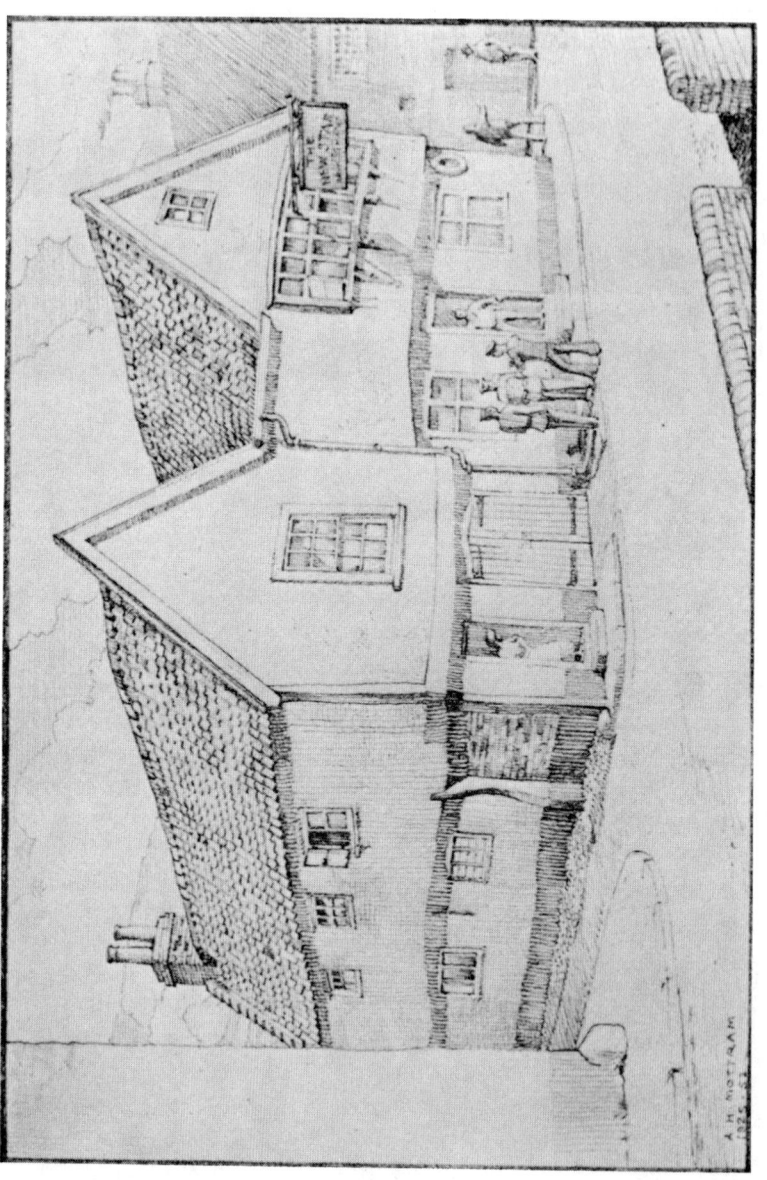

15. THE NEW STAR INN, QUAYSIDE

16. MOUSEHOLD HEATH

17. ANOTHER PART OF MOUSEHOLD HEATH

let a little daylight in, but, as has been pointed out, St. Stephen's is so ridiculously incapable of carrying modern transport that it is a one-way street. It leads to precisely nothing. Its north-eastern end receives Surrey Street, a professional street full of fine Georgian and neo-seventeenth-century buildings. Then, on its west is Rampant Horse Street, now being rebuilt as an important shopping street, at what is called St. Stephen's " Plain " and used to be the " slough " in medieval documents, through which meandered the little stream from " Jacque's Pit " to find its way along the " Back of the Inns " to the Wensum near Blackfriars Bridge. As the highway from London, in fact, it just peters out in what was, in my boyhood, a narrow, cobbled lane lined with public-houses and fishmongers' shops with oyster-rooms. Today, one side bombed flat, it is still lined with hotels and a superlative fish restaurant. The odd-shaped triangle with a bus-control box in the middle looks incredibly awkward, and most people who see it today attribute its appearance to the huge hole that Hitler digged, where a hundred cars now park below street level. The joke is, that before 1942 it was already awkward, uncouth, what you like, though it did afford a back entry to some important shops. Its western corner leads to the Provision Market by a dangerous angle. Its northern continues in a slanting " plain " called " Orford Hill " after one of Robert Walpole's relatives, still cobbled, with a coffee-cart in the middle, before the fine ancient front of the Bell Hotel. Two-line traffic alleys leave it at three points. The busy modern roadway was shorn clean through the Bell and its yard, to make the trams possible in 1900, and now, continued in what were once " Castle Ditches ", does make a kind of approach, after skating round the semicircular northern side of the Castle Mound, to Prince of Wales Road and the railway.

It is bad enough today, with all these modern " improvements ", but when Elizabeth and Charles II had to negotiate this rookery it must have been well-nigh impassable, especially with a rowdy crowd filling it. St. Stephen's Plain was a swamp, Red Lion Street a slum (no Mayor or prominent citizen ever lived in either), Orford Place was the Goose & Gridiron inn yard, partly occupied by a bell-founder's establishment, and Orford Hill was virtually the front yard of the

K

Bell Hotel. What did these monarchs, with their cavalcades of horsemen, their lumbering coaches and train of wagons, and riff-raff bringing up the rear, do to negotiate it? For they were bound, Elizabeth for the Bishop's Palace, and Charles for the Duke of Norfolk's, both half a mile away on the other side of the City. There was no means of tacking across the Cattle Hill as we know it. That was still strictly enclosed and not accessible to wheeled traffic. They must have turned half left, and by sheer shoving, reached the Provision Market. Beyond that fresh difficulties confronted them, but they may have got rid of some of the crowd. Charles, moreover, had the advantage of the two hundred livery-men and the seven hundred of the City regiment, who may be presumed to have kept some sort of order. But Elizabeth must have been sorely tired by the time the great gates of the Bishop's Palace closed behind her. She had ridden over ten miles, and her arm must have been stiff from waving and kissing her hand. Charles was comparatively fortunate. He had only the length of Dove Lane from the Market Place to the Maddermarket. After that the Norfolk retainers could make a way for him into the Duke's Palace. He was only forty, and must have been a man of fine physique. Elizabeth was five years older.

So the tumult and the shouting died and there was no more Royal Progress until 238 years later, when Charles' remote descendant, Edward VII, dressed as a Field-Marshal, came to open the new cavalry drill-ground on the outer rim of Mousehold Heath in 1909. He rode in a carriage, as a man of sixty-seven may well do. We are left with the old streets of Norwich, as they have been perambulated by ordinary people; and what a diverse company those streets are!

Let us go back to that Goose & Gridiron knot in the midst of them that still ties up the access from London. Imagine those two royal occasions, pushing, as I have said, past an inn yard with its muck-heap and cheering, beery, taproom crowd, and past the bell-founder's yard, with its muddle of earth, its smelly furnace, and its blackened bare-armed workers, all waving. As they turned into the Provision Market, with Brigg's Lane on their left, opposite to it was a very different place.

If one looks today one sees, sandwiched between a big store and a big office building, a rather diminutive and ordinary house called Orford Chambers. There is an inscription on a plaster panel, not too easy to see, but which can be made out to state that on that site lived Sir Thomas Browne, M.D., author of *Religio Medici*. I do not know who lived there when Elizabeth went by, but I expect Charles had the tact and sense he always showed to wave to the crowd in the windows, not of the present building, of course, but in a far more stately one that stood there until the brink of the twentieth century. The family crowd at those windows may well have included nine daughters of Sir Thomas, as well as a son or two, for that is how that sort of man, the new grandee of those days, lived. He was, it is true, a landowner on a modest scale, but his real eminence consisted in his professional status, for he was what was just beginning to be called a Doctor of Medicine, and not a " leech " or " apothecary ", and thought of as a useful if humble member of the Barbers' Guild or Company. Thomas Browne was a good deal more than that. I have said that Charles II's interest in him arose from the notorious fact that, in Roundhead Norwich, the centre of Cromwell's Eastern Association which created the Ironsides, at a moment when the Parliamentary cause was triumphant and that of the Stuarts more lost than it was to be for half a century, Thomas Browne refused to contribute to the fund for the raising of a new army to recover Newcastle. The mere fact that he was not molested shows how high was his local prestige as well as his international reputation. No wonder Charles knighted him in the New Hall that afternoon. He remains today one of the most deservedly famous of all the sons and daughters of Norwich whom one picks out, if asked to name a dozen such. In that house stood the splendid, elaborately carved, timber mantelpiece, all inset with semi-precious stone, which, after many wanderings, is now safe in Norwich Castle Museum. Anyone can go and look at it and imagine, without much strain, the whimsical and learned (according to the lights of his day) doctor and collector.

Behind the building which has replaced the house is the yard of the Lamb Inn, through which can be seen some traces of greenery and the gable of a very old building with a fine plaster ceiling. This was the site (now encroached upon by centuries of intensive building) of that wonderful garden where Evelyn walked with him; admired his Quincunces or groups

of rare shrubs, five in a group, which has no equal that I know
of in the modern world save in the public square of the same
name and pattern at Bordeaux. There he kept his queer birds
and his stuffed " dolphin ", and there proceeded from his pen
the lesser works that followed his *Religio Medici,* his *Garden of
Cyprus,* his *Christian Morals,* his *Common Errors* and his *Urn
Burial,* for he had the overmastering curiosity which is the mark
of the liberation of the human spirit. Anyone who takes the
trouble to get leave to penetrate through adjoining shops and
offices will find one great old fig-tree remaining, and can admire
the ceiling of the garden house, if that is what it was. And com-
bining the sight of that majestic mantelpiece with the sound of
the bells of St. Peter Mancroft opposite, which still ring in-
finite changes on their peal of twelve and a great tenor bell, one
can step into the shoes, almost into the skin, of that great figure
to which I am so sure Charles waved.

Alas for human greatness! Those who really want to understand the seventeenth century must not only look at the statue
of Sir Thomas Browne that stands in the centre of the Haymarket, contemplating a skull. They must also remember that
the same man gave medical evidence at Bury St. Edmunds
against two wretched old women accused of witchcraft so that
they were done to death. That is how the centuries overlap.
Browne could be all he was and that too. And as if to under-
line the peculiarity of human fate, his fine wall monument in
St. Peter Mancroft must not dazzle us so as to forget that his own
skull was found to be missing from his coffin and was, or was
said to be, retrieved from the museum of surgical curiosities at
the Norfolk and Norwich Hospital. But I only say here, look
at the contrast in a few yards. Slum, inn yard, bell-founders'
yard, the house of Sir Thomas Browne. They stand next each
other like that.

Not all the associations of Norwich streets with each other,
however, are so indiscriminate. On the whole, the Middle
Ages (prior to the Reformation, that is) were rather definite in
fixing the character of streets. Most of the main thoroughfares
were named after the saint to whom was dedicated the church
of the parish through which they mainly ran. Thus we have
St. Benedict's and St. Andrew's, one continuing the other, St.
Giles', St. Stephen's, St. Martin's, St. Peter's, St. George's and

Botolph Street.   Or the conventual establishments that are now only remembered by the names that have stuck to the highways they dominated, Blackfriars, Greyfriars, Whitefriars, The Chantry, Palace Street.   We have St. Catherine's Plain, St. Mary's Plain, St. Paul's Square; Magdalen Street (in Norwich pronounced long—Mag-da-len) led to the hospital for lepers outside its gate, still standing, used as a Branch Public Library, and called for centuries the Lazar House.   That combination of an Eastern disease brought back from the Crusades with the notion connecting Lazarus with a charitable or welfare activity, the whole dedicated to the figure which, of all those surrounding that of Christ, makes respectable Christianity impossible, is characteristic of Norwich streets, which contain no lepers, no Lazarus and no Magdalen.   On the other hand, there were three streets in pre-Reformation Norwich which were of ill-repute; they are marked Turpis Vicus, Way of Turpitude.   I need not point them out, the name has long been forgotten, but on very old maps can be found, with additions and remarks so shocking that most editors of old records render them ———.   How nineteenth century that is, as if to say: "Shocking! Don't let anyone know."   In fact, as we shall see, "the dangers of the streets" of Norwich today are more likely to be a drab, ill-planned, ill-built monotony than any scarlet sin.

That was not the case in an earlier Norwich.   If you were a goldsmith you lived and kept shop in what is now London Street.   If you were a whelk-seller, you were domiciled in what we call Wensum Street.   If you were holy, there were plenty of churches, convents, colleges, chantries right down to little stone rabbit-hutches or dog-kennels, called Anchorages, where you might exist.   There are specimens of the latter against the north wall of St. Julian's Church, the north wall of Blackfriars' Hall, and a bit of one, just north of Whitefriars' Bridge.   How any human creature maintained life in such places taxes the imagination.   So do the will-power, control of the imagination or lack of it which led people to do so, when across the street in many cases, others had what I think I have shown to be literally palaces.   When I say that, I mean establishments in which Royalty might be received and on occasion was.   I once horrified a party of intelligent Americans by describing Blickling as a Palace. They had the idea, I think, that the word meant a permanent residence of the sovereign. I doubt if they grasped that earlier majesties were peripatetic. The Tower and Windsor were occupied intermittently, St. James', Westminster and Buckingham Palace and the rest so infrequently and so lately. However, my point is plain. The hermit or anchorite lived opposite the Palace, and bore no grudge. Yet again, if you were a bad character, there was the Turpis Vicus in which you could ensconce yourself comfortably in the deep and presumably welcome mire of iniquity.

And finally there was a whole category of streets that were not streets at all in the sense in which we use the word. They were paved passages, in which wheeled traffic of today (that is, since Elizabeth) is not expected, and posts were put up to stop it—" bars " to keep traffic pedestrian. The task was easier in early days, when there was no wheeled traffic—nothing heavier than a pack-horse. The one exception is Ber Street, which in the oldest documents is so described, not as a " gate " or, as I should prefer " gait ", going or track. That old highway was always paved with rammed earth, of course, and wise people attribute that to the Romans. The oldest " street " otherwise, in Norwich, is that now known as Lower Goat Lane, after the sign of an inn. But in the oldest documents it is Stone Street, plainly a markedly exceptional thoroughfare. Why it was so, whence and whither it led, no one seems sure, unless it was to Coslany Bridge, an early crossing of the river. The other one was what we call Bishopgate, and was once Holmstreete, where the rammed gravel has been seen several feet below the surface, during road repairs within living memory. The uncertain use of this street and meaning of its name I have discussed elsewhere.

All along the crowded centre of the City (the mathematical middle of walled Norwich is St. Andrew's Church), the matter needs no arguing; there are a series of churchyard alleys, mostly paved for pedestrians today. Bridewell Alley next St. Andrew's; St. John's in the Maddermarket, which goes through the tower of the church; St. Gregory's next it, westward, where the alley, still cobbled, goes under the altar, while its main stem runs across the churchyard and along the west front. The markets were semi-enclosed, I have never discovered if this were to prevent theft or to facilitate taxing of goods. The fact is plain. All Norwich markets are deliberately difficult of access and all devoted to special commodities—hay, madder, timber, horses are still named, while Swine Market, Hog Hill and the rows of stalls in the Provision Market, though still existing, have lost their names. What a diverse company! How odd, forgotten, misunderstood, misnamed! That is why I called this section after the Goose & Gridiron, the central muddle to which the London road leads.

XVI

ST. GEORGE'S, OR THE REWARD OF MERIT

WE now leave the Middle Ages behind and come to the younger members of the family, to streets properly paved and lighted, or as properly as the Commissioners empowered to levy rates for this purpose were able to compass. We see people who wear trousers and carry umbrellas, who know that the earth goes round the sun, and are able to take sufficient care of themselves, so that in the third quarter of the eighteenth century they no longer died nearly as fast as they were born. Of course it wasn't so simple as all that. There is no sharp line dividing the Middle Ages from modern times. One might take Henry VIII's assumption of headship of the Church, Parliament's insistence on a constitutional monarchy, and the introduction of washable underclothing, each as dividing the Age of Faith and Helplessness from the Age of Rational Welfare. But those three events are each a century apart. Still less is it true that any street in Norwich was pulled down and built up afresh overnight. Ber Street was always as wide as any modern Minister of Transport could wish. On the other hand, we can find plenty of houses in the streets of Norwich that are little altered since 1600, and some from even earlier than that. So the change we note is very gradual and the work of centuries.

There is one district, however, which bears the marks of a new feeling about life, that no one had before A.D. 1700, and has left a decisive mark on its appearance today, as well as upon our national history. It is those parts of Colegate and St. George's Street, and Magdalen Street, in which dissenting merchants of woollen and silken goods conducted their business, built their Meeting-houses and for about two generations carried on a life, among a few privileged families, as highly civilised as can have existed anywhere. It had its parallel to some extent in Bath and Edinburgh, but is somehow particularly distinct in Norwich. To take three of the names significant of the place and time: if one could somehow subtract the influence of the Gurneys from the world of finance, that of James Martineau from theology, and that of Sir J. E. Smith from science, would there be a gap or not? I think there would. Now all those people lived part of their lives in, and were in the basic truth of the word, natives of north Norwich, of the Ward of Over-the-Water. True, something very akin in architecture and feeling can be found in All Saints' Green, Surrey Street, and in Bethel Street–St. Giles', for similar reasons. Yet the greatest concentration of what was no less than a new up-welling of the human spirit, limited in place and time, but sufficiently distinct to be seen, took place in those streets just beyond the river, and not to the same extent even in the Cathedral Close, where there was always, of course, a centre of piety and learning.

Why in St. George's? Well, as one looks at the first maps, it is clear that north of Colegate, and between Pitt Street and Magdalen Street, lay a large portion of open ground, not intensively built upon since the Blackfriars had vacated it in 1320. Count Calvert of the Holy Roman Empire had something like a park there, and trees of forest size today still lurk in the gardens of many a house that has seen better days. Here was a chance for something new to develop that did not exist south of the river, where the enclosures of the Castle and Cathedral, then so inaccessible, the exigencies of the Provision Market, the closely-built-up area along St. Andrew's and St. Benedict's did not afford similar scope. Moreover, in the early years of the eighteenth century, Quakers, Presbyterians and Jews and other " non-Christian " sects felt safer here because farther from the prejudiced centre of government in the Guildhall and the mobs of the market-place. It can be no accident that the Gurney families began to be noticeable in Pitt Street and Magdalen Street, the Martineaus in Magdalen Street, and the Smiths beyond Stump Cross. Mrs. Barbauld kept school in Black Boy's Yard, and Amelia Alderson, destined to be the bride of John Opie, lived opposite St. George's Church, near which too, the Taylors, especially Sarah Austen, congregated. She ran a non-scandalous salon to which members of the Government of that day would drive down. Near her lived her relative Henry Reeve, the clerk to the Privy Council.

Yes, those are the people, not unknown to our national and

even to international history. Who were they, why did they congregate in St. George's and round about? Above all, why is there still, in the nineteen-fifties, an unmistakable character about the district? In spite of great modern factories, in spite of great holes blown in the façade by the air attack of 1942, there still exist scores of old houses, two Meeting-houses and several green gardens, which mean something. What do they mean?

To find that out one must go back to the bitter partisan feeling of the seventeenth century. The Restoration of 1660 was a superficial affair, a patching up of a hasty decision about things that cannot be decided like that. People liked Charles II better than many of the Major-Generals who had defeated him. It may be that they liked the sort of peace Charles meant, better than the kind of military occupation Cromwell left behind. The disturbance of national life was outwardly political, but going deep enough to affect religious observance. Among the immediate effects of the Restoration, the learned Dr. Collings, who had become what was called Presbyterian in his views, was driven out of his cure of St. Stephen's, and took his congregation with him, to worship, as obscurely as possible, in two cottages in the vacant lands in Colegate. The Rev. William Bridge, whose particular shade of nonconformity was called " Independent ", had to take refuge in Rotterdam, and only came to build himself a Meeting-House in 1694. There it stands, in Old Meeting Yard, very mellow and beautiful, and in it are a Cromwellian preacher's chair, a pitch pipe (for starting hymns, before organs were thought of), and tablets to Letitia Brightwell and other later worthies. The Presbyterians' cottages were pulled down in 1760 by the congregation in the leadership of which John Taylor had succeeded Collings, and replaced by the Octagon Chapel, the work of Thomas Ivory, who also built the Assembly House and many a mansion for the rising merchant and dissenting class. A little farther west, on St. Mary's Plain, is the Baptist Meeting, with which Daniel Bradford, one of Cromwell's Ironsides, was associated. It has been rebuilt, but its name and associations still deeply tinge the feelings of this quarter of the town, and the new suburb beyond. And these buildings, one must remember, are only the relics of those who stayed to face the vacillations of James II's politico-religious policy. The less patient people of this sort had long sailed to America, where religious creed and church architecture bear them witness.

Most important of all, perhaps, were the despised and ridiculed Quakers, Gurneys and others, who built their first Meeting-House more obscurely still, in the Gildencroft. The Quakers were not born rich. They became rich because they were honest. The Presbyterians were not originally endowed with educational advantages. They became an intellectual aristocracy because they possessed a gift of lofty concentration. The members of the Independents' and the Baptists' meetings became the heads of the City, producing a long succession of Mayors and other notables, among them the Colmans, because they possessed integrity. That is what the new England was like. The workings of a free spirit produced a high spiritual courage and enlightenment. It stood fast until it had stared ignorant persecution and brute intolerance out of countenance. Many of the original members of these sects may not have been pleasant people for a drawing-room tea-party. They were mixed up with psalm-singing, image-smashing " levellers " and others, whom everyone was glad to see the last of. But even at their worst there were two things about the Puritan ancestors of what were destined to be the richest and most cultured groups in Norwich. First, out of a very motley Home Guard organisation they built up a body of troops that defeated the finest professional cavalry in Europe. How? Why? Because there is some secret strength in moral conviction that outweighs material advantage of weight or numbers. Napoleon was wrong (as usual) about God being on the side of the big battalions. He is almost invariably on the side of the small semi-volunteer ones. That was one thing. The other was that the Puritans were proved right about the Stuarts. For years the verdict was uncertain, but at long last, in 1745, it was given. The Stuarts disappeared. There supervened the seventeen-fifties, which I always feel to be a significant period in English history. The dynastic threat and all it implied was lifted. For a few years there seems to have been a sort of breathing space. The figure of George II on the throne had nothing to do with it, save that he was still sufficiently a foreigner on sufferance not to interfere. It was in that brief space before the endless

contest over the Far East and Far West was resumed, before
the break-up of the first British Empire, that several of the
houses in this quarter of the City were built, and these streets,
anciently Colegate, Gildengate, Fishergate, acquired a new
importance as the centre of the flourishing trade in woollens
and in silks.   The skill and initiative were there.   The water
transport, indispensable for moving any bulk or weight of
merchandise, lay ready to hand.   And there was coming into
being in Gurney Court something more important still.   The
Quakers were trusted with other people's money.   Finally, in
1775 the Gurneys opened their " banking office ".   That is
what these houses, and the people who built them and lived in
them meant.   As one looks at Colegate today, the much older
house in St. Clement's churchyard alley, the ancient " Hall "
of the Bacons whose stone frontage fills all the space between
Calvert Street and St. George's Street, the old parish churches,
can be seen to belong to another age.   A new light had come
to shine through high sash windows, under neo-classical
cornices.   No longer were light and air safely obtained only
by an enclosed courtyard in the middle of the house.   Here
were great carriage entries, with ironwork gates, opening upon
green lawns and arbours which no one thought of as needing
defending.   The counting-house was built in or on to the
dwelling.   Some at least of the workpeople " lived in ".   The
dye-stuffs were no longer a concoction of roots.   William Stark,
the father of the painter, was a chemist who invented " Norwich
Red ".   A new era of internal peace and overseas success
began to favour a new kind of person who was something else
besides being rich.   So gradually there came to float on this
basis of material prosperity something without which money is
dross and success but a burden.   It began perhaps with John
Taylor, minister of the Presbyterians who composed a Hebrew
Concordance which was subscribed by all the bishops of
England and Wales save four, and by fifteen Irish bishops.   It
was under his guidance that the congregation using the dismantled cottages determined to build that peculiar eight-sided
building, the Octagon Chapel, the main contractor for which
was Thomas Ivory.   It cost £5,000 in the money of those days.
Bartlett Gurney the banker deviated sufficiently to subscribe to it.
William Smith, M.P., who strove so hard for the liberation of

the Dissenters, and aided Thomas Fowell Buxton in the Abolition of Slavery, frequented it, and has his portrait hanging within it. John Taylor, the grandson of the minister, musician and scholar, and the charming and decorously famous women I have named used its pews. Later, little Harriet Martineau was to sit with her littler brother James beneath that ornate dome and fancy that the angels were riding down the slanting rays of the sunshine from those high windows, to fetch good little girls to Heaven. Both this and the equally distinguished Old Meeting of the Independents next door were surrounded by graveyards in which, from sentiment, the members of such conventicles were buried rather than in the parish church-yards which might, earlier, have been refused them. We have seen how the Quakers buried their members in their plot in the Gildencroft. But by 1800, at least, the sort of dissenter who used such places had won his way and was often Mayor, as the stands for the civic regalia in the Octagon show. The Old Meeting preserves also some unmistakable Dutch bricks in its forecourt to commemorate its congregation's long ago exile.

Nor was it only divinity and political eminence that flourished in such streets as St. George's. John Crome had his studio at No. 83 (as it is today), where he lived with his sons, pupils and friends. Cotman gave his lessons a little farther off, on St. Martin's-at-Palace Plain, but the house there might as well stand in St. George's, as far as its plan and appearance go. Nor can psalmody have been lacking, for in St. George's also was born the infant prodigy William Crotch, " who at the age of ten (in 1777) could play ' God Save the King ' and the ' Minuet de la Cour ' ". He must have been a terrifying child, but had a longish, useful, uneventful life as a not-too-distinguished musician. This queer, completely informal group produced as by-products Luke Hansard, destined to become the printer of Parliamentary debates, and one Fransham, the Norwich Poly-theist, who wore a hat like a great mushroom and used to sleep on Mousehold Heath. I have said that something parallel to the atmosphere of St. George's can be found in Surrey Street and All Saints' Green. It was in his house in the former, one of those tall houses near the modern bus station, that Sir J. E. Smith kept the Linnean Collection for some years. Yet another branch of this group of streets can be found in St. Giles' and Bethel Street.

Where has it all gone? Why are these fine houses now turned into offices? The Meeting-Houses are still open, but no members of the Cabinet now drive down from London to visit anybody's salon in St. George's. The Mayors and Aldermen live far out in suburbs and housing estates, not in Colegate. There is nothing like Crome's studio, or Cotman's, and while Norwich is still a famous place for music, it breeds no William Crotch. As for the Divines whose sermons used to attract crowds and become theological battle-cries, all that energy seems to have gone into welfare. Why? Well, one can see something, if not quite all of the reason. For there is always the inscrutable element of human mutability. Man must change or die. At best he can steer a little. How did that affect the people in St. George's, who deserved so well of their fellow-citizens?

I saw just the tail end of the tradition. Taylor of the Octagon and Kinghorn of St. Mary's were gone before my time, of course. But there were still, living in those streets like St. George's, professional people of an older generation, the men dressed in black, the women, particularly the older maiden ladies, wearing white, frilled caps and semi-uniform black gowns, who greeted a young man semi-parentally. They were not Quakers, but they approximated in type, and would have been and looked quite at home at Elizabeth Fry's meetings, Harriet Martineau's literary evenings, or decorously approving the Abolitionist and Emancipation campaigns of W. P. Smith, Clarkson, Buxton or Wilberforce. It is easy to laugh at righteousness plus five per cent, but it is not so easy to pass these people by. Their achievement is taken as a matter of course today, and many a modern politician talks as if his party had invented Welfare, universal franchise and native rights. It was, however, as a matter of sober fact, which can be checked by the dates of legislation, these earlier pioneers who faced the disagreeable, unpopular and even dangerous tasks. Like all battles, once they are won, this one, too, seems now so unnecessary.

That was not how it seemed, even fifty years ago. Although, as I have said, the glamour had departed, there were Sunday

Schools at the Octagon and St. Mary's and the Old Meeting, which were much more than pious devices for making children who then existed in the yards of Norwich in conditions of squalor now incredible, read the Bible, and strive to imitate the decency that their professional middle-class teachers exhibited. Every form of what is now National Health Insurance was already being practised by volunteer enthusiasts, and clothing and housing as well. The first talk in Norwich about Garden Cities and better housing was heard at the Octagon Chapel. There was very little of the Welfare State that was not anticipated at St. Mary's and the Quaker Meeting. These people could and did foresee the twentieth century. Having abjured violence and many pleasures of the flesh, they became rich and powerful, and turned riches and power to the uses of their less fortunate neighbours. As the framers of the Education Act of 1902 and the People's Budget of 1909 found, they had to take over, not invent, vast social services which were, on the whole, of nonconformist inspiration. I am trying to be quite fair, and indeed the explanation is not far to seek. Many a wealthy Chapel-goer in North Norwich had handed down to him a dim recollection of what poverty and helplessness were like, and how some far ancestor had been hunted through the streets by the soldiers or the mob. The churchman, while often of exemplary vision and devotion, would be a little less liable to such memories, a little more settled—a little more orthodox, in a word. Does anyone now realise what fury that word still kindles instinctively in my breast, just for a moment, until I remember how long ago it all was, and how far we have gone since such differences mattered?

Anyhow, it is now done. The little schoolrooms have become part of a great system, the teachers drawn from leisured homes have been replaced by Organisers of everything, who are far more efficient. Moreover, there were too few of those prosperous, benevolent folk of St. George's. A score of families bore a burden that is now national. It could not go on, especially in Norwich when the collapse of the wool trade removed the material basis on which that early naïve philanthropy rested. Not only it, but the artistic appreciation which demands spare time and spare money was equally cut off. Crome and Cotman today would have taken classes at the

City College. Crotch would have been an organist. The literary ladies would now be dons of women's colleges. No doubt the changes have been for the better. The great housing estates and their amenities are the result. But in places like Norwich it is not possible to forget who began it. There is no need to read the mortuary tablets, some still bearing armorial blazonry, on the walls of old Meeting-Houses, which tell how so and so was once a member " of this society " and has become at death, by " catholic candid and exemplary conduct ", " a member of the blessed society above ".

The real memorial to those who built these Meeting-Houses and mansions lies in the appearance they still present to the eye. Their windows were meant to let in light, they were not loopholes for defence. Their ample hearths and fine marble overmantels were built wide to accommodate a circle of people who appreciated Grecian architecture and Roman history, and were ready, in the generous ease of their hearts, to welcome anybody and give anything they had.

Of course it could not last. Nor, if it had, could those small coteries, and the similar ones at Clapham and elsewhere, have given, as they proposed in theory to do, to every human creature a mansion and a garden, a library and a foreign tour, and the heavenly equivalent of all those things, in those other and better worlds in which they so firmly believed. Laughable? I am not so sure. Sighable more likely. If we had a few more of those people, or their like today, we might sleep easier at night. Perhaps they, from whatever " blessed Society above " they now frequent, are arranging all that. Meanwhile it is clear to me, as I look at the traces they have left, generations after most of them passed away, that these people deserved what they had, and the streets round St. George's bear the visible impress of those deserts, in spite of gaps and patches.

XVII

THE BACK OF THE INNS AND BONIFACE

IN many families you will find a good-humoured, round-faced member, patient, discreetly jolly and knowledgeable about a variety of things to the point of cunning. He is generally allowed to play host.

The street in Norwich which plays that part cannot be mistaken. Castle Street, a short, truncated offshoot of what is now the main shopping thoroughfare, and which does not lead to the Castle, receives typical Norwich alleys, paved for foot-passengers only, and ends in one. It is called The Back of the Inns, and that is what, for centuries, it was. It is a little less so today, though it retains signs of its original conviviality amid the modern shops that line it. If you pursue its narrow, generally crowded course, you emerge in the ganglion that used to be called the Goose & Gridiron.

It is now, as you might think, one of the elder members of the family. Its greatest fame came to it in the eighteenth century, when Parson Woodforde mentions familiarly one of its inns and made it nationally famous. For it did contain most of what Norwich has of that romantic piece of stage property, the " good old coaching inn ". Half a dozen of them had their long yards running from a front entrance on the Gentlemen's Walk, back to its rather overshadowed intricacies. That is why this alley is called The Back of the Inns. For once the name means what it says. It is regarded as rather a nuisance by Town Planners and those who are used to symmetrically laid out towns of Continental, American or Garden City pattern. And rightly. It grew up, as all things grow up, by idiosyncrasy as much as reason, and remains today picturesque, slightly impeding but too valuable in site value, too much a part of Norwich to be abolished and made convenient. There is in fact a reason for its presence and character. To find out what it is, one has to know what the " inn " of other ages was like, why it was like that, and how it has been modified by changing habit. The original hospitality quarter of Norwich was not here at all. We know very little of the early days of inn keeping, and much of what we know is legendary. Such documents as we have show that a large amount of housing and feeding the stranger, the guest and the traveller, was done by the monasteries. The late Canon Hudson, who delved so systematically into the early history of Norwich, said that the great hall of the Cathedral Monastery which I have described might well have been called the County Hotel, because of the scale of the provision it made for the reception of the visitor, as distinct from the Almonry, where the poor were the object of charity.

Yet we also know, from the police-court records of the thirteenth century, that there was, outside the monastery walls, some provision for the traveller. It seems to have stretched from Fye Bridge, then certainly the principal, and perhaps the only bridge over the Wensum, on the east side of what is now the short Wensum Street, as far as Tombland. It was known as Cook Row, and apparently consisted of eating-houses, which sold food cooked or uncooked. From the source of our record being what it is, we do not hear the best about those engaged in this occupation. Naturally enough, they only came before the Bailiffs when they had been caught selling bad whelks mixed with fresh, or serving up " porcinas superseminatas ", measly pork, drowned sheep and other comestibles which the surprisingly particular inspection of the thirteen-eighties considered as " contrary to the laws of our liege, the King ". These deplorable cases must surely have been exceptional, for the Cook Row persisted a long while and was perpetuated— much improved, one gathers—in the present Maid's Head Hotel, which is mentioned in the Paston Letters. Its earlier name was " The Myrtle Fish ", a species unknown to me and apparently to modern makers of inn-signs. At least it has been the Maid's Head for many centuries, and I should like to meet anyone sure enough of himself to declare with certainty that the sign was derived from the Virgin Mary by association with the Cathedral, or from what other Maid who struck the popular imagination sufficiently to have inns called after her. A little farther south, where what is still called Prince's Street leads the highway from west Norfolk into Tombland, there was a Prince's Inn, during the reign of Henry VII (a fine timber lintel carved with the name has been moved to King Street for some reason long forgotten). I think the hospitality of the town lingered here, as the market lingered, in Tombland, despite all efforts to concentrate it in what is now the Provision Market. There is no mention that I can find of an inn in that quarter until the old formal rows of shops, one row to each trade, began to break up after A.D. 1500, with the growth of the town, the export trade and the general disinclination of the new Protestant England to stay where it was put and do what it was told. After the monasteries were gone, or so changed that they no longer undertook the housing of man and beast, there must have been a considerable increase in public accommodation, for people certainly did not move about less than they had done before A.D. 1500, and they began to move by wheeled vehicle. Perhaps we can see the change taking place in the fact that Elizabeth, in 1587, still stayed at the Bishop's Palace, but Charles II, in 1671, stayed with his Grace of Norfolk. What, then, did inn-keeping become? We can see something from the first map that pretends to be a map, and not a " prospect " or view from the highest neighbouring hill. In 1766 Samuel King dedicated his " plan " to the Mayor, Recorder, Steward, two Sheriffs, twenty-four Aldermen and sixty Council men, with the rest of the worthy citizens of Norwich, and it was a plan, or map, showing Norwich not as a distant view, but as a more or less measured plot, on a scale of about 1 in 4,000, but so neatly engraved that he is able to show the inn yards, or many of them, leading from the main streets, to the stable end in some obscure lane, such as The Back of the Inns, the principal one. For that is what we have now to try to imagine. The inn had developed from the sort of establishment we hear of in the classics and the Bible and which can still be seen anywhere east of the Adriatic. This was a square enclosure, with some sort of roof running round one, two or three of the walls, not often over the entrance, keeping fairly dry and more or less sheltered a raised platform on which humans camped amid their baggage, while the animals were tethered, or at least could not run far, in the " yard ". A fountain or well is the extent of its convenience. From this it came to be a usually rectangular yard, with one or more galleried stories looking down into it, public rooms on the ground floor, bedrooms above, stables out of sight

—the sort of inn in which Samuel Weller cleaned boots in the open, indulged in badinage with the maids answering bells in the galleries, or the carters whose loaded wagons stood in the yard all night. That Dickensian type of inn was a London establishment of some pretensions in the eighteen-forties. The Norwich inns were older and simpler, a narrow passage into which the vehicle drove or horseman or pedestrian entered, accosted the office, in a little built-out bay, and was accommodated in the buildings running along each side, while his means of travel was led away by the ostler to the back. Here, beside the stables, were a heap of manure and a taproom for the humbler frequenters. The front rooms had some pretension to style. The first floor had a gallery, probably open to the sky, from which the bedrooms were accessible. The back had a smell. In 1766 there were half a dozen inns of this pattern along the Gentlemen's Walk, their faces to the Market Place, their feet, as it were, in the deplorable gutter " Back of the Inns " must have been. An ancient stream or cockey ran there covered over and, I have no doubt, used as a sewer.

These eighteenth-century inns can be traced today. Starting from the north end of the Gentlemen's Walk, next the wall of what is now Lloyd's Bank, is a passage containing a bar called by the pretty name of " The Walnut Tree Shades ". It was the Half Moon Inn, and still runs through to the Back of the Inns as described. On the south side of the Bank is a widish paved alley, now a prosperous shopping centre, and known as Davey Place, from a fairly recent owner. This was the King's Head Inn, and the sign of the King's Head still hangs above a licensed house at its eastern end. This was what Parson Woodforde says: " Nancy's Brother Willm breakfasted with us, and soon after breakfast, he set off for Somersett. My brother went with him in my little cart so far as Norwich. Willm set off in the mail coach about 4. They dined together at the King's Head." So that was it. The London mail ran from the King's Head, with much clatter, halloing, waving and general fuss. As late as Parson Woodforde's time, a journey to " Somersett " or even to London was one in preparation for which one said one's prayers, if any, put flannel next one's skin, gulped a strong dram of brandy, and wound one's " comforter " round one's neck and over the mouth, to keep the fumes in. Dickens has so described the precautions, and for more than half the year they must have been of the first necessity to the " outsides ", passengers who from lack of cash or mere casual toughness booked those exposed seats on the top of the coach. If that was so for the young and bold, or at least insensitive, what can it have been like for the ill and infirm, and those going to the death-bed of some relative in reply to a frantic summons? At their best—that is, for about ten years when the railways had begun to run but were still too dangerous, inconvenient and incomplete—the " outside " traveller put up with what the wind and wet, frost and fog did to him for an hour, at about which time the end of the stage would be reached (that is, an average of ten miles), when there would be a hurried, noisy halt, and just time for another brandy-and-water. My own father went by one of the last coaches, from Norwich to Chelmsford, and often described to me how the art of changing the horses had been brought to a fine point, the fresh ones already harnessed, standing waiting. The instant the exhausted, smoking team had been unhooked and withdrawn, this relay was run out, hooked on, the " ribbons " handed up to the coachman.

" All right, Joe?"

" Way you go, Ben! "

Click, chirrup, rattle and strain as the well-trained beasts took up the weight and found the rhythm of their sharp trot. Any bold " outside " who had lingered from dire necessity, from desire for an extra drink or a smile from the young woman in the snug, had to run, catch on and clamber up. And so on for no less than twelve changes (including the final dismounting in Lad Lane, Lombard Street, or wherever it might be. Rather less, of course, to Chelmsford.). Sometimes that sort of journey at its best had moments of exhilaration, as Dickens showed. Who does not remember how the Pickwickians, escorted by Mr. Jingle, left the Golden Cross in the Strand (now pulled down, but I have dined there) : " ' Heads, heads, take care of your heads,' " cried the loquacious stranger, as they came out under a low archway, which, in those days, formed the entrance to the coachyard. " ' Terrible place—dangerous work—other day— five children—mother—tall lady, eating sandwiches—forgot the arch—crash—knock—children look round—mother's head off—sandwiches in her hand—no mouth to put it in—head of a

family off—shocking, shocking. Look at Whitehall, Sir—
fine place—little window—somebody else head off there, eh
Sir?—he didn't keep a sharp look out enough either—Eh, Sir,
eh?'" I have made this apparent digression because it
emphasises a point about the sort of inn which had a yard
opening upon Norwich Market Place and a " tap " in the Back
of the Inns. You will not appreciate the point in Davey Place
—that is, the King's Head yard, which has been enlarged and
rebuilt. But you will if you follow the Gentlemen's Walk a
little farther, when, between Nos. 23 and 24, there appears what
is now a narrow entry. But by boldly following this, the old
Bear Inn Yard, and turning to look upwards and backwards,
you will see a portion of the timbering, staircase and gallery of
the original building. The yard no longer goes through to the
Back of the Inns, but its ancient egress can be traced there,
between the Post Office and the Royal Arcade. Now, as one
looks at Bear Yard, the point of Mr. Jingle's story becomes plain.
How did any good-sized coach ever get in and out of these rat-
holes? Have the surrounding buildings been altered, or has
the century-old accumulation of filth raised the roadway?
This difficulty is not peculiar to the Bear Yard. The same
question arises in the mind when one tries to picture a coach
entering or leaving the yard of the Bell (which has been turned
into a lounge but is quite discernible in spite of the swing doors
that now close it) or that of the Maid's Head. Were the coaches
very low, swung between their springs? Or have the buildings
been altered out of recognition? Could either of them have
been, where so much is plainly Elizabethan, if not older?
But one understands Mr. Jingle better. One could easily get
one's head knocked off, if one entered either yard as an " outside " passenger on a coach.

Passing along the Walk, the next inn was what is now the
Royal Arcade, and was for long the Royal Hotel and, a hundred
years ago, the Angel. Here there is space to spare, and an
enlarged alley beyond the Back of the Inns, leading up into
Castle Meadow, rather destroys the illusion of a cramped lane
full of dirty straw and horse-droppings. What wealth of
manure those old places must have disposed of! A cousin of mine
who farmed on the banks of an Essex estuary used to buy
manure by the barge-load (delivered at his quay) from the

General Omnibus Company at ten shillings a barge. What wonder the land was well farmed! A few yards south of the Arcade (as it now is) narrow White Lion Street does not, I am told, represent the yard of the White Lion Inn, which merely branched out of it. The street itself is now thought to represent the original way from the Castle to the Market. In its latter days the old White Lion became a soldiers' house, and was affectionately known to the Victorian long-service enlisted man, in his garrison—Bermuda, Capetown, India or beyond—as the " Blue Monkey ".

The last of this range of inns whose taps or backs made the Back of the Inns was the Star, now very roughly represented by the present Lamb; the Bell, a very old sign fronting Orford Hill, through the yard of which the new street which continues Castle Meadow was driven, and the Castle, which has migrated, face away, with their backs to Back of the Inns, completing its course. Beyond this, where Orford Place and Brigg Street bring the Gentlemen's Walk to its conclusion, there remain the site of the Rampant Horse, facing north, with its back in Rampant Horse Street, and Abraham's Hall, an inn now completely submerged by the Haymarket Cinema. I suppose it dimly recalls some Jewish owner, before A.D. 1290. The ghetto lay approximately on the site of the Star, adjacent.

In the corner of the market enclosure next the great tower o St. Peter's Church, a garage has now displaced the old White Hart, whose yard ran back to Theatre Street. It had a proper eighteenth-century office, a little half-octagon bay built out on to its ancient cobbles. When the Norwich Philharmonic Society gave its concerts at what is now the Assembly House, my father, who played the trumpet in the orchestra, used to say that there was just time to get from his place, during the interval, drink a glass of stout, and get back. I remember it as having the last of the old underground skittle alleys; I have hurled a wooden " cheese " there.

Almost next door, a fine timber lintel, heavily carved, surrounds the door of the old Swan, where Parson Woodforde went to see the play. On this, the western side of the Market, the new City Hall, an admirable building and urgently necessary improvement, has abolished the Pope's Head and the Wounded Hart, whose long yards used to run where its stately corridors long rang to the tread of exasperated mothers seeking emergency ration cards. St. Giles' Broad Street, as it was called, used to display the signs of one of the principal coaching inns, with connections for the west of the county, the Norfolk Hotel, and of the Black Horse and the Dolphin. The first of these was frequented by John Sell Cotman. Also on the north of the Market, but stretching into Little London Street, was the ancient sign of the Tuns, whose yard was made the entry of Exchange Street.

Such was the front which the inn-keeping of the eighteenth century made to the Market Place. That was by no means all. Down beside Coslany Bridge was the unusual sign of the St. John's Head and in the main western thoroughfare of St. Benedict's Street the not too usual one of The Hand. Down in Colegate, next St. George's churchyard, appropriately set in the midst of the old textile trade, was and still stands the Woolpack, now entertaining clickers and lasters. The Blackboys, also in Colegate, in the yard of which Mrs. Barbauld set up her remarkable school, is now gone, but no less than two White Horses, with full-scale thoroughfare yards, are to be found surviving, one in Magdalen Street and one on Palace Plain. This latter may well be the last place in which your footsteps still crackle on sanded flagstones, and where after sundown the gas is lit.

These conditions are a necessary reminder that Boniface, the inn-keeper, whose half-dozen middens made the Back of the Inns, was not always the comfortable host of Early Victorian days you meet in the *Pickwick Papers*. That was his heyday. The railways were running, but they had not pushed him aside into the mere tavern-keeper he became in less fortunate circumstances, or the proprietor of the Railway Hotel if he were intelligent and lucky. The changes the railway wrought I will show directly, when we meet the street which was made by and for the railway and gave the whole aspect of the streets of Norwich a new twist. I only need here to show how late the " old coaching inn " organisation lingered in Norwich. It is still to be found in the first street directory of Norwich, compiled by Blyth in 1842, just at the moment when my father, as a boy, taken for a walk along the river-bank, asked *his* father what those men were digging up so much gravel for, across on the

other bank, in the pleasant suburb of Thorpe. He was told:
" They are making ready for the new Railway, my boy." He
seems to have been satisfied with that.

In these pages of Blyth's " Directory ", in which trades-
people and " private residents " have as yet no numbers to the
houses in the streets in which they lived, there are five coaches
to London, three making the up journey at night and two by
daylight. The night coach by the Newmarket " and northern
and eastern railway " route is described as " setting out " every
evening from the White Swan, St. Peter's and Rampant Horse,
St. Stephen's [this means the parish, not the street, the inn
actually stood in Rampant Horse Street] at eight o'clock.
The return was made from " the White Horse, Fetter Lane,
London at seven; Bull Inn Bishopgate, Swan and Shoreditch
Station half past seven, and arrives at Norwich at seven o'clock
the following morning ". There it was, twelve hours by road.
Or, alternatively, one could take the railway from Shoreditch
as far as Cambridge, or even, if a first-class passenger, have one's
carriage hoisted on to a float, and lashed there, to clatter along
between the tall-funnelled engine and the lower-class trucks.
The design of the private carriage was in fact copied in the early
first-class railway coaches.

All the towns and many villages were served by coaches,
wagons and " fly vans " down to the humble once-a-week
carrier, whose tilted cart (sometimes printed by Blyth as a
" caravan ") was to be found parked in Ber Street or St.
Benedict's, on its appropriate day, until the First World War.
That is how the transition from road to rail came about.
Before the last horse-drawn carrier's carts had ceased to run,
the process was being reversed, and traffic was going back to the
roads, by 1914.

Let us not forget that I have shown Boniface, at his latest and
most gentlemanly years, before he became extinguished, or
rather, converted. What coaching was at any time up to
Waterloo can be judged by the words of Hudson Gurney I have
often quoted, about my own great-grandfather: " Mottram
has gone with £80,000 in gold in parcels beyond number and
compass, which I cannot but feel to be a very hazardous dis-
patch, by the times we live in." The old gentleman continued to do so until he was over eighty, sustained, one hopes, at

that age, for those twelve hours, by his sense of duty—and brandy and water. Once the coach was attacked, or at least threatened, by an individual who rode up to it, holding out something at the coachman. A fellow traveller of my ancestor's shot the intruder dead. He was found to be a ragged wretch riding a stolen horse, his weapon a brass candlestick. (Possibly this was to escape the extreme penalty if caught.)

So take farewell of the Back of the Inns. The modern hotel (h. & c., lift, garage, N.P.), the roadhouse and the Country Club have replaced the old inn-keeping. But the name lingers. Indeed, the new inn-keeping would never have existed without the old.

XVIII

EXCHANGE STREET, AND WHAT WAS CHANGED THERE

THE time came—of course it did, for if times did not come no one of us would ever arrive here—when the streets of Norwich, which had sufficed for so much and for so long, were no longer adequate and new ones had to be made.

New ones. Let us distinguish. The Gentlemen's Walk was not new, it became an eighteenth-century street. There was no compact body of gentility before that. There were aristocrats, and there were humble craftsmen and labourers, but the Gentleman was one removed gradually by birth (and by money) from necessity. He didn't have to fight, administer great estates, or enter the professions. He could do what he liked, be as idle as he pleased, and so long as his money lasted, would always find people to supply his whims as well as his wants. He was an eighteenth-century phenomenon.

Now, the street called the Gentlemen's Walk had been there for centuries. It became, grew up to be the Gentlemen's Walk, after being called the Cordwainery for generations. The Back of the Inns got its name in the seventeenth century. It had not originally been a street, but the bed of a little stream. And so on. Hundegate became Elm Hill, and Upper Newport, Bethel Street. The names of streets changed with their uses, the direction in which they gave access, the parish through which they ran. These names they assumed down the ages were just the signs of growing up, of the passage of time and the achievement of adult status, or old age. Just so the baby becomes the boy James, who goes to school, the apprentice Jim, young Mr. James, a married man, James Esquire, and finally old gran'sire.

We now come to something different, to new streets deliberately and consciously made, not old streets repaved and enlarged and called by new names. The walled city, with gates closing the main thoroughfares where they led out into the open country, had sufficed from the great upheaval of the Norman Conquest. It had even resisted the changes the

Normans tried to make, partially succeeded, and then quietly incorporated what could not be reversed. I know nothing more dramatic than the emergence of the English nation, some time between A.D. 1200 and 1300. Before the former date there had been three sorts of people in Norwich, speaking three dialects, dedicating their churches to different saints. In 1002 Danes and Saxons massacred each other. In 1066 the Normans must have killed a good many of the other two nationalities. By 1300 the three sorts of people had forgotten all about their origins and adopted a common tongue, roughly the English of Chaucer, and began to call themselves " English ", as distinct from French, vassals of the same Lord though they and their French counterparts might have been. They kept their early records in Latin, of course.

This momentous change is like nothing else but the enormously larger similar process now going on in the United States. Come whence you will, speak what is your native tongue, but in a few generations you will be a citizen of the great Republic and speak its variety of English.

So in Norwich, this great solidification lasted until about A.D. 1790. There was the walled City; you could see it, a clear-cut entity, visible from the London or Lynn or Yarmouth roads. Between 1790 and 1840 all that was changed, and new streets, many new public buildings, appeared. The wall was built upon, the gates were demolished. The citizens began to go about their business or pleasure by ways which, a few months earlier, would have led slap through slabs of masonry, shops and dwellings that had succeeded one another on the same sites for ages.

It all seems to have begun at a meeting of a " Special Assembly " or, as we should say, of the City Council. On 15 August 1792 it was resolved that " in consequence of the recommendation of the conference at the last Assembly, it is ordered that a case be stated by the Town Clerk, and laid before the law officers of this Corporation, for their opinions respecting the power the Corporation has under the Tonnage Act, to take down any of the gates, without risking the loss of revenue arising from that act, and thereby rendering insecure the mortgages on that fund; and that such case be submitted to the Speaker of the Corporation for his approbation."

Such was the cumbrous procedure necessitated by the fact that the Gates had, as one has suspected, for centuries been of less importance as a fortification than as a means of controlling the movement of goods in and out of the City, for taxation purposes. The repair of these masses of ancient masonry and rubble had been a continuous drain for more than four centuries. The walls no longer seemed likely to be assaulted, the Gates impeded the wheeled traffic that had greatly increased in bulk and in the size of vehicles and number of cattle that had to pass through narrow and dilapidated stone portals. Some of the walls and towers were dangerous. All blocked the expansion for which the City was ripe. The Corporation, however, were a little nervous of abandoning landmarks of their taxing capacity, especially as they had borrowed money on the security of the revenues collected at the gates and the river-bank towers. But legal sanction was obtained, and at the next quarterly Assembly it was ordered that the gates closing St. Stephen's Street, those called Brazen Doors closing All Saints' Green, Pockthorpe or Barre Gates, St. Giles' Gates and St. Benedict's Gates be taken down. A Committee of worthies was appointed " or any five of them, to receive proposals and contract for doing and finishing thereof in a handsome manner ". It took all that to disembarrass oneself of the Middle Ages.

And at the next Assembly there had evidently been trouble with people who, one may guess, had already built on to the wall and round the gates, for " the Committee . . . are hereby empowered to treat with the proprietors of the houses on the north side of the opening where St. Giles' Gates stood, for so much of the houses as will accommodate the passage into that part of the City ". They seem to have come to terms, for " at the Quarterly Meeting on 22nd January 1794, Ordered that St. Augustine's and King Street Gates be taken down ". The other five followed until, as we saw when we followed that oddest of Norwich streets, the Way under the Wall, they were gone. Nor do the revenues of the City seem to have suffered. Of course the local Octroi became, a generation later, merged in the modern rates levied on the value of property and not on imported goods. Yet until the First World War the signpost at the junction of the Ipswich and the Newmarket Roads to

London bore the inscription " Erected by the Tonnage Commissioners ", which shows that the Authorities of the Middle Ages did achieve something, although the first Directory of Norwich describes the work of yet another *ad hoc* body in these terms: " The Pavement is generally bad. An act for paving the City was passed in 1806, but the work had suffered long interruption. The entire paving of the frequented parts of the City would be a great improvement as well as a convenience; indeed there is scarcely any place of importance in England, in which the streets are in a worse condition." That was written actually after the Municipal Reform Act of 1835. Cobbles were frequent in 1900. They now remain only on Orford Hill and Elm Hill, I think deliberately preserved to impress visitors. Yes, I fear our historic streets were shabby.

Into such a company came the first new street for five hundred years. Let us follow the family image for a moment. It sometimes happens that elderly parents, or perhaps a remarried widow or widower, produce new offspring after an interval. They surely cannot avoid knowing more about how to bring up this little stranger. They have had so much practice that the attempt to look as if they didn't know would appear hardly sincere.

Even so, the determination of the Assembly of the ancient Corporation of Norwich to make a new street (for the event took place before the great clean-up of the Municipal Reform Act of 1835, and the Corporation had had four centuries to arrive at this determination) was the result of practical experience in the management, or often mismanagement, of the public highways of the City. This was to be no enlargement of some old track trodden out rather than planned or paved, by the barbarians of centuries before, as all the other streets of Norwich were. It was an attempt to facilitate the increased traffic of the nineteenth century and to provide public buildings which were lacking.

From the time of its enclosure within its walls, until the morrow of Waterloo, Norwich had been incredibly inconvenient. In fact, convenience of access seems never to have been contemplated. As we have seen, when Charles II, approaching from the south-east, required to reach the Duke of Norfolk's Palace, he seems to have skirted the outside of the walls from

Ber Street Gates to those of St. Stephen's. This may have been partly to show some belated courtesy to his patient Queen, who was approaching by the latter route. But it may also have been that, had he entered the City by Ber Street Gates, he would, after that wide old street, have found himself faced with the choice of various narrow lanes, avoiding the enclosure in which the Castle stood, or, alternatively, have had to edge his way through encumbered old subsidiary market-places, like Timberhill or the Swine Market. As it was, he had to use the Goose & Gridiron, about as convenient as some village cross-ways with a pound in the middle. That was how Royalty fared. The lot of the simple citizen was no better. Anyone living and working in the increasingly important industrial (weaving) Ward of Over the Water had no direct means save one-track lanes of arriving at the Market Place. Either those had to be used—and there must have been continual traffic jams as the wagon of the period stood probably for hours, un-loading or loading at some warehouse—or there were long detours to make to attain the main arteries running from Tombland. Even so, it must have been nearly as quick to go round by the walls. For, to tell the truth, the Market Place had never been planned to be accessible. As we have seen, the reason for its position was to be under observation from the Castle, and near the garrison, which needed food.

So, at length, in the eighteen-twenties the plan took shape, to drive a new street from the Market connecting directly with the Ward of Over the Water. The provision of a proper Corn Exchange was perhaps an additional incentive, and the members of the Corporation obtained the necessary Parlia-mentary sanction. The spot chosen for this project was the north-east corner of the Market Place. How right this choice was can be seen by the fact that the crossways thus created is today perhaps the busiest in the City, although one could hardly foresee that modern London Street, then called Cockey Lane, would soon become the principal shopping street. For ages it had been an obscure by-way leading nowhere in par-ticular. On the northern flank of this corner (Cockey Lane alias London Street being on the eastern flank) there used to stand the old inn known as the Tunns, with a long yard, which, however, turns at a sharp angle away from the direction in which the Corporation had determined to drive a way through. They seem to have used the southern end of Tunns Yard. This brought them to Pottergate, through the courtyard of the fine mansion of Sir Benjamin Wrench, an eighteenth-century physician, a spacious Elizabethan building in which John Crome and his party of friends, relatives and adherents had held their exhibitions of paintings which they called " The Norwich Society " and which may be said to have founded the Norwich School of Painting. The progressive spirit of the time made short work of this relic of past glories, and led the new street into old Pottergate. In line with the direction taken was yet another narrow, paved passage, left over in the Middle Ages from the abandonment of the old parish church of St. Crouch, which had once stood in St. Andrew's Street.

Now they found themselves blocked by the bulk of the Duke of Norfolk's Palace. We have seen how, only a generation after the great festivities in which Charles II had been so splendidly received, a queer quarrel, of which no one seems to know the exact point, between the Ducal family and the Corporation had led the Howards to abandon this edifice. Part of it had already become a City Workhouse, and the impression it still made on the public mind a century after the last Howard had inhabited it was such that the youth of Norwich of the less fortunate classes, who desired to find themselves a job to render them independent (and we may be certain they were en- couraged to do so by their parents), would station themselves opposite the long-closed doors in the little square known from its ancient use as the Maddermarket. Here masters and mistresses who desired cheap domestic or odd-job labour would repair, and inspect the groups of likely or unlikely grown-up boys and girls. The process was known as " going on the Palace ", and it is always said that it was by this method of recruitment that young John Crome became the errand-boy of the famous Dr. Rigby.

Now, the part of the Palace which stood in the way of the Corporation's new street was the " offices " let to the work- house authority, together with a Roman Catholic chapel and priest's house. These latter had been let to the Norwich Public Library. Unwilling, one must conclude, to disturb either of these occupants, the Corporation had to make their street deviate several yards to the west, where the old forecourt of the Palace had long been demolished. Here was an unencumbered site, opposite the Maddermarket, and across this, northward, the new street was planned, taking whatever extra traffic it attracted from the Market Place, by this short right-angled deviation and the immemorial stream of vehicles and foot passengers from Dove Lane to a bridge erected across the Wensum in 1822. Once north of the river there used to be one of the numerous " waterings " or alleys of access to the river-bank by which the water was dipped and carted for use, one hopes not, at this date, for cooking or human consumption. This led out into Colegate. Across Colegate yet other gardens were found which pointed at the corner of the churchyard of St. Mary's Coslany. Here Tooley Street (St. Olave's Street), as it had been, ran a little east of north to the junction of St. Augustine's Street with Botolph Street. Thus the new line was complete, from the Provision Market, to the main northern and north-western quarters. The Committee of the Corporation must have heaved a sigh. The cost of the new " Duke's Palace " bridge, the first to be erected for at least three hundred years, in its permanent form (cast iron) was no less than £9,000. Some of this was recovered by a toll levied upon the users.

This, then, was the first of the great " improvements " by which the old City within the Walls was given some degree of light and air, some diminution of the jostling in its narrow, ill-sited or rather unsited roadways, a good deal of saving of time and temper in the movements of its citizens. They were not content with the street. They now determined to have their Corn Exchange, and that name was given to the new way, and can to this day be seen inscribed on the brickwork of one of the houses on the western side, near the entrance to the Market Place " Exchange Street 1829 ".

To further this project the Norwich Corn Exchange Company proceeded in 1826 to erect the first Corn Exchange, which lasted until 1861, when it was replaced by the present one. It cost £8,000, of which £2,000 was subscribed by prominent agriculturalists. Nor is this wonderful when we realise that its chief promoter was Thomas William Coke. The splendid house of the great physician, Sir Benjamin Wrench, whose portrait hangs today in the Council Chamber of the Guildhall

M

and who practised in that place for sixty years, afforded ample scope. Yet Exchange Street never became quite the north and south highway the citizens hoped. The crick in its neck in St. Andrew's, with the awkward corner this created, may be the reason. It had to await some spectacular destruction in 1942 to be rebuilt in a manner to give it any great distinction. The advent of penny postage had brought it the Post Office, but it remained somehow a street that never quite found itself. Perhaps the members of the Corporation were too optimistic or the citizens too stubborn—a lesson in what can be done in forcibly changing the daily habit of men who have long been accustomed to tread certain ways and will not easily or quickly be made to tread others, even when the reasons are excellent.

This " improvement ", as it is described in Blyth's Directory for 1842, was accompanied by the widening of Briggs' Lane, named after Alderman Briggs (a local politician who owned land in the vicinity), which did something to prolong the Gentlemen's Walk southward. Another was the drastic widening and paving of the old King's Head yard, turning it into its modern use as a shopping highway for pedestrians. This was done largely by Alderman Davey, who had acquired the property. Hence its present name " Davey Place ". Admittedly this was a private venture, but Blyth listed it in his Directory, along with Briggs' Lane and Exchange Street as an " Improvement " directed to making the approaches to the Market Place more convenient.

With better access came better light. A company for the manufacture of gas was formed in 1820, and shortly four chandeliers appeared in the Market Place, throwing what can have been but a soft and feeble radiance over the old housefronts, the flush-work of the Guildhall and the then far more homely outline of the massive roof and tower of St. Peter Mancroft. But it was a brighter light than they had ever known. One wonders now how far some feeling of inferiority this illumination produced gave birth to the urge to tear down so many of these buildings. They had been there so long, like elderly and disapproving relatives. Moreover, in 1836 was instituted the New Police, " twenty-four policemen and eight supernumeraries, who are appointed by the Town Council, and are dressed in the same style as the metropolitan police. They are under the control of a sergeant whose duty it is to see that the men attend to their beats. At eleven o'clock p.m. they are relieved by the night watch, who are thirty-eight in number, including supernumeraries. They are compelled to go round their beats, some every quarter of an hour, some every half-hour. To ascertain whether they are attentive to this order, registers with clock faces within various houses are placed in different parts of the City, and each man is provided with a key with which he marks the time of his round. There is likewise a River Police with two boats."

So Norwich was lighted and opened up, policed and emancipated from its ancient walls, even if the paving and cleansing left much to be desired. It began pumping water, too, into a reservoir into which the public park, now known as Chapel Field, had been converted, and from which the water incontinently burst.

As one looks back at Exchange Street, the Exchange and all these other changes, one sees that modern thoroughfare as a harbinger, a kind of coming-of-age, belated and incomplete, but symbolic. Norwich had left the Middle Ages behind. The dark, odorous uncertainty, dominated and modified by a few large and shapely buildings of stone, was gone. With a confidence we now feel rather naïve, the streets of Norwich prepared to undergo changes, even the greatest change.

XIX

THE GENTLEMEN'S WALK, AND WHO WALKED THERE

WE now come to the younger members of the family of Norwich streets. As anyone knows who has the acquaintance of a large family, the elder children are dismissed to "make themselves useful" while the nursery is teeming full, and the back-kitchen one continual procession of baskets of washing and small toddlers getting under everyone's feet. Then, as time passes, if all goes well and the family has prospered, those same toddlers grow up in a state of comparative comfort and leisure their elders never knew. There is time, and by good luck money, to give them a better chance. Better education, that may mean, or it may mean leisure that their big brothers and sisters never had. Education itself may have moved on, meanwhile. Very often the younger children reflect their parents' increased maturity and are fit for more intelligent occupations, and likely to demand better conditions. Just so with the streets of Norwich. We have seen how the eldest of them fared in the rough world in which the life of the Norwich streets began. It was little more than an extended trackway, purely utilitarian. Its airs and graces were such as arise from usefulness and situation.

Not so these later additions to the family, renamed in the eighteenth century and showing what were the ambitions and the achievements of that epoch of new super-civilisation.

The visitor to the family with these facts in mind will not be surprised when he finds the wide pavement that lines the eastern side of the Provision Market, labelled " Gentlemen's Walk ". It begins, at its northern end, in what had been Hosier Gate and had become " London Lane " because it contained some of the best shops, particularly those dealing in wearing apparel. It ended at the inn called the Rampant Horse, which abutted on the Horse Market, where the gentlemen would meet the dealers who supplied their steeds. The intelligent visitor will say immediately :

"But this is not what the street, or rather pavement, was always called. A name like ' Gentlemen's Walk ' belongs to the Age of Gentility, when, for the first time, there were people whose means permitted them to walk about during the working hours of the laborious, quizzing each other, and ogling what they probably called the Fair and Frail Sex! "

Quite right. The term occurs only in the middle of the eighteenth century, and for good reason. Only then had reasonable safety from invasion been assured. The ghosts of a Stuart Restoration and complete upset of the Protestant mercantile society that had supplanted the Stuarts were not quite laid. But they were by then ghosts, and ghosts only. It was not any longer necessary to spend one's life looking jealously after such land as one had acquired, lest perforce one might have to summon one's tenants and defend it. In the City itself, a certain number of the younger men were no longer inclined to put in the whole day behind their father's counter or in his warehouse. A club was opened at the corner of Walnut Tree Shades yard, from the high and wide first-floor windows of which young men who had not quite learned to call themselves " Bucks " but had begun to lay aside their swords in everyday wear, leaned out to survey the passers-by. Even today, entertainment (which used to mean inns, and now means cafés) and clothing (largely men's) occupy most of the shopping space. A wide roadway separates these from the market stalls, which anyhow had by then been dominated for centuries by the premier parish church of St. Peter, where the best people had themselves baptised, married and buried, and the Guildhall, where the best people governed themselves and the others, not so best.

Now much of the sentiment which caused this pavement to be called " Gentlemen's Walk " has disappeared. The feeling of security and leisure, then so novel, has long departed, and indeed, been reversed. But the name marks an epoch. When it was first used, it did show that something had happened. Progress had permitted the gentlemen to discard weapons, and become gentle, in very fact. But progress was wildly irregular. What had actually happened was what happens when a loosely coupled goods-train stops and starts again, what happens when a marching column halts and proceeds. The wagons pull apart, the ranks open. That is what was happening socially in those latter years of George II. The old drive against outward pressure had been eased, the stresses and strains of society relaxed and changed. Within a few yards of the Gentlemen's Walk were courts and tenements, unlighted, unpaved and undrained in which the less fortunate citizens existed in conditions differing from what they had been five hundred years earlier only in their congestion and their segregation. Five hundred years earlier the hosiers and goldsmiths, the innkeepers and saddlers and spurriers along that pavement, had dwelt, if more sparsely, under the same threat of war and pestilence, famine and drought as any workmen in their lofts or cellars, any tenant of a market stall, the wagoner or pack-horse man who transported their goods from Quayside or St. Anne's Staithe, the mariner who shipped them thence or thither. But not from about A.D. 1750. There then emerged a new type. He was not necessarily noble or learned. He had money, not necessarily land. Tradesmen whom he despised and hired built his house and furnished it, brought his food and drink to a side door, leading to the portions of his house in which it was prepared for him. He had time to burn. Where did he burn it?

If he had had enough of the Club at the corner of the Walnut Tree Shades and had walked along to look at some possible horse in the Horse Fair, he could then turn west by the churchyard of St. Peter Mancroft and through White Hart yard, or by the parallel street called Chapel Field Lane, and in a few yards he would come to an imposing building that was never more alive in his time than it is today. It was the Assembly House. How did it come to be there?

As he saw, those who take the Veil had been numerous in Norwich. One of their most splendid churches and one of their most flourishing establishments had been the College of Priests and Hospital of St. Mary, with a chantry attached, abutting upon the walls of the City between the St. Giles' Gate and the St. Stephen's Gates. At the Dissolution its land and buildings had come into the possession of the Hobarts of Blickling, who had built a great town house with its forecourt set upon the foundation of the conventual cloisters, and its park extending over what is still called " Chapel Field ". When the Hobarts wanted to change their town residence it suited very well to dispose of this property to what we should nowadays call a syndicate, which employed the great local architect, Thomas Ivory, to build an Assembly House. Here, then, on the graves of the chaplains and their servitors, the gentry, if not the nobility, met to dance and play cards, to hear music and to hold banquets, and very fine they must have looked. For they represented a mobilisation of money and materials to produce elegance. Thomas Ivory, who never called himself an architect, but rather a builder, Wilkins the plasterer, who did the lovely mouldings, other tradesmen in their degree, were employed to make something they themselves would not have dreamed of using, any more than Chippendale would have made his chairs for himself, or the large catering and caretaking staff of such a place would have proposed to eat the viands or take part in the minuets and card-parties they made possible. The humble chairmen who carried the guests to the entertainments did not dream of entering those portals of the privileged, but (this is one of Time's revenges) left their initials cut in the bricks around the front doors where they stood, stamping their feet and cheering each other with the humour of their kind, so that today we know more of them than of the patrons they laboriously bumped thither.

So there arose between the two wings of the Hobart mansion, along what had been the southern side of the Cloisters, a suite of Assembly Rooms in the finest style of George II. Its front had that simplicity of solid brickwork which is the glory of that era, pierced by wide sash windows and a handsome double door. Within, beyond an imposing vestibule with steps and niches, was the magnificent tea-room (*foyer* as we should call it), all neo-classic, with pillars and panels, a coffered ceiling whence hung great glass chandeliers before a gallery to the north and a bow to the south. Westward, a fine entry gave upon the Ballroom, 66 feet by 23 feet, with its shapely balcony for the musicians; eastward was the Banqueting Room or smaller ballroom, with lovely fireplaces, and great swags and festoons of elegant plaster mouldings between its portraits and mirrors. The vista across these two main rooms with the tea-room between them was no less than 143 feet. In the corridor were card-rooms, withdrawing-rooms and such resources, and more above stairs.

There, for a generation or two at least, splendid in their apparel and choice in their deportment, the wealthy and well-born from the City and County moved to the sound of music and happy laughter, chatter and scandal, the delicate scrape of feet and swish of skirts, while the candle-light gleamed on satin and brocade, on uniforms and high head-dresses, and smiles and powder hid Heaven knows what hopes and jealousies, and the servants scurried discreetly in the background.

What must the ghosts of the monks of the Chapel in the Fields and the Chaplains of the College and Chantry have thought of this parade of fancy dress? Not only in clothes. The lane that had once led to the north porch of their great church, and had been designated, very properly, " Our Lady's Lane ", now served to give access for carriages and chairs to this very different community. It became " Lady's Lane ", and early directories think was named after Lady Frances Hobart. The sign was subsequently changed to " Ladies' Lane " and obtained a slightly altered significance as the Gentlemen invited to the entertainments, not their wives, but those who would have liked to be. Then, in the eighteen-thirties, Norwich lost its textile prosperity and the brilliant society that had floated like coloured foam on the surface of so much arduous industrial activity dwindled and sank, and finally the Assembly House was closed.

Yet it was too commodious a place to fall out of use for long, and by the eighteen-seventies the Girls' Public Day School Trust occupied it, and turned its rooms to the new uses of female education and something of the air of *Love's Labour's Lost* and Tennyson's *Princess* seeped into the ageing, if still comely building. The great panels of the ballrooms bore the long list of those who had gone thence with distinction to such novel establishments as Girton and Lady Margaret Hall. The cellars in which wine had winked became laboratories, and Lacrosse was played in what had been the garden, so that the ghosts of its eighteenth-century devotees may have been more astonished than those of their predecessors, the chaplains, except that dancing was taught by the Noverres, a family descended from French aristocrat refugees, in a new room added to the western Hobart wing.

But by the nineteen-thirties, after sixty years, the centre of the City was no longer the place for the education of the daughters of gentlemen. They had gone to live a mile or more away. There was no room for expansion, and industry hemmed the place in. The school moved. Perhaps it was just as well, for the Second World War was no respecter of Girls' Public Day Schools or Assembly Houses. The streets were machine-gunned, and the place itself narrowly missed destruction. But what likelihood was there of anyone ever repairing its sagging roof and broken windows? It was then that Providence, if that is what it is, stepped in, to the rescue of all that is gentle and happy in life, as it never had to the professedly religious or frivolously genteel occupation of the site. It was no visionary Providence either, but took the figure of Henry Sexton, Norwich born, and one of the heads of the footwear trade that had grown up on the ruins of the old weaving industry. He, with exemplary munificence, poured out the necessary thousands, and today anyone can go to the Assembly House of Norwich, at any hour from eleven to eleven, and find food for the mind and refreshment for the body, a cinema and a restaurant and much else, and not an inch to spare. The place was probably never so thoroughly used or so well kept. And the moral is, Never despair, not even of so abandoned a shrine of what many thought such ephemeral or outdated activities.

So there you have them, very much alive today, these younger members of the Norwich family, Gentlemen's Walk, Lady's Lane, and the Assembly House. Not quite so famous as their equivalent at Bath, not better perhaps than their like at York, but still a living witness to something else in life than the crude getting of the wherewithal to live. Music and the spoken word, pictures on canvas and films on the screen, meeting of friends and nodding of acquaintances have superseded the stark devotions and the frivolous display of other times. These perennial streets of Norwich are at least more sophisticated than their elders. While they are used as they are, reason and reflection and recreation will not quite desert us.

XX

PRINCE OF WALES ROAD AND THE RUDE MECHANIC

THE younger members of the Norwich family belong to the nineteenth century. This means more in Norwich than in most places. Many a town in England is almost entirely of this generation, with only a hint here and there of all the long centuries of eventful life that had preceded it. Not so Norwich, where a continuous national predominance from the fourteenth century at least, to the eighteenth has never been obliterated.

Early Victorian Norwich is therefore all the more striking. The streets that belong to this period are distinctive. They bear witness to something new, and more startling than anything that had happened since the half-animal creatures that ranged the glacial and other deposits where Norwich now stands first pushed a log into the lagoons and streams, and tried to govern the direction in which it floated, as they bestrode it. Or since the day when one of them caught and tamed the wild four-footed creature of the primeval woods and heaths, and made it carry them or their loads.

That is what primly prosperous Prince of Wales Road and, to a lesser degree, other new streets meant in Norwich. They were not new streets deliberately planned by the City Council. They were made at the urge of a new idea of locomotion, coming from outside, and had no direct relation to the old City, left irrelevant by the distance that intervened between it and the newly important coal- and iron-fields beyond Peterborough. These influences gave the final twist to the complicated knot of Norwich traffic, the most decisive alteration that had taken place since the Normans failed to destroy Tombland, and almost the last of the changes that created the Norwich of the twentieth century.

Prince of Wales Road was created to serve the needs of the new railway. It is named after that particular Prince of our Royal Family who stands as a symbol of the new financial and mechanical world, and who attained his majority and was

186

married to his beautiful Danish Princess just when that street was made in the 'sixties. Norwich, a little later than other parts of England, by creating this new street, showed that it, too, was to forsake the time-honoured methods of moving about, horse-drawn or water-borne. It built Prince of Wales Road to get to the new railway. It was so shy of this snorting monster men had called into being by their creative powers, that the actual line, on which the belching engine and clattering trucks ran, not to an inn, but to a " station ", was excluded, outside the enceinte of the old walled City, and to the east of the river. This was in 1843. For twenty years it came no nearer to the heart of Norwich. The people of the old City were a little alarmed by this new invention. When the first cuttings were dug and bridges made, the railway amounted to a twenty-mile stretch, from the old Vauxhall Pleasure Gardens, just outside the north-west corner of the walls of Yarmouth, to the spot in the parish of Thorpe next Norwich where the old Yarmouth road, issuing from the City by Bishop's Bridge, climbed the pleasantly wooded southern side of Mousehold. Here, on the flat " rond " that faced all that part of Norwich defended only by the river, was built the " station " of the " Yarmouth & Norwich Railway ", a one-storey weather-boarded affair, with a dovecote clock-tower, to look as much as possible like a big stable, for travel was still indissolubly connected in the public mind with horses. This small length of line joining the two main towns of East Norfolk was able to support " an engine with ballast trucks running from the Yarmouth end to assist the excavation " by the month of October 1843. Norwich flocked out to see, much as one would now go to a circus. The local paper said : " Its marvellous facility in whirling along any number of loaded waggons elicited exclamations of astonishment from many hundreds of Norwich people who went out to see it ". On 12 April 1844, Major General Pasley, Government Inspector, accompanied by the Lord Bishop of Norwich and several of the Directors, proceeded in a train of carriages from the Norwich terminus to Yarmouth. On the 30th, the extension of the Northern & Eastern Railway from Cambridge had reached Trowse. Guests were carried to Cambridge, where they met " a like contingent ", presumably from Shoreditch, and " luncheon was served ".

There had been for half a century at least a short cut from the Yarmouth road, leading to a wooden bridge across the Wensum, from which ran a narrow lane which my father used to call " the path through the hop gardens ". For, along the whole riverine defences of Norwich, from the Boom Towers where King Street ran along the river-bank and formed the southern termination of the City, northward to Bishop's Bridge, there never had been a road entering the City. All the land between the Cathedral Close and King Street on the river bank had been the property of the Greyfriars, and at the Dissolution had been cut up into market-gardens, orchards and hop-fields. It was the least-developed part of Norwich, and it took twenty years of what must have been acute inconvenience, before any body of persons in Norwich made up their minds that the new railway had come to stay and that a proper approach from it to the centre of the City would be to the public advantage and the profit of whoever took the risk of making it. Accordingly a company was formed, old derelict properties were bought piecemeal, and the work began.

It was, however, severely circumscribed. The new railway station stood opposite the least accessible part of Norwich. There could be no question of driving a new street through the Close to bring traffic from the railway to Tombland, still the natural centre of the highways. Nor could a thoroughfare be driven under the Castle mound to connect with the Provision Market. There was, however, just room, and only just, between the two. By using part of an old alley that descended from King Street towards the river, known as Rose Lane, and part of " the path through the hop gardens ", the new traffic artery from the wooden bridge could be directed, with a sweeping curve to mount the gentle gradient, so that it entered King Street, which then ran uninterrupted from Tombland to its Gates, opposite Blue Boar Lane. This picturesquely named alley gave north-westward upon the little " Redwell Plain " where the Gurney's Bank, housed in an old mansion, had begun to give a certain dignity and usefulness to Cockey Lane, straggling from the Market Place, so much so, that that obscure byway, which could barely take two lines of traffic, had changed its name to London Lane, and finally London Street, in a rather self-conscious endeavour to improve its position among the streets of Norwich. It had never been important. No Mayor or Alderman lived in it. Issuing from the Market Place as part of ancient Hosiergate, it led nowhere in particular, but petered out on Redwell Plain in Redwell Street and in Queen Street and Blue Boar Lane aforesaid. This may have been why Bartlett Gurney, with Quaker reserve and diffidence, had moved his Bank there.

How unconscious are the actions that produce such remarkable results! The Bank only began to be important in 1785, and rather more so after 1815, when it became concerned with the efforts of Government to clear up the state of the coinage. Even so, who was to foresee that the traffic from the unimaginable railway would ever need to pass that way? But as one looks at the map today it is plain that what had happened was that, by a set of completely fortuitous circumstances, the new street built through the hop-gardens would lead to Gurney's Bank, and so to London Street, and so to the Market Place. Without meaning it, Norwich had linked the great discovery of the nineteenth century—travel by rail— with the Guildhall that held its reformed Corporation, in the Market Place which was now the focus of the retail trade. That is how, as late as 1860, town-planning chanced to happen. Of course London Street was always inadequate for its new role. Not so Prince of Wales Road. It is the one street in Norwich that can take four lines of traffic, even modern buses, and does so. How little any of that was foreseen can be told from its architecture.

Here, then, for the first time for eight centuries, the circulation of people in the streets of Norwich was violently wrung from its previous general direction, into a new one. Hitherto, old King Street, lined with its town houses of the country gentry, had run uninterrupted from Tombland to its exit at King Street Gates. The new street suddenly tore a hole in its eastern side, and gave the current vehicles and pedestrians a new direction, at right angles to the old. Moreover, this happened opposite the ancient enclosure of the Castle bailey, to which various obscure lanes had led, but which was now thrown open by the destruction of a section of the western side of King Street, opposite its new tributary. (In doing so, the planners, if they can be so called, of that day destroyed the

Griffin Inn, in which John Crome was born.) How unnatural
was the whole proceeding can be seen by the steepness of the
gradient from Prince of Wales Road to modern Castle Meadow.
The original earthen bank of the bailey that enclosed the yard,
or outer court of the Castle, has been smoothed away, but not
much, and in 1952 buses have to mount a steep incline (the
hump of the bailey bank just where it joins the Castle Mound)
and then to descend again into the deep ditch which lay under
the non-bailey western side of the Mound, from which much of
its earth must have been dug, and which made this side of the
ancient fortress impregnable to the assaults of those days. This
dark and narrow, tree-shaded lane, ending in the yard of the
Bell Inn, bordered by the back yards and gardens of the houses
in London Street, now lost its old name, Castle Ditches, which
described it accurately, as what it was, and became Castle
Meadow, a kind of off-shoot of the newly-opened-up Cattle
Market, that had drifted piecemeal into the Castle bailey as it
outgrew Tombland. Until 1900 and the coming of the trams
its chief use was for " running " horses at the big horse sale that
occupied the present car park behind the Bell. But that is a
later story. Let us see what this new interloping street did to
the feelings and outlook of Norwich people.

It was a rather parvenu street, built to facilitate traffic and
commerce. The days of old textile Norwich sending away its
woollen goods by water or " the heavy wagon to Birmingham "
that ran from what is now the taxi station next Ethelbert Gate
on Tombland, were gone. Norwich was just picking up the
miscellaneous packing and domestic trades that depended on
the skilled fingers of the handloom weavers whose livelihood had
been wrenched from their hands. Colman's mustard, starch
and flour, Caley's chocolate, crackers and mineral water,
turn-shoe work, weaving of wire-netting were all trades that
depended on movement of goods, and not the stately movement
that had once taken Norwich cloth to the ends of the earth by
time-honoured means. Even today, Prince of Wales Road
looks and is new. Harvey, the banker, became impatient of his
stately old house, with its small " banking office " built on to
it, which can still be seen at No. 19 King Street, and built
himself a grand neo-classic one, not in King Street at all, but
on the alignment of the new street. After his collapse and

suicide in 1870 as a result of unwisely backing France in the Franco-Prussian War, it became the General Post Office, and many people are unaware that the sculptured crown over the pediment does not signify Government Service, but is the device of Harvey and Hudson's Crown Bank. A few years later a grand new Agricultural Hall was built next it in red brick and sandstone. On the northern side a long row of lofty, inconvenient villas replete with areas and attics that must have shortened the lives of a whole generation of maid-servants extends its frontage in the worst style of Islington architecture. In the main, however, the new street outran the impulse that had engendered it. For many years, between the new Bank and the villas and all about, lurked dismembered gardens, behind rusty-coloured palings. In 1952 nearly half the street remains, lined with the one-storey buildings that were all the less venturesome speculators it attracted could compass. Trees of forest size still obtrude, where it incorporates Rose Lane, and others can be glimpsed behind cinemas and offices, showing incongruously how the street had shorn, with mid-Victorian (or was it second Empire) cocksure vulgarity, through what had been a quiet corner of a big village that had never quite forgotten the monks whose great abbey once stood there. In my boyhood its pavements were thick with leaves every autumn, and the Castle and the Cathedral dominate its skyline still.

Yet Norwich was proud of Prince of Wales Road. There was a rather pathetic self-consciousness about the crowds that made it their new promenade. People who had been born in the 500 yards and courts of Norwich, who never had any certainty of health or employment, among whom an eighteenth-century fatalism lingered and who took refuge in rivers of cheap and good beer, came out, in the late evening, after work, and especially on Sundays, and sauntered, giggling and chattering, from the new iron bridge, named Foundry Bridge, after one of the neighbouring establishments, up to the new Bank and Agricultural Hall, then turned up Blue Boar Lane, where an enormous ash-tree stood in a private garden, and so by a slight deviation, past the older Bank, down London Street to the Market Place. They had never had such a promenade before. It lay along the fronts of big new public offices that had none of the sheltered dignity of the private houses of the gentry. The railway and the market at either end were fitting termini to a stroll undertaken in a new spirit. " Here we are," they seemed to say, " the other three-quarters of Norwich. You never saw us before, never thought that we might need fresh air and leisure, a wide street, and a little silly, innocent respite from our laborious lives. Few of us ever travelled by coach, but any of us might go by rail. It is not dignity and security we want, the Cathedral and the Castle, not holiness or authority, but a little more comfort, opportunity and relaxation." It was a portent, the new Prince of Wales Road, little as its originators dreamed it. One can sympathise with the motives that brought such a street into being. They need all our sympathy. For there was a callow, unstable quality about all that sudden new Victorian prosperity, rebuilding, space and leisure. The houses look it. The façade they make is not so much ugly as childish. Compared with Georgian St. Giles' Street or Colegate, with Elizabethan Elm Hill, and the fifteenth-century flint-faced dwellings, the houses on Prince of Wales Road have an air of being built in a hurry, by people who did not expect them to last. As late as 1923 numbers 47–51 on the south side did, in fact, collapse. A less spectacular change— a social collapse, if you like—overtook the lofty range of " villas " opposite. Built for family residences of the newly settled professional classes, they have become offices. Most of the doctors and lawyers who originally occupied them have gone, the latter to the comparative quiet of The Close, the former to the new districts in which their patients live. It is significant that, as late as the 'sixties, such people expected to live over their surgeries or consulting-rooms. The workshop of carriage-builders who once found Rose Lane a convenient place to carry on a business which is always likely to spread out from the workshop into the roadway, has become a great motor mart and included what was the Skating Rink. Nor is this singular. There are half a dozen of the big motor firms occupying the place in society that used to be filled by coach-builders, job-masters, cab proprietors. Cycles are here to be found. A photographer or two linger, to remind one of Tanzy, the great American photographer, whose one-storey, wooden-walled shack used to have here the Stars and Stripes flying, and to invite a new public, hitherto unused to being photographed, to have a dozen or so reproduced, by the appealing consideration " They've all got sticky backs ". Here flocked the members of the old professional, long-service army, to leave with as many of their female friends as they could remember a queer presentment of themselves (for the yellow-and-red of the uniform would not come out in the photographs of those days, although the high-light on the " quiff " or forelock, sedulously curled over the edge of the cap, did) before they departed to Egypt or Afghanistan.

It was not merely in plan that Prince of Wales Road stood at right angles to the older streets of the family. It stood at right angles socially, morally, spiritually. There was an appealing pretentiousness about it. The very licensed houses called themselves after the Prince of Wales, the Duke of Connaught, the Duke of Beaufort, in the flush of mid-Victorian ostentation. Beyond the new Foundry Bridge the short cut to the Yarmouth road blossomed out into substantial villa-residences behind green palings on flint walls tarred to keep the frost from their joints. That is characteristic. The glory of the flint is its black-diamond translucence. The new Thorpe Road had just arrived at the degree of sophistication at which one is conscious of, and admits that one must wear a waterproof to avoid, rheumatism. That is exactly what tarring a flint wall means. It spells the sacrifice of appearance to the needs of health, and that is just what the new street did. Alas! In a few years the new railway was so successful, ran so many trains, created such clouds of smoke that doctors began advising the residents to live at the other end of the town. There might have been an embarrassing collapse in the property market had not that social movement coincided with another, the need of a whole new set of administrative offices demanding accommodation that the Regency Shire Hall could never afford them. The County Councils began to take over the duties that had devolved on County Magistrates in the 'eighties. All that had been done, or left undone, in the " stewards' room " at every manor house, had now to be done by properly appointed officials. Education and Health, Police, and Transport now operate from the ghosts of the bijou boxes to which the successful, if weary, business or professional man hoped to retire. Telegraph Lane,

N

and the inn called The Redan, the long-disused Cremorne Gardens, Salisbury Road and Stanley Avenue, show what were the topics of the hour when the extension of Prince of Wales Road became the eastern outlet of Norwich.

Finally, Prince of Wales Road begot other changes. Half a century after the railway opened, the working population of Norwich lived so far from its work that some public means of transport was a necessity. The fashions of 1900 were for trams, with overhead trolleys carrying the current from wires that netted the main streets. Or as many as they could compass, for opposition was strong. The City might sell the concession to the company, but up rose the doctors, the residential gentry and some of the shop-keepers to protest that the new means of locomotion deprived them of their ancient right to have carriage or van standing before their door, whirled their customers past to other shopping centres, obscured their daylight and needed drastic street demolitions. It was to accommodate the new trams that Castle Meadow, alias Castle Ditches, was made into a thoroughfare, a wing of the Bell Hotel demolished to give the new cars a straight run into the Goose & Gridiron, which became their incongruous and always inadequate centre. Yet another consequence of Prince of Wales Road, the only street really fit for trams, was a new cut in the quiet old residences of Redwell Street, to bring the lines into St. Andrew's and the western traffic artery.

Even so, the demolitions were insufficient. The trams ran for some thirty-five uneasy years, but the plain fact was that Norwich streets are too narrow, its corners too abrupt. The tram-cars had to have a specially shortened wheel-base that would have outraged Manchester or Liverpool, to navigate at all, and the cost of renewals was ruinous. Finally omnibuses, more manœuvrable, took the place of the trams on their lines of rails, with their sparking trolleys overhead.

So it may be justly said that Prince of Wales Road, the new cocksure Victorian member of the family, was not so much an improvement as a portent.

XXI

GROVE PLACE. THE FAMILY BREAKS UP, OR BREAKS OUT

ALL families break up. This may sound a harsh and unnecessary saying. But is it any kinder, or more honest, to pretend that a human institution is more permanent than a human individual? Of course it is a little more permanent, not much. What would we have? A family that is permanent, that never changes, never gives way to others? Surely not! That is as bad as the most awful nightmare ever conceived by the human imagination: that of the individual who cannot die. The familiar title to this inconceivably hideous conception is that of the Wandering Jew, a piece of medieval anti-Semitism that is best forgotten. But the threat remains. Unless we school ourselves in all humility to face the fact that we, and our family circles, are transitory, we are left with that awful alternative. Just imagine a Norwich which never changed. Imagine yourself, gentle reader, unalterable. No, families must go the way of all flesh, because they are human.

Yet we are permitted to be wistful about it. A family can be such a happy thing, we can hardly let it pass without a sigh. The family of the streets of old Norwich was a happy thing. For centuries its members allowed the people of Norwich to go about their pleasure and business, and just because those streets answered in a rough-and-ready, inconvenient, familiar way the needs of those who used them, the day came when Norwich, grown larger and more prosperous than ever before, outgrew those familiar thoroughfares, and broke out into others. It was inevitable. Had it not happened, Norwich might easily have dwindled to a museum piece, like some little Cotswold or Suffolk wool town, or silted-up East Coast seaport, Chipping Camden or Dunwich, Cley, or Bradford-on-Avon, Lavenham or Dunmow. It didn't. What is the result?

We have seen that the gates were demolished, or rather the gateways that confined them, the Wall built over, and the people passed out to live beyond the walls. The first to go were wealthy merchants who had made their money and who were tired, or whose families were tired, of the confined air, the built-over garden and courtyard (I expect their females nagged them. The girls became tired of the inner rooms and the solar where they sat sewing.). The surrounding hamlets, conveniently included within the City boundaries by the Act of 1556, became sprinkled with fine houses and gardens. But they were few. Eaton and Lakenham, Thorpe, down the river; Earlham, that became, from a semi-fortified blockhouse, the ideal English home, under the Gurneys; Catton Hall, Mousehold Hall were all the seats of the new gentry, whose success in trade made them into additions to the flexible landed class, that very gently moved up to and married into the ancient titled aristocracy. That movement left hardly a trace, except that it made room for people like their clerks and managers to occupy splendid rooms they would never have built for themselves.

In the wake of this fine spraying out came the main movement. The land outside the walls between St. Stephen's Gates and St. Giles' Gates became covered with little, ill-built, dingy streets of " cottages " (for it was not possible for the builder of the eighteen-twenties to think of anything outside the walls except in terms of the country), often with no name, but just a number: Row 20 and so forth. This was called the New City, and anyone who knows France intimately will recognise the *Nouveau Monde* that will be found on the outer boulevards that have replaced the fortifications of the old garrison towns in that country. There can be no mistaking the place or its purpose. But Hitler knocked most of it flat (it was not of the substance of the old stone-and-brick-built Norwich that stood up well to bombing). The first thing that strikes anyone who goes to examine it, is its anonymity. It has no proper names. The older members of the family were known by what they did. Conisford led to the King's Ford, Fybriggate to Fye or " Slush Bridge ", Pottergate and Cowgate need no explanation. In contrast, the New City, built as a dormitory for people who had deliberately moved away from their work, had to find a name for itself. Vauxhall Street dimly recalled some little garden with arbour and bowling-green behind a public-house, Rupert Street commemorated

Rupert. Who can he have been? Not the Fearless, surely? Rupert Street never looked like a dashing cavalry soldier! Others were less lucky. They were called Norfolk or Suffolk or Midland Street. (Imagine the depth of inarticulateness that forced one to name one's place of abode after an abstraction like the Midlands!) Shadwell Street may be called after someone who remembered, perhaps had been born at Shadwell, next Thetford, or equally, in Shadwell by the docks of London. Henry of Henry Street must have been an Irish builder. But who was Johnson? Or Nicholas? They had streets named after them. No one remembers, and it doesn't matter. These names were mere labels; certainly Crook's Place was named after some small owner, long before his patronymic had gained an unenviable association. Then there came an era of pathetic snobbery, and the new little streets, rather better built as they neared the outskirts of Colonel Unthank's Park, that stretched across an undulating piece of land along one side of the Earlham Road, received such names as Ampthill Street and Walpole Street to signify some knowledge of worldly greatness, even if it were dim with distance. But these fade off again into a maze of little residential thoroughfares, lined with identical prim little front doors, and " best-room " windows, called after all the counties of England: Essex, Cambridge, York, Gloucester, Leicester. Where the old mill stood at the top of the rise was naturally Mill Hill Road, but around a yet better quarter came a change of feeling. This was, after all, the best end of Norwich. " Park Lane " was the obvious choice for those who had moved out of the obscurity of New City, just as their fathers had moved out of that of some alley behind a great merchant's house. " West Parade " the tale continues. There was a little confusion when " Mount Pleasant " was given to the pretty lane that then led through to Newmarket Road. Mount Pleasant recalls East London and railways and the G.P.O., but must originally have meant that the new suburb round the Mount was pleasant. (The original Mount in London was one of Oliver Cromwell's forts built to guard the capital; Mount Street, Mayfair, is another. But Norwich of 1840 wouldn't know that.)

After New City and its development, it was the turn of that quarter of Norwich which lay a little to the east of New City, between the junction of Ipswich and Newmarket roads on the one hand and the highway which issued from Ber Street Gates on the other. Here Trafalgar Street and Cherry Street show some hasty builder's attempts to dignify a row of squalid cottages with the one name all English people remember. But he couldn't think of a second, and had to fall back on some dim memory of a cherry-tree that had once beautified the lane to Harford Hall. The district was known as Peafields, and perhaps once produced that vegetable. Nowadays, bombing and clearance have made an end of a suburban slum of which Norwich could never be proud, and new houses of various categories are replacing, but fortunately not reproducing, what stood there. But any concerted and deliberate idea of adding new streets that would house adequately the dense, ill-paid, often unemployed section of the population that still sheltered where it could in the five hundred courts and yards within the City walls was still far beyond the imagination of the Norwich of the first half of the nineteenth century. It was a matter of common belief, almost a principle of morality, that one lived where one could afford to live; that in general, setting aside exceptions, one got the sort of house in the sort of street one deserved. It was equally true to say that one deserved what one got. If one's labour was worth but a pound a week or less, one or two rooms up a yard seemed natural enough, and there was no great outcry among those who lived so, or even among those who did not live so, and did not like the idea that anyone did. To see what the early Victorian considered to be the natural, and even admirable kind of street that was worthy to be added to the family, one has only to look at Unthank Road.

The actual road, I believe, is the drive across what was Colonel Unthank's park, the stable buildings alone of which remain opposite Clarendon Road. The whole place, park and mansion have been " developed "; the outlying fields where my father used to play cricket, the old mill are gone. In 1824 the Fathers of the City of Norwich did a dreadful thing. They had reason enough to think that the old Guildhall and the Bridewell (so called after the one in London, and now the Craft Museum) were inadequate for the prison needs of a civilised town in the nineteenth century. So what did the members do? They built a gaol outside St. Giles' Gates, just against the Colonel's park. I wonder if it were that which led him to develop his estate and move out into the country? I just remember that gaol, which lasted until 1900, when, its use having been long superseded by the fine new building on Mousehold Heath behind the Barracks, which dates from 1880, the Duke of Norfolk bought the site at St. Giles' Gates and built thereon the new neo-thirteenth-century Roman church of St. John. It cost a million, it is said. The gaol had cost £30,000. So now we have Unthank Road, the second residential road in Norwich in pride of place. That is how cities develop. Just anyhow. Look at the handsome row of villas (1860 in date, and in the Torquay style of architecture) with which it begins as it leaves the City Wall. They must have stared at prison walls for a generation or two. But Unthank Road never succumbed, largely because of the fine forest trees surviving from the Colonel's park. Beyond the abrupt escarpment on which his house stood, and which must have had a good view south westwards, was the " rose valley ", a dim recollection of the gardens that became a market-gardener's place of business. The long road grew and grew, all my father's lifetime and mine, until it reached out and met the Newmarket Road at Eaton Village.

They have gone, one and another, the great estates that lay just beyond the walls of Norwich. Some have been preserved intact, like Earlham. Others have been built over. It was all part of the same nineteenth-century process, the great break-out of the citizens confined within the walls of the City. First went the very successful and wealthy Pastons and Custances, Gurneys and Harveys. After them came the modest professional class. Only after the First Great War did the artisan and the operative have whole new suburbs planned and built for him and his wife and family, and the teeming yards with their common tap and privy have now been emptied. That is a later story.

Let us pause here to accord a sentimental smile to the modest professional class. There was something so demure and decorous about their emigration. Not for them new Housing Estates of a later dispensation. Only after a long life of self-denial and saving did they venture to leave the comparative obscurity, almost rural with its garden and trees about it, of Castle Ditches, or Gildengate, Chapel Field or the Close. Elderly and settled, it seemed that they would never move, but they did. Something the doctor said, some vigorous protest from their grown-up children, caused them to take a halting walk, or even to hire a chaise, some fine summer evening and go out to Lakenham, above the Yare, or Catton, beyond the busy northern ward in which, likely enough, they had spent most of their days in some counting-house or study, or out on to the Earlham Road. Gentle and reserved, they considered the step thrust upon them by relatives or skilled advice. They were to be uprooted, displaced. I remember the sudden drop in the voice, the silence, the dumbfounded consternation of my own father when he was told he must retire. It was outrageous, unheard-of. No one of his name or kind had ever retired. It was a new state of being; he did not care to contemplate it. All his forebears had died at the desk at which they had spent their working lives. Perhaps they did not expire there actually, but the day came when they collapsed, fell down, dropped the accustomed quill, had to be carried out by bewildered juniors who could not conceive of the office without them. My father was the last to live over the place in which he worked. Never shall I forget the day when he came up those familiar stairs from the office, and sat down, as if he could no longer stand : " My dear," he said to his wife, " they say I've got to go ! " She, capable and devoted, undertook the heavy task of finding a little house in the suburbs and moving him, and as much of the accumulation of three generations in those high rooms over Bank Street as would go into the new home, in which he was to die.

As with him, so with all the others, Managers, Head Clerks, often only " old Mr. So-and-so ", who had run the businesses of their masters for so long. One can trace the process. In all the " better " suburbs, beyond the City gates, there sprang up between 1820 and 1860 little single houses, or terraces, so often called " Grove Lodge ", " The Grove ", or " Grove Villas ". In solid red brick, or stucco-covered, these hid decorously behind evergreens that screened them from the road. In the centre of the front elevation would be the door, often with a charmingly designed fan-light above. Right and left of it big, square, sash windows lighted the dining-room and drawing-room. Often little pilasters ran up to the parapet, above the first floor, with Corinthian capitals. Sometimes a modest pediment would frame the façade. There would be three windows on the first floor, of course, and one knew that the middle one lighted the stairs. Against the walls, between the windows and door, would be trained a magnolia or camelia, virginia creeper or variegated ivy. A small side gate concealed by a trellis over which roses were trained led to the tradesmen's entrance, at the back out of sight. For people of this sort, at least the first wave of them, still had maids, sometimes a man, at the very least a regular gardener once a week or oftener. He would see that the little semi-circular drive leading from one white-painted gate in the wall next the road, round the lawn and before the front door, to the other, was kept hard and smooth and weedless as marble; he would trim the lilac and laburnum that filled the corners flanking the gates. He never grew vegetables—that would not have been quite seemly. For this class of retired person who had moved out of the City represented, in those days, the lowest layer of the upper division of society, which consisted of those who worked with their heads, the other, lower division contained those who could work only with their hands. Within doors, the dining-room and drawing-room opened left and right from the hall, which contained the stairs and some monstrous article of furniture, often surmounted by a stag's head, on the antlers of which, or on pegs, the garments of the family and their visitors hung. Beyond this was the green baize door, as inevitable as the class distinction it symbolised. Beyond it were the back stairs, the kitchen and offices. It shut off their sounds and smells, hardly permitted a glimpse of their sights. If there were, occasionally, a nursery in such a house, it was approached by the back stairs, up and down which clean water and fuel, and down which slops and cinders were carried. Under the front stairs was a door that led down precipitous steps to the cellar. It might well contain wine properly binned down in racks, but the portion of it next the street would hold the coal that was shot in, by a removable grating beneath the dining-room window.

The extent of the back garden varied. It was sometimes

large enough to be " grounds ", and often small enough to be
with difficulty screened from the domesticities of the back yard
behind the kitchen. The conditions of work in that region,
though better than in older houses in the City, were bad enough
to account in some degree for the present dearth of domestic
servants. It is not merely the relatively low and uncertain
pay and lack of organisation that make young men and girls
avoid the occupation nowadays. One kitchen I knew, well
enough furnished, had windows so contrived that only the
sky, and not much of that, was visible. But the London
suburban type of villa, with a whole basement devoted to
domestics, who lived, worked and slept in it, half buried, is
rare or later in Norwich. From 1860 to 1914 this state of thing
lasted. After that there was a shortage of domestic service,
of money—one might almost say, of retired people. Above
all, there was a shortage of the sentiment that made " The
Grove " possible. Too many people were moving out, and of a
slightly different kind. They had not come outside the walls
to linger a little on their savings before some fell disease, then
thought of as a dispensation of Providence, swept them away
(cancer and less obvious sorts of tuberculosis, many functional
and dietetic diseases were unrecognised and unclassified, and
described, as late as the seventies as " a decline ").

These new people had come there to live and to journey to
and from their offices four times a day, twice in, twice out.
There were too many of them to have a " Grove " built for
each, nor would they have appreciated its miniature stateliness.
They liked ornamental brickwork, encaustic tiles, doors with
panels of coloured glass, zinc-roofed verandas supported on
cast-iron pillars with more or less Corinthian capitals. They
had bow windows and basements in order to get more for their
money; their tradesmen's entrance was not concealed, and they
had less use for laurels or rhododendrons. Their one maid was
not shut off by a green baize door—they wanted her within
call; they had no decorative bell-pulls in their drawing-room,
which they did not always remember to call by that name. It
became the " front " room. The only one, for while " The
Grove " was either a single house or at most one of a small
block of two or three, the newer streets ran to scores, each with
one window beside the front door, and eventually with a

common passage way between every two, leading to " the back ". While the occupants of " The Grove " affected not to know whence the joints and sweets placed before them upon the dining-table came, and expressed surprise that the trades-men had sent a new suit, dress or piece of furniture, these later arrivals, who lived in " Florence Villas ", knew well enough. The " lady of the house " might still like to be called so while her husband was at the office, but in fact she spent her morning in the kitchen and her afternoon shopping, not genteelly knitting in the drawing-room or being driven in a hired cab on a round of visits. With them there began to disappear the gilt-framed oil-paintings, the piano with accordion-pleated silk front, the cabinet with glazed doors, in which lurked fine old china of a previous century and well-bound volumes glittering with gilt. No, the new generation had process reproductions of celebrated works of art, or photographs, perhaps a cottage-upright piano or a shelf of books. And the difference was more noticeable upstairs, where a bath had to be fitted, beginning with a zinc coffin filled by a dangerous and smelly " geyser " and ending with white enamel that stained under the taps and a boiler behind the kitchen stove.

On the heels of this second emigration came the final break-out, and all the major roads into the City became flanked by little streets of incredible monotony, in which a hundred numbers on the little gates that opened into pocket-handker-chief-size gardens indicated one door, one window, two windows above, and a passage, no longer a hall, leading to a kitchen where the family lived and ate, leaving the front room to antimacassars, horse-hair, china dogs and views of the promenade and the watering-place at which the honeymoon had been spent.

Such was the state of the new streets when the planners were given, belatedly, a chance. I cannot help a little sentimental feeling about " Grove Place ". It was what is now, I believe, called " twee," whatever that means.

XXII

LOSINGA CRESCENT, "HOUSING" AND
THE PLAN

So at length we come to the infants of the family. A family without infants is plainly doomed to give way to others. That may provide a certain feeling of satisfaction in having infants. Yet an infant is always a phenomenon, if not always an infant phenomenon. Perhaps more so to men than to women. Perhaps the infant is more the woman's job, and she is specially qualified to deal with it. The most devoted of husbands and fathers cannot help being a little nonplussed, if abundantly gratified, by the " new arrival ". It is not hard to see why. We like to think we have evolved in these islands, and are evolving all the world over, a state of civilisation better for man and not unacceptable in the sight of God. And then along comes this new little atom of humanity-to-be, and reduces everything to those bare essentials without which human life cannot exist and develop. Food and sleep mainly. These demand warmth (or at least control of temperature) and shelter. Noises must be hushed and the routine of years altered to make things easy for the new little creature. And so on to the first walk, holidays, sport, education, a career, religious observance. Differences in religious observance have been the cause of many of the tragedies humanity has suffered.

What has this to do with Losinga Crescent? With " Housing " and the Plan, by which the infant streets of Norwich, like Losinga Crescent, are coming into being as these words are being written? The answer is: Everything. All the new streets of Norwich, now growing up under sedulous controls and with all the difficulties of a maternity home full of infants, owe their origin to religious teaching which called attention to the immense contrast between the conditions of those who could move out into the fresh air, space and amenity outside the wall, and those condemned, generally by sheer inability to get anywhere else, to live all their lives in some ill-built, ill-ventilated, damp and ugly cottage at the back of one of the old yards, too glaring to be borne. Hence Losinga Crescent, "Housing" and the Plan.

I have not traced the origin of the term "Housing" back through the dictionaries to see when it was first used, in the sense we now use it. My own father would hardly have understood it, as it is printed today, my grandfather would have misunderstood it, and wondered what it had to do with the streets of Norwich he knew so well. Someone might have reminded him of the rebuilding of St. Paul's Square, which took place, by special Act of Parliament, in the 1860s within the old walls of Norwich. He would have nodded.

"St. Paul's was a disgrace. Of course the City rebuilt it!" But even then, the notion that that sort of Housing activity could ever become the major means of finding shelter for the growing population, by adding to the family of the streets of Norwich, would have seemed to him quite mad, a reversal of the processes of the universe. St. Paul's was dilapidated, verminous, disgraceful. A new St. Paul's Square had replaced it. Well, fortunately he views the matter from so exalted a state of being today that we suppose he understands. For it has happened, the thing he thought impossible, and Losinga Crescent is the result. The Corporation Handbook for 1951-2 says:

Houses and flats erected and occupied:

Under 1919 (Assisted) Scheme	332
Under 1923 Housing Act	48
Improvement Schemes (1923)	96
Under 1924 Housing Act	3,742
Non-subsidy Parlour Houses 40, non-Parlour Houses 50	90
Under 1925 Act (T.B.)	50
Under 1930/36 Housing Acts	3,388
Under 1935 Act (Overcrowding)	170
Under 1946 Act	2,452
Prefabs.	499
	10,867

There we have it, the additions to the Norwich family that we owe to the new twentieth-century Welfare State. It is now clear that in this new Norwich we are not housed according to what we can pay, or according to what we deserve in respect of what service we can offer that community. We are housed according to an agreed minimum standard, below which the daily life of the citizen is not to be allowed to sink, whoever he is and whatever he does. Taking the average household as four to five persons, something between a third and a half of the population now live according to this standard. All these houses have been built and occupied since the First World War. The five hundred yards and courts within the walls, and the squalid little " rows " in Peafields and New City have been emptied, and largely demolished, some, it is true, by the air attacks of 1942, but in a large measure as the result of a deliberate policy. A certain number of these houses and the new streets they form lie within the walls and replace the courts and yards of other days. But the vast majority of them stand in half a dozen Housing Estates, dormitory districts, inhabited from breakfast to tea-time by housewives and children, the very old and invalids. They form not only new streets, but a new sort of street. There is seldom any industry in it, unless you wish to class housekeeping, child-minding, schooling and recreation as industry. This combination is of course the oldest and largest industry, but it is not what we usually mean by the word. So has come into being a new Norwich street, and a large fraction of the 120,000 people now living within the City boundaries (a decrease of 5,000 since 1932, largely due to people moving out into the country) live here. Schools, shops, a public-house or two, places of worship and amusement have followed, until the 8,165 acres to which Mary Tudor and Philip of Spain enlarged Norwich in 1556 is nearly all built over, save the 564 acres, or one-sixteenth of the total, which form Public Parks, wisely set aside. These range from the 190 acres of Mousehold Heath and the 118 acres of the Municipal Golf Links next Earlham Hall, to the half-acre of Stuart Gardens in St. Faith's Lane. It is nothing less than a social revolution. I can remember the very beginning of it. I hear my mother's voice :

" How is Mrs. Blank's little boy, Doctor—the one I asked you to go and see? "

" As well as anyone can be in the situation in which they live in Whosits Yard. Damp, airless, insanitary. The husband has no work, and when he has he doesn't bring the money home ! "

Or again: "Willie, why isn't your brother Johnnie at Sunday School?"

"He hasn't got no boots, ma'am." (Sometimes this was not true. There were parents before 1914 who knew the value of bootless children.)

Or, once more: "Why is Walter Botts crying, Miss Smiffham?"

"He didn't make enough attendances to go to the treat at Yarmouth on Thursday next."

"Well, I should let him go. It's the only day out he'll get this year, and there are ten of them in that awful room they inhabit in Pigg's Court, mostly feeble-minded." (Again, there were times when she was imposed on. Children went to one Sunday School in the morning and another in the afternoon. Even so, they enjoyed only two days at the sea per year.)

Finally, to her husband, who had mildly remonstrated: "I don't care, James, it's unChristian to let anyone live as the Ponks live in Water Lane. Someone ought to do something about it. What's the good of my taking the girls into my class and teaching them how to make up their clothes and cook and sing part-songs, when they go back to conditions like that?"

We may say: "She need not have bothered." But she did, and the result of her bothering and that of a whole section of the population like her, is what we see today, in all the new streets of the new sort in Norwich. As can be seen by the table of Housing I have quoted, it was not all done at once. It began just within the ancient Mile Cross, where Sweet Briar Lane joined the River Wensum above Woodlands Park (Woodlands was where old Mr. Fitch the antiquary and chemist from the Market place lived out his retirement. Father used to take me there on a Sunday afternoon. My little legs ached, for it was two miles from the Bank House, but I was solaced by a glass of ginger beer, poured out for me in a little champagne glass with a hollow stem, while my elders sipped their port.). It was here, alongside the Aylsham Road, opposite the brickfields, that the first squares and crescents were laid out and built up with nicely designed, easy-to-run houses, in small blocks and rows. I have chosen the one called Losinga Crescent because it shows the good-natured irony of history. Herbert de Losinga was a Norman who formed part of the conquering party that settled

the southern portion of these islands between A.D. 1066 and
1100. It is disputed if he derived his name from a lozenge in
his armorial device. He was a priest by profession and a
politician by inclination and career. He built the central
arches of the Cathedral church of Norwich, having obtained
authority to incorporate a good bit of what had been the market-
place of the Saxons, obliterating some half-dozen parishes and
appropriating whatever they were worth. He lived in the
fortified manor house of the Thorpe hundred which became the
present Palace of the Lord Bishop of Norwich. I do not think
he was a bad man; if he had not been a ruthless one the Saxons
would soon have disposed of him. But it is a little comic that
his name, that of a potentate who installed an army of occupation (for that is what it was) composed of Benedictine monks,
foreigners and enemies of the barely subjugated population,
should now be the label of an innocent residential street of
Welfare Norwich. I wonder if the clerks and operatives, City
Councillors and electors who live in it, in conditions so much
more pleasant than those in which they were born, and which
they have planned for themselves, ever meet, as they come home
from their day's work, a commanding figure in robes, with a
tonsured head, holding a great crozier. I wonder if he tells
them severely in Norman French that they are neglecting their
God and being unbearably bumptious to their King. Fortunately they will not be able to understand the language he uses,
for if they did they would be even more perplexed by the idea
he was trying to convey to them. Losinga, and all his con-
temporaries, lived in an atmosphere when survival to adult
age was in itself an achievement so remarkable that one thanked
God for having permitted it to happen, so far was it beyond
human power to ensure, so rare was it. To a man of Losinga's
outlook, the purpose of the Christian religion was the anni-
hilation of non-Christians, under the leadership of the Normans.
(Losinga was a Norman.) Anyone who got in the way of the
Normans had to be dealt with. That is what the Normans
did to Norwich, a Saxon town with a strong Danish flavour.
The Norman theory of human existence was well exemplified
in the Crusades, which were ill-managed expeditions to the
eastern Mediterranean with the purpose of hitting with long
swords, people of skins of a different colour, and a religion of

similar but conflicting objects. Fortunately the Normans
quarrelled with the other Crusaders, and the project petered
out. But what would have astonished Losinga more would
have been to know, as we do, that in about a hundred years his
language had ceased to be spoken in Norwich and that in
four hundred other years the Cathedral he built would be
presided over by a Protestant Dean. So I consider the use of
his name to indicate a street of Welfare Norwich a wonderful
piece of irony. I wonder how many people who live in that
street realise it. I do not blame the committee of the Corporation which has had the difficult task of finding names for the
new streets of Norwich, because they used Losinga's. I think
it was an excellent idea to commemorate a man of whom we
can hardly approve, but who did leave us one of the principal
objects that make up the pleasant and inspiring townscape of
Norwich, the Cathedral. We should have been worse off
without Losinga. The only remark I would make about the
use of his name for this purpose is that I hope every inhabitant
of Losinga Crescent will realise how odd he and she will look
in a few generations, to those who rebuild its houses and live
in them. They will look, in fact, as queer to succeeding
generations as old Losinga does to us.

In choosing the name of this otherwise nearly forgotten pre-
late, the Committee of the Corporation was hounded on by
necessity. I have pointed out that the old streets of the walled
City had their names by reason of their uses. What people did
in them, and whither they led, gave them the name by which
they were called. But these new streets, on the outer rim of the
enlarged City, led nowhere and were not inhabited by any
special body of people. The qualification for living in Losinga
Crescent was to want a house. The street in which the house
stood wanted a name. Within the walls were some hundred
and fifty streets, not counting non-thoroughfare yards. But
by 1952 there were 164 miles of streets, and something had to
be done. In the years that followed, as the rehousing of
Norwich progressed, every citizen in the least notable, and
some not in the least, had their names utilised to denote the
places in which the people of Norwich had gone to live.

Mile Cross Housing estate of 769 houses was, I think, the first,
and had the great advantage that it lay along what had always

been a main thoroughfare, and one on which were already established places of worship and of amusement, shops and some industry. The next to be developed was between Earlham Road and Unthank Road, which were joined by a continuation of Mile End Road, called Colman Road, with some point, for J. J. Colman was one of the makers of modern Norwich. Here some six hundred houses were built, largely in fields taken from agriculture. This meant that a " community centre" (I do not know if that name had been evolved by the mid-1920s when Colman Road was built, but the thing indicated by the name) had to be planned for, and intending shop-keepers had to be induced to rent shops in a district which had none. It was perhaps an advance in planning that a site for a Branch Library was given a very central position, almost opposite the new Anglican church, and the estate seems to centre round those buildings. This is perhaps an advantage, giving a civic sense to the new and rather inchoate dormitory district, better than that which obtains in Mile Cross, which is plainly an " improvement" tacked on to an old thoroughfare, the Aylsham Road, the natural outlet of St. Augustine's, a main street of the City. The Mile Cross Branch Library is therefore rather less of a feature of the estate, and the newly erected and dedicated Anglican church of St. Catherine again simply falls into line with other places of worship longer established on the Aylsham Road. Many readers may differ from me, as they have a perfect right to do in a free country, in thinking, as I do, that a Branch Library somehow sets the seal on a Housing Estate. A place of worship probably preceded the planning, and in any case a church or chapel comes into being at the instance of aspirations which are older than the Welfare movement of the last half-century, that has produced rehousing. Or it may be that, to a member of the Libraries Committee, it seems to be important that the inhabitants of a new Housing Estate should at least be able to read. So I give it merely as my point of view.

Colman Road Branch Public Library was the first to be opened. This ceremony was performed by the Lord Mayor in 1929. Mile Cross followed in 1931. Finally Thorpe, the next estate to be developed, got its Branch Library in 1939. The Housing Estate at "Thorpe", as the Branch is called, lies along the south side of the road from Norwich to Yarmouth, by the old coaching route round the north end of the Broads. This means that the houses of which it consists lie along the southern slopes of Mousehold. There are altogether a thousand of them. So Norwich expanded, west and north, west and east, and then south, where a thousand houses have been built in Lakenham on the fields that used to descend from Ber Street Gates and the older suburbs, down to the River Yare, where the road to south Norfolk crosses it by the old prize-fighting inn, Lakenham Cock. Here fifty years ago I have seen the police, in couples, waiting to prevent Jem Mace's adherents from entering the City for the purpose of holding a sporting contest forbidden by the magistrates.

One would hardly believe it today, to see the streets of neatly planned, pleasantly situated little houses. Lakenham has not yet got its Branch Library, though the site is designated. Later developments are not so easy to see and to define. A thousand houses have been built in Catton Grove, east of Mile Cross, bringing the City to the very palings of the Catton Park that Humphrey Repton planned. These use the old north Norfolk highway, leading into the City by Magdalen Gates. North Earlham, Larkman Lane, and finally West Earlham, bring the westward extension to the Gate of Earlham Park. Then Tuckswood Estate has sprung up between the Ipswich Road and the river, and within sight of Lakenham's new houses. Finally the list closes with 499 " prefabs."

So out of 36,741, the total number of houses in Norwich today, 10,867, or nearly one-third, have been built in thirty years, and the streets in which they stand—crescents and closes, avenues and ovals—are now part of the Norwich family as much as the main thoroughfares of the old town that have been there thirty times as long. I have pointed out the peculiarity of these younger members of the family—namely, that they are part-time streets. Most of their male and many of their female inhabitants spend only half their lives in them. For five and a half days a week and who knows how many evenings, they are half-empty, and their inhabitants are occupied with work or play elsewhere, and generally in public buildings. The young streets of Norwich are like the young people of Norwich: they do not belong, as their elders used to belong, to one spot of earth, one outlook or the lack of it. They no longer speak the local dialect, but one largely influenced by the precise " Oxford " of the B.B.C. or the jargon of the Middle West heard at the Picture-Houses.

I hasten to add that this is natural, and to a certain extent right. It is right so far as the people who live in those streets do not come to think that they have achieved the best possible way of life. Our age, the twentieth century, with its many virtues, its inculcation of a civic sense, its immense advance in the attempt to make physical life better worth while, has somehow engendered a curious reaction. The old Liberalism (I mean of course that of the mind, not that of the political platform) has been largely ousted by a curious return to the totalitarianism of the Middle Ages. The Dictators talk just as the Medici and the other tyrants talked: " Do what I say, believe what I tell you, or I will oppress, torture and possibly murder you." We have not seen the worst of it in these islands, but odd symptoms of the disease are visible. It is a kind of recurrent fever, generated by moving too fast. The Renaissance gave rise to it. Welfare, apparently, engenders it. It remains to be seen if what is said and done in these new streets can deal with it.

XXIII

THE GREEN MAN, THE WILD MAN, AND THE
RURALISING OF THE CITY

AMONG the inn-signs which give us slight if profound glimpses of the thoughts and feelings of the people of Norwich down the centuries, who have lived in these streets, is that of the Green Man. One such sign used to hang in King Street. A variant of it, the Wild Man, stands where ancient Pottergate, here called Bedford Street, is engulfed in modern London Street. This was the famous place at which the beer-filled toughs of the Norwich of my childhood used to settle their differences, in the days when drink was sold as long as anyone had any money to buy, or could stand up to drink it. Many a time have I been roused from my infant slumbers to be told: " Go to sleep. It's only the fight on Wild Man Hill! " There are other Green Men or Wild Men outside in the county.

Generally the Green Man is portrayed as a mountebank and tinker, leading a donkey, on whose back were carried the wares he had to sell, but he was equally willing to lead a dance or frolic. The essential characteristic was his Wildness. He never was and never can be part of a settled urbanised civilisation. It is not possible to imagine him incorporated in a National Health Service, hardly even in our system of Education. At this statement incredulity generally breaks in: " What . . . people living wild . . . not insured or letting their children attend school . . . nonsense." Nonsense it is of course, a mere sign-painter's fancy. But it is no more mere fancy than the Red Lion, or the Blue Boar, the Man with a Load of Mischief, or the Swan with Two Necks. Something lurks behind those simple-minded grotesques. The sign-painter did not invent them because he thought they were pretty. He did not invent the Green Man. He portrayed an idea, too indefinite to be called a memory, too factual to be called a superstition. A colourful misconception is perhaps the nearest we can get to definition. Someone had seen a Lion and had been struck agape by the thrilling strangeness of the sight.

Someone was chased, or had heard of someone being chased, by a boar, when boars still were wild in Sherwood or Arden, the Weald or Wales. Since lions and boars are dun-coloured beasts, the sign-painter who was bidden to use the memory of them for a sign gave them a good striking colour. Red for the lion, Blue for the boar. The Swan had two nicks in its bill, its owner's mark. Swans are still so nicked at St. Helen's or the Great Hospital in Norwich. But those tiny, almost secret marks were too insignificant for the sign-painter's effect, and knowing his job as well as any newspaper or billposter, he gave the Swan two necks. No one was likely to forget that. So, when told to paint the sign of the Green Man or the Wild Man, the sign-painter scratched his head. He had never seen one, of course. He had heard of such a creature, equally of course, for all Norwich people have. The notion of some other kind of human or semi-human being, not exalted above our kind, like the angels, but fractionally below our level, a little more real than a fairy, not an evil spirit, or a mere revenant or re-visitor, a disembodied soul returning to the haunts of its sometime body, is many centuries old. What the sign-painter produced, when he had done scratching his head was something of the gipsy, something of the show-people of Tombland Fair, something of the pedlar, a good deal of the poacher, even the smuggler, perhaps. He painted this figment of his imagination Green, because that was how the tradition had been handed down. Before the Romans, before the Belgae or whoever they were that nineteenth-century history-books took to calling " the ancient Britons ", there had always been occasionally visible in the woods figures of human form, dodging between the trees, living, it was supposed, on fruit and refusing to be incorporated in any tribe, named and numbered and administered.

All sorts of reasonable explanations have been given. These were the last nomads. They were gipsies. They were outlaws. They had good reason to keep outside of the constraining ring of civic settlement. Perhaps the most imaginative explanation of all is that the human spirit, conscious of its limitations, not to say its shortcomings, is always hungry for some other state of existence. In its more chastened moods, not feeling bold enough to challenge comparison with angels, it finds some satisfaction in believing in these other, lesser, but still non-

fabulous populations, lurking somewhere beyond the limits
of verification but within those of credulity. Let us hesitate
to brush it all aside. Some years ago, when I had to look after
a farm, I was met, as always, with a request for new gates. The
local custom is for the landlord to indicate the timber and provide the irons, the tenant to do the work. I told the farmer:
" You can have those two oaks in Tuddenham Gorse."

" Oh no, Sir. I couldn't do that."

" Why not? " [It took the best part of an hour to drag out
the answer.]

" Not Tuddenham Gorse. There's rum folk about there. I
daren't touch them trees."

Did he believe it? Had he some deep conspiracy to sell the
trees when I was not looking? Was the Gorse a gipsy lair, and
if he disturbed them, would they put their horses in his meadow
(or put the evil eye on his cattle, or rob his hen roosts or whatever was the particular enormity he credited to the gipsies)?
Or was it some part of the Scandinavian superstition that
peoples the lanes of the East Anglian countryside with " Old
Shuck ", the Headless Hound? Or merely the secretiveness of
those who are the children of a score of generations of smugglers
and poachers and look on the darkness, the close cover, the
secrecy, as a perquisite? I don't know. I doubt if anyone
does. But, entirely without superstition as I am, I can't help a
little twinge of awe when I tread the Drove Road, or even the
comparatively modern Peddars Way. Who made, who used,
who perhaps still haunts those grassy tracks? Why do they
not disappear, with lack of use? Is there some quality, impressed so deep in the non-human structure of the earth on
which we balance ourselves, that it has a memory of its own and
will not forget our first meanderings across it, just as we can
never forget certain scenes of childhood, unimportant, long ago,
because they are that?

Lately, I have been told, when some great works were instituted in the Waveney Valley, the constructional authority,
among whom were Americans, noticed that the fruit-drinks they
brought to work were consumed without explanation. None
found out what happened. Those who set up to know say
that creatures of more or less human shape, visible only when
the sight is directed elsewhere, could be seen, out of the corner

of the eye, moving soundless and intent along the edge of the clearing where the work was going on.   At a word, movement, attempt to visualise them, they vanished.   So did the fruit-juice.

What has all this to do with the streets of Norwich?   Why, as I come to the end of my survey of that family of almost human beings those streets are, I cannot omit those in which Nature, excluded, one would have thought, from the hard pavement of a City closely built up these many centuries, re-enters—nay, is called back by—the will of man.

Perhaps this curious reversal is more noticeable in Norwich than in many towns.   I have said Norwich has 564 acres of public parks.   By far the oldest and largest is Mousehold Heath, of national celebrity, the Heath Crome painted and Borrow sang, for his prose grows lyric about it.   Note that Mousehold Heath, where you may still find rare plants and butterflies and where the kestrel will hover over your head as you thread the half-wild track along Dussens Dale, is not some remote resort.   It is within the City boundaries and touches the walls, or rather the river that takes their place on the north-east of the original enceinte.   True, the fine infantry barracks and the modern prison have taken one corner, new urban development is over-lapping one side, industry is near.   But in Dussens Dale it is possible to lose sight of the lot, and to find oneself tripping over the heather, entangled by briars, fenced in by gorse, and overshadowed by that very scrub of young oaks and alders, birches and mountain ash which covered this island of ours as its gradually warming climate, after the Ice Age, began to make life possible for the human creatures from whom we are descended.   There is one good metalled road now, right across Mousehold.   I have said, urban encroachments hem it in. Its completely wild state, in which Crome painted it, with City children herding miserable little sheep (before the careful breeding of Coke of Holkham and other experts had produced our present heavy, wool-covered animal), has been broken into. No longer will you find gipsy camps, inhabited by people as picturesque as Isopel Berners and the Flaming Tinman. Well-meant plantations of conifers have altered its appearance, and wartime needs for sharp gravel have pitted it with workings. Yet not many weeks ago I found three spots in different corners of it in which not a chimney-stack nor church tower of the near-by City was visible, and one might have been miles away in empty Breckland or the remote fastness of the Broads, instead of less than two miles from Norwich Market Place. Mousehold Heath, by law and public sentiment, is protected from encroachment, and there are nearly 200 acres of it. What is perhaps more remarkable is that the modern City has tried to re-duplicate it, on a much smaller scale, and necessarily, therefore, with a different texture. At the other end of the City, the Corporation had the good sense, in the nineteen-twenties, to purchase and preserve the historic home of the Gurneys, Earlham Hall, with its park of thirty acres. Here is a contrast indeed to Mousehold, for the park is a gentleman's demesne, full of well-grown and properly-tended beeches, chestnuts and oaks. The lawns and walled gardens, shrubberies and rockeries have been kept intact. The walks where young Joseph Fry courted Elizabeth, most beautiful of a family of beautiful girls, can still be traced, and the house in which little Percy Lubbock, who wrote its history, was the darling grand-child, is still there to be seen. The main rooms are devoted to many excellent public purposes, but the kitchen yard is worth a visit. Nothing like it, one may say with confidence, will be built again. Arranged round a square, and screened from the gardens, are bake-house, brew-house, laundry and well (worked by a horse walking round). In a corner, a splendid peacock displays his glittering colours. Tall trees guard it from the north-east wind. It is the perfect English home, a self-contained unit, requiring a " garrison " of about a dozen domestics, inside and out. Church, rectory and the few cottages of the hamlet are visible from the windows. South-ward, occupying most of what was the farm, is the Municipal Golf Course of 118 acres, bordered by the infant Yare, that runs under the bridge, at the foot of the park. This in turn connects with Eaton Park, that continues the green belt within the City boundary, southwards, here marked by the Yare. Eaton Park is again a complete contrast. It is no gentleman's park, but a series of sports-fields, intersected by formal gardens and a ferro-concrete bandstand with a ring of changing-rooms. Beyond this building lies a considerable toy yacht-basin, used by a flourishing club, and few prettier sights are to

o

be seen on a fine afternoon than the weaving of miniature sails across this piece of water.

Here, then, we have the Green Man of Norwich streets or open spaces, not in his wild native state, as we meet him on Mousehold, but as the modern Municipal Counsellor sees him, the sporting character, exhibiting himself to cheering crowds. During the Festival of Britain in 1951, the main open-air Fête of the proceedings brought a crowd of twenty thousand people to watch a beauty contest, acts of skill and daring and all the fun of the fair. The wide, grassy space that is continued by market-gardens and a bit of wild gorse, up to the backs of the houses on Newmarket Road, is also the pitch of those mammoth travelling circuses that come from time to time to set up their " Big Top " for the delight of the youth, and also, make no mistake, of the adult population of Norwich and Norfolk. It is hard to believe, until one gets under it, that these gigantic circus tents hold an audience of 4,000 persons, as well as the ring for the performers—that is to say, twice the capacity of any public hall in Norwich. Nor has a whole generation of cinema and radio blunted the thoroughly English appetite for the entertainment of the Circus Ring. Both in 1951 and 1952 the huge audiences have been collected for a week of performances, much of them by bus coming from villages over twenty miles away. It is one of the paradoxes of our age, that as the mechanical vehicle monopolises our roads and takes over many agricultural operations from the horse, the interest in what a horse can and will do, with a little encouragement, seems, far from flagging, actually increasing. I scanned with interest the composition of the programme I witnessed, carried out here by the performers of a certain world-renowned Circus. There were twenty turns. Elephant and lion, trapeze and high wire, juggler and jolly little dogs playing football with gusto—they were all there. But no less than five turns—a quarter of the whole number—were by horses, and some of them by horses alone. Against this preponderance there was only one turn that brought on an automobile, and that a comic one, and only one involving the cycle. Clowns were ubiquitous and all-pervading, of course, but the horse had the bulk of the programme, and next in order of popularity was the dog turn. One must admit, of course, that turns by elephants, lions and tight-rope walkers are breath-taking and make the applause fitful. Yet I still think my main conclusion is right. The more people live in carefully-arranged streets of houses, opening on to paved and tarmac'd roads that take them by motor bus to occupations largely dependent on machines, the more they flock, even at considerable inconvenience and expense, to see horses in action. The seats are not cheap, the journey may be long, but come they will. So do not dismiss as a mere fantasy that weatherbeaten sign of the Green Man, leading his donkey, and lifting his foot, in invitation to the jig. That is a dim presentment of a permanent and apparently growing sentiment, at least among the people of these islands. A strange travelling figure, not native, not easily accountable, a four-footed beast, preferably a horse, a mystery, a performance, an occasion that makes a sharp, sudden contrast to our schooled and regimented lives, is more popular than ever it was when the juggler and acrobat did their simple turn before the crowd in the fairstead at the Monastery Gate. Churches may frown, the law may rate the Green Man and all that lies behind him as " a vagabond ", outlaw. Public feeling is with him, making little of the strictures of morality that class him as a person unlikely to keep the rules, or the dictates of prudence that declare he is, at best, but a waster of time, from whom can accrue no permanent profit.

And now Welfare, and Hygiene have come to the aid of the inveterate human instinct to laugh and waste time, to gape at the unusual, and be thrilled by the mysterious. The Green Man among the streets of Norwich has become the green belt on the Norwich Plan that is to govern the development of our City.

Resuming the circuit of the City boundary in an easterly direction from Eaton Street, there comes next the wide fairway of Eaton Golf Club, that runs down to the marshes of the Yare, as far as Harford Bridges. Here the Housing Estate of Lakenham and the recent development of Tuckswood reach nearly to the water-side, but the Cricket Ground, Recreation Ground and paths and the open space of Long John's Hill still maintain a chain of green-sward and open air, as far as the trees of Bracondale and the wide grounds surrounding the offices of Reckitt & Colman, which were the garden and park of the Colman family. These take us opposite the junction of the

Yare and Wensum, on the northern bank of which lies Mousehold, separated from it only by the railway. North and west
of Mousehold the ring is completed by Sewell Park, Catton
Park, Waterloo Park and Hellesdon Park, Heigham Park and
Wensum Park. These range from three to thirty acres, and
with Woodlands Park, on the south of the Wensum, we are in
sight of the trees of Earlham, and the circuit is complete.

Such is the twentieth-century satisfaction of the insatiable
demand for fresh air, green grass, trees and water. As one
looks at it, one realises how comparatively recent it is. The
conventional statement that our towns are growing is less than
half true. Our towns are being ruralised. The Green Man is
invading the streets, even becoming a solid, respectable
citizen. Of the five hundred acres of Norwich, about 6 per
cent—nearly a square mile—is never going to be built on at all.

This is a great contrast to the state of affairs when I, a little
city-bred boy, looked out from the windows of the Bank
House. My father's idea of exercise to keep him fit (though he
never called it that) was to tramp round the path that surrounds the Castle Mound. Below him lay three acres of what he
considered almost extravagantly luxurious public garden. It
had only been laid out in the 'eighties, and had been, most of
his life, in the state in which it is shown in all older pictures of
the Castle, a dishevelled slope, correctly called Castle Ditches,
covered with coarse grass, trampled every Saturday by the
beasts of the market that had long overflowed Tombland.
That was the daily walk of my childhood, varied by the green
silences of the Close. There was always the 8½ acres of Chapel
Field, already described, but rather far from us. No, in my
young day you had what you could pay for, or make other
people pay for—a private garden behind your house. If the
Green Man had broken in there, dancing beside his " dickey ",
my father would have sent one of the maids to give him a
penny and tell him to go away. The garden behind the Earl
of Surrey's Palace where my aunts kept school was not even
accessible from the street. Nor can I imagine the Green Man
invading the pleasaunce surrounding the Bishop's Palace. So
far from being a hardly credible figment of the imagination, he
is becoming more and more present with us as we progress.
The strict attention to business of the Victorians, the life-time

spent in close confinement, semi-darkness, complete airlessness, was one of the many things that their courageous and devoted spirits could endure. We are a weaker generation. We have been seduced by that flitting and indistinct figure of the nomad of the woods, the half-human who was never to be wholly civilised. He has invaded the enceinte of the walled City. We have let in the Green man.

XXIV

THE STONES THAT DO SPEAK, EARLHAM
AND THE ROSARY

So I come to the last streets of Norwich, which make up the family. And fittingly, for these streets have a special function. They are no highway leading from Norwich to other parts of the Kingdom and the world. They lead, we like to believe, to another Kingdom. They have the usual Norwich complement of trees, in good measure, perhaps more than the average. Considerable effort is made to render them gay with flowers. But their most distinctive feature is that they are lined with stones that do speak. They are the streets, avenues, paths of the Rosary Cemetery on the high ground of Thorpe Hamlet, and those of the Municipal Cemetery on the Earlham Road.

It is an arresting thought (at least, to the thoughtful) that for eight hundred years, in some cases a thousand, Norwich got itself buried in the old churchyards of the City. There are certainly churches that were established before the Norman Conquest, and though most of the thirty-odd that remain today within the walls have been wholly or partially rebuilt, the enclosure in which each stands is the original one. A City, or burgh, such as Norwich, was, until it received its great Cathedral to distinguish it and its walls to enclose it, merely a collection of parishes, more populous and closely connected than the parishes of the countryside. It had a market, the local Eorl lived in or near it, but otherwise it was just a bunch of parishes at some important spot. Its churchyards were its public open spaces. There the parishioners met and did what little public business was done, until the Toll-house and finally the Guildhall concentrated public affairs at some central spot (the Market Place). The parish churchyards were then left to the task of containing the mortal remains of the citizens. Presumably those who could, put up some sort of stone to mark the spot and crave a memory. Later, we know that the more distinguished (and wealthy) had themselves buried inside the church itself, and very handsome many of the family tombs are, with their knights in full armour, burgesses in ruff and gown, and ladies in the robes of fashion then current. Earlier than that some few had a memorial in brass, and later, wall tablets, elaborate, heraldic and coloured in the seventeenth and eighteenth centuries, severe and dignified in the nineteenth.

But taking it all in all, of the hundreds of thousands of burials that have piled many Norwich churchyards high above the surrounding streets (and street levels seldom fall, they usually tend to rise, which makes the height of the churchyard all the more remarkable), how few have left any trace! Shakespeare knew his England, and the now famous grave-digger scene must have been, apart from the magnificent rhetoric with which it is ennobled, a slice of common life. Probably any Elizabethan sexton digging a grave unearthed some unknown and unknowable bones, and stored them (if he did so much) in some shed or the all-purposes crypt, if his particular church possessed one. Often the bones would be fairly recent. The gravedigger in *Hamlet* knew Yorick's skull. That must have been unusual. At Norwich there was a special institution for the reception of surplus bones, a Carnery, or Charnel-House Chapel complete with staff of monks, etc. It is now the building occupied by King Edward VI Grammar School. Most bones must have quietly disintegrated, unknown, unrecorded.

I do not know when tardy justice will be done to the nineteenth century. Its lack of grace, or of certain graces, its serious virtues, its insistence on duty, are all against any just appreciation of it. In this matter, the necessary human task of getting oneself buried, one's carcase, that has been so precious and vulnerable a thing, disposed of when it is of no further use, the nineteenth century was the first to show any sense of comprehension of what was involved. Princes and priests had had spectacular memorials, squires and dames, merchants and mistresses had at least a name, sometimes a carved or engraved figure to commemorate them. But in the main, the recognisable relics of most human existences had been shovelled, in ever-increasing quantity, into the same patches of ground, with all the ineptitude which is the enduring mark of the Middle Ages. It was not until the year 1819 that a certain retired Dissenting minister, one Thomas Drummond, who would nowadays presumably be called a Unitarian, set out to provide something more seemly for the last resting-place of mortal remains. The official institution of modern cemeteries under local control did not take place for a whole generation later. Drummond purchased, apparently with his own money, a plot of ground in the parish of Thorpe called " The Rosary " on what was then the Yarmouth road, leading from Bishop's Bridge, to skirt the southerly side of Mousehold, and so away eastward to the sea. Modern Thorpe Road, issuing from the City as a continuation of Prince of Wales Road, joins it at the very spot. In a short time Drummond was able to interest some friends, and a small company was formed, plots sold, interments undertaken. In 1821 the Lord Bishop of Norwich gave his sanction to the undertaking. Honorary Trustees, elected by the shareholders, have carried on the work ever since.

This " Rosary " was something else besides an attempt to reach decency and hygiene in such matters. Incredible as it may seem, at that date Nonconformists, Dissenters, Quakers, Jews could be buried in the parish churchyards only according to the rites of the Anglican Church. Most of such communities had therefore their own graveyards. But as these were not protected like churchyards, by law, there was little certainty of permanence. In the Rosary, at least, with characteristic honesty, you had what you could pay for, and it was yours until the crack of doom. How right Drummond was can be tested by the fact that after his death the nation at large, indeed most civilised nations, followed the example. What was publicly thought about the Rosary Cemetery is voiced by Blyth's Norwich Guide of 1842 in these words:

" This extensive cemetery, for persons of all religious denominations, is pleasantly situated in Thorpe Hamlet, on the side of a hill, commanding a fine view of Norwich and the adjacent country. From the inconvenient state of most of the churchyards of the City of Norwich and from want of accommodation for dissenters, the Revd. T. Drummond urged the necessity of a cemetery on Freehold Land, to be so vested in Trustees that it could not at any subsequent period be devoted to other purposes. This truly philanthropic plan, as regards the physical economy of a large City, was first ridiculed as visionary, but the projector succeeded in its establishment in 1819 and it was registered at the office of the bishop of the diocese in 1821 for persons of all denominations. It occupies about five acres of land, and the ground is sufficiently capacious for the interment of 30,000 persons, without disturbing the ashes of anyone. It is divided into sections, separated by plantings of trees and shrubs, and contains a small oratory or Chapel. Since the establishment of this cemetery many other large towns have imitated the example of Norwich.''

Norwich itself did not imitate the example of the Revd. T. Drummond until, on 1 March 1856, the Cemetery on Earlham Road was opened under the care of the Burial Board. After that, for the first time down the ages, all and sundry had graves of their own and the possibility of memorial stones, if their relatives felt like it, so recent are what we call the decencies of civilisation.

There it lies, the Bygone Norwich that has been, ever since it recovered from the loss of its textile industry and became the home of milling, packing, wire weaving, light engineering and the footwear trade. The families that made Norwich— Gurneys, Colmans, their relatives and co-religionists—are all in the Rosary. The great bulk, unnamed very often, lie in the pleasant walks of the Cemetery on Earlham Road. Only the Deans of Norwich, if they die in harness, have now the right to be buried in the Cathedral Garth, in the midst of the cloisters, but quite recently the Congregationalists, at the Old Meeting, found that the authorities had no objection to the burial of ashes in the old historic graveyard in Colegate, behind their seventeenth-century Chapel, and it may be that, with the aid of the Crematorium, some four miles out on the Aylsham Road, we may once more see our City churchyards in use. As for the past, one can only take refuge in the thought that it may not matter much. Orthodox people still have a certain prejudice in the matter of laying what is left of them, in what they call consecrated ground. But orthodox people, those at least who attend some place of worship on a Sunday, are a mere ten per cent of the population, and that includes nonconformists, who are, today, " orthodox " in that matter at least. Who really believes—I mean believes after examination of the facts:

I do not consider repeating what someone or other claiming some authority or other tells one to believe as " Belief "— that at the Day of Judgment, whatever that is, God is going to divide the orthodox from the less or non " orthodox " ? So perhaps we need not grieve over the fact that half the original churchyards of Norwich (there were once sixty) cannot now be traced. Who knows who was buried in St. Winnaloy's, or St. Botolph's, St. Anne's or St. Mary Magdalen's, that perhaps gives its name to what used to be Fyebriggate and is now Magdalen Street. Nor was this work of obliteration the result of the Reformation. The churches and churchyards were let go, allowed to fall down, or built over or sold away. It is most questionable if orthodoxy is wise in such matters.

Let us take our final walk through the streets of Norwich along these pleasant alleys. In one thing at least the Burial Board of 1856 was somewhat wiser than the Rosary Trustees, and foresaw that the splendid forest trees for which the Rosary was remarkable would prove a certain inconvenience as they flourished, grew large and then old and decayed and had to be topped or taken down, amid plots of graves ever more and more closely congested. When the Trustees of the Rosary enlarged it in 1924, they wisely took the hint, and have planted only ornamental shrubs since. But that is not the vital point. It is that to nearly every plot there is attached a memorial of some sort, ranging from miniature mausoleums, through ample family graves with inscriptions and so on in varying shape and design, to the humble bunch of faded flowers, renewed while relatives or loved ones remained, and then, as the last to remember dropped off, forsaken, unchanged, to disappear with the leaves of so many years. It has long been the fashion to find epitaphs funny, and the various crosses, obelisks, columns, figures of angels and railings to keep dogs off the graves in most cemeteries do give rise to a wry smile sometimes. " Curious Epitaphs " were collected by William Andrews, and very curious some were. But one never knows if the persons who thought such inscriptions comic, when they described the virtues or deplored the loss of others, were equally amused when they, who laughed, reflected that they themselves had also to be interred, with some doubtless equally feeble or ineffective human words to keep some trace of them alive for a generation or two. For that is the fact, inescapable so far as human intelligence goes. Even if a name or some signal deed survives, it does so by virtue of the peculiarity that impresses history. It is the peculiarity that is immortalised. That is why, for four hundred years, the obscure nobleman who was killed on Palace Plain in August 1549, as he attempted to suppress Kett's Rebellion, was remembered by the unlettered inhabitants of that street, by a simple S in the pavement. It is within only this last twenty years that the Corporation, careful of its tourist trade, put up a plaque in the wall of an adjoining house, describing Lord Sheffield and perpetuating the whole incident. What is commemorated there is the astonishing fact that a heavily-armed nobleman could be unhorsed and brought down by a set of:

> Country knoffs, Hob, Hib and Dick
> With Clubs and clouted shoon

as the old rhyme says. There is some doubt if they did bring him down, or if his horse was frightened by the " new " cannon going off pop, pop. To frighten horses was the tactical value of artillery, it may be that this then novel fact is the one really recorded. And so on. Henry the Eighth is remembered because he had six wives, Charles II because he was " merry ", that is, verbally witty, Queen Elizabeth because no one knew what she would do next. They are remembered for such items of gossip, not because they founded the Anglican Church, the Royal Navy or the British Empire. They are better remembered than the saintly Edward the Confessor, Henry the Sixth who founded some of our more important educational institutions or Edward VI who organised others.

So we must take the mortuary inscriptions on all these stones with a charitable conviction that the inscriptions on ours will look no better a hundred years hence. Fortunately, in many cases Time has lightly passed his hand over the lettering. In others, the good sense of relatives and relicts have confined the words to a brief statement of name and age and perhaps a dutiful and doubtless heartfelt sentence from Christian or other scriptures. The one I like best is on the slab beneath which rests my great-aunt, Jenny Mottram, in the graveyard of the old Octagon, "Beloved and lamented": what more can one ask? I do not know of any inscription which says in so many words:

" Gone from this imperfection to something nearer perfection."
It would be refreshing to find it, or some of the million possible
variants of such a theme, instead of the repulsive assumption
that somebody or other knows all the answers, and that some
particular answer is full and final, and the poor wraith who made
it will have some privilege, somewhere or other. As if one
wanted to be privileged!

Too much to ask. Norwich and its streets are a fair example
of what the mean average of western European civilisation has
managed to accumulate, these thousand years and more, since
its various components took on roughly their present shape and
texture. In these streets you can see what it amounts to, for
there has been less complete clearance and rebuilding, even
allowing for the destruction of the nineteen-forties, than in
many places. Here you can see, piled slab on slab, by faint
allusion here, by complete change of purpose there, the
infinitely various and flexible life that these streets have contained. So much so that I have felt emboldened to cast this
book in this form. These streets, as I have said and I hope
shown, have become so soaked with essence of humanity that
they have become something like conglomerate human beings,
holy or disreputable, busy or forsaken. What claim can I make
to justify the undertaking? None, except to those who, like
myself, are enthralled by life, think it a precious thing, ours, to
do the best we can with, so that we may leave it with some small
addition of our own. For, indifferent, even deplorable, as some
of it will be, no one can deny the streets of Norwich the quality
of possessing a character.

INDEX

I. *Streets, Roads, Railways, Gates, Bridges, Rivers*

229

II. *Churches and Parishes*

III. *Personalities*

IV. Buildings, Districts, Open Spaces

V. *Inn Signs*